A SURVEY OF

General equilibrium systems

BENT HANSEN

University of California, Berkeley

McGRAW–HILL BOOK COMPANY

New York   San Francisco   St. Louis

Düsseldorf   London   Mexico   Panama   Sydney   Toronto

798,780

This book was set in Monotype Baskerville, and printed
on permanent paper and bound by The Maple Press
Company. The designer was Marie Carluccio; the draw-
ings were done by Basil C. Wood. The editors were
Robert D. Bovenschulte and Ronald Q. Lewton.
Charles A. Goehring supervised production.

A SURVEY OF

General equilibrium systems

Printed in the United States of America

Library of Congress catalog card number: 74-115142

1234567890 MAMM 7876543210

26063

To *So'ad*

Preface

The purpose of this book is to give a cross-theoretical survey of the most important general equilibrium systems encountered by the student in contemporary economic literature. A comparative study of these systems requires rather extensive readings, and how intimately they actually are related is not always clear from the specialized, technically more or less advanced works in which detailed analyses of the systems and their properties have been undertaken. The original authors of the systems have often, for obvious reasons, been inclined to exaggerate differences rather than emphasize similarities; perhaps they may not always have been aware of the similarities. All the great general equilibrium systems, associated with the names of Walras, Cassel, Lindahl, Keynes, Hicks, Samuelson, Patinkin, Leontief, von Neumann, and Solow are, however, species of the same genus—the theory of demand and supply. The present juxtaposition and comparison of these great systems, and of some minor ones, too, aim at demonstrating this relationship.

The emphasis of this book is therefore upon the general structures and specifications of the systems, their economic interpretation, and their common origin and kinship, rather than upon detailed analysis of the properties of the individual systems. When the specifications of the systems are found to differ, more often than not the explanation is simply that their authors have asked different questions. The coexistence of disaggregated and aggregated systems, short- and long-term systems, open and closed systems, and so forth, illustrates this point. When genuine conflict is involved, it is related to the precise formulation of demand and supply relations rather than to the problem of whether economic theory should work in terms of demand and supply. Even Marx slipped back into demand and supply theory when, finally, he began to inquire into the concrete economic phenomena of capitalist society. If this book can convey to the reader the basic view that all these systems belong to the same family of theory, and that in many cases the choice among them is a question of the problems to be solved, then the book has served its primary purpose.

It is difficult, and in any case inefficient, to discuss complex systems of relationships without using mathematical symbols. All the models surveyed here are formulated as systems of equations. Nevertheless, this is not a book in mathematical economics. The reader will find relatively little pure mathematical analysis, and the little he will find is quite simple. Mathematics are mainly used for expository reasons, which, of course, is closely related to our preoccupation with the structure of the models and their economic interpretation. It is usually in the analysis of the solution of a system that high-powered mathematics may become necessary; but for this purpose the reader should turn to the more specialized literature. Despite all the mathematical symbols used, the mathematics required do not go beyond simple calculus. Indeed, the book has deliberately been written to make the material accessible to readers with relatively limited mathematical equipment.

Some knowledge of "positive" economic theory is, on the other hand, indispensable; welfare aspects of general equilibrium theory are not dealt with. The reader should be well acquainted with both micro and macro theory corresponding to the level of good intermediate textbooks. It is taken for granted that he is well versed in production, cost, and demand theory on the micro side, and Keynesian economics and national income analysis on the macro side.

It is preferable to read the book consecutively. Chapter 17 may, however, be read with advantage immediately after and in connection with Chapter 3; and Chapter 18 could be studied with Chapter 11. Each chapter concludes with a list of references to works quoted in that chapter. In most cases only original contributions have been quoted, but in some cases reference has also been made to later expositions.

During the years in which I have taught this material, I have benefited greatly from critical remarks and positive suggestions from students whom I take the opportunity to thank for their helpfulness. Some of the material was included in my *Lectures in Economic Theory*, Part I, published by Student-litteratur, Lund, Sweden, in 1966. I also want to acknowledge my indebtedness to the editorial staff of McGraw-Hill's College Division at Novato, California, for their help in transforming my poor English into good "American" and otherwise improving the presentation. The responsibility for whatever mistakes and deficiencies remain rests, of course, with me.

I have dedicated the book to my dear wife, So'ad Ibrahim Ref'at.

BENT HANSEN

Contents

Chapter 4

A simplified Walrasian system

Chapter 5

Money and the Walrasian system

Chapter 6

Budget restrictions,
homogeneity, and demand for money

Chapter 7

Assets and debts,
intertemporal theory

Chapter *8*

Patinkin's system

Chapter *9*

Investments and savings, price level and activity level

Chapter *10*

Inflation, general equilibrium, and *quasi*-equilibrium

Chapter *11*

The Keynesian system

Chapter *12*

Alternative interest theories

Chapter *13*

General equilibrium
and foreign trade

Chapter *14*

Leontief's input-output system

A SURVEY OF
General equilibrium systems

The concept
of equilibrium

1

General equilibrium theory is, in this book, conceived of in a very broad
sense, including those dynamic models to which the concept of equilibrium
is applied. For this reason, and also because to some the word "equilibrium"
may connote political harmony and ring of apologetics, it may be helpful
to begin by explaining exactly what is meant by equilibrium, and how it is
used in economic analysis. First, however, we will define a few concepts.

1 / Some concepts

About 35 years ago, Ragnar Frisch (1935–36) suggested a terminology that
has now become generally accepted. Following Frisch, we say that an
economy is in a stationary state if over time nothing changes in the economy.
A stationary state repeats itself unchanged indefinitely unless it is disturbed.
An economy is said to be in evolution, or development, if something in that
economy changes over time.

    To describe and analyze an economy we need an economic theory;
that is, a model. Economic theories, or models, may be either static or
dynamic. In a static model the variables are by assumption independent of
the passage of time. In a dynamic model time enters in an essential way so
that, by assumption, the variables are made dependent upon the passage of
time. This circumstance does not prevent some, or even all, variables in a
dynamic model from being constant over time, inasmuch as a dynamic model
may have a so-called "stationary solution." That a model has a stationary
solution means there exists a set of numbers such that if we allow the variables to take on values equal to this set of numbers, the model will repeat
itself unchanged indefinitely, and thus describe a stationary state. We speak
about an "equilibrium solution" of a model if time does not appear in the

solution. Thus, the solution of a static model is always an equilibrium solution. The same applies to the stationary solution of a dynamic model. Dynamic models may have equilibrium solutions, however, where certain features of the models repeat themselves unchanged over time, and other features exhibit changes.

A dynamic model is said to be stable in the large if it has an equilibrium solution and the model will finally reach, or approach, equilibrium no matter what initial values are attached to its variables. A model that is not stable in the large may nonetheless be stable in the small; it will then reach equilibrium if the initial values are sufficiently close to the equilibrium solution. The problem of stability is more complicated, however, because several equilibrium solutions may exist, and stability may be one-sided (P. A. Samuelson, 1947, Chapter X). A model that is not stable is said to be unstable.

A static model can only be used (1) to describe a stationary state, and (2) to analyze the differences between alternative stationary states. The latter sort of analysis is called "comparative statics." It happens occasionally that static models can be used to describe and analyze important properties of evolutionary economies; examples will be given in Chapters 10, 15, 16, 17, and 18. This is possible only when the evolutionary economy has certain features that remain unchanged.

Dynamic models are much more flexible. They can be used (1) to describe the time paths of economic variables, and (2) to analyze the differences between alternative time paths of variables. The latter is called "comparative dynamics." A dynamic model may also be used to describe a stationary state, and to analyze the differences between alternative stationary states provided the dynamic model has a stationary solution.

A given stationary state may thus be described either by a static model or by a corresponding dynamic model having this stationary state as its stationary solution. If the corresponding dynamic model is stable, interesting conclusions can be drawn from the stability properties of the dynamic model to the equilibrium properties of the static model. This relationship is the "correspondence principle" formulated by P. A. Samuelson (1941, 1947, Chapters IX and X). The principle extends to stable equilibria in general, whether stationary or dynamic.

Thus, far from belonging to alien and irreconcilable worlds, statics and dynamics are closely related, overlapping branches of economic theory. Statics appears as a special case of dynamics. Results obtained by static analysis may always be conceived of as the longer-run tendencies of some dynamic model. In this sense, static analysis may also be relevant to evolutionary economies.

2 / Equilibrium and economic theory

Equilibrium plays an important role in economic theory, and although many economic problems cannot reasonably be dealt with in terms of equilibrium theory, it remains an indispensable tool. It has often been criticized as being a purely static concept with no relation to the evolutionary world in which we live. This criticism is entirely beside the point, however. Even in a disequilibrium analysis the concept of equilibrium will often be needed as a frame of reference and modern theory has shown its great usefulness in dynamic analysis (examples will be given in Chapters 10 and 15 to 18). Modern growth theory, for instance, has been cast largely in the form of equilibrium growth, and even inflation theory may apply the concept of equilibrium with advantage.

First, it should be understood that equilibrium is essentially a dynamic concept, and sometimes problems in static equilibrium theory can be answered only if the dynamic nature of the equilibrium is considered. Such an example will be given in Chapter 12. The concept of economic equilibrium has been taken from classical mechanics, where it belongs to the theory of dynamics. It is loosely defined as a state wherein the forces that operate on a point (or body) "cancel each other out." A more precise definition states: "Any configuration of a rigid body, or of a system of bodies, is said to be one of equilibrium if the body or the system can remain indefinitely in this configuration under the forces acting upon it" (Rutherford, 1957, p. 119). The concept of economic equilibrium also requires specification of the forces working in or upon the economic system.

The dynamic nature of equilibrium has not always been clear to the economists who used the concept, and it is only thanks to R. Frisch (1935–1936), J. R. Hicks (1939), and P. A. Samuelson (1941, 1947) that it has been fully comprehended. Probably, the most common definition of economic equilibrium is equality of demand and supply. A market is said to be in equilibrium if the quantity in demand is equal to the quantity in supply. An alternative definition states that demand price and supply price must be equal. Both of these seemingly static definitions are actually based on implicit assumptions concerning the forces that work on economic variables, such as prices and quantities. Indeed, the first definition is based on the hypothesis that if quantity in demand does not equal quantity in supply, the price will tend to change. This hypothesis has found an explicit expression in Walras' excess demand hypothesis for price changes (Chapter 2). The second definition is based on the hypothesis that if demand price does not equal supply price, producers will change the quantity in supply. This is Marshall's excess price hypothesis for quantity changes (Chapter 2). These definitions or, rather, conditions of equilibrium, thus presume some law of motion for prices or quantities. A third definition of equilibrium, developed by proponents of the Swedish *ex ante*, *ex post* analysis (E. Lindahl, 1939) states that equilibrium prevails if all plans and expectations of all economic subjects are fulfilled so that, at given data, no economic subject feels inclined to revise his plans or expectations. This definition of equilibrium obviously calls for laws of motion governing the revisions of plans and expectations.

To generalize, we can say that if we have an economic model that explains certain variables, and if there is no tendency for these variables to change, given the data of the model, then the system of variables is in equilibrium. To determine whether there is any tendency to change, however, we must first study the forces of the system. Such study may then lead to equilibrium conditions similar to those mentioned above. In this book we shall stay largely with the traditional static equilibrium condition: quantity in demand is equal to quantity in supply. We shall bear in mind the law of motion behind it, however, and now and then we will be compelled to bring it explicitly into the discussion. In Chapter 10 we shall see that modern theory and development have cast some doubt upon the appropriateness of both the traditional laws of motion and equilibrium conditions.

Second, equilibrium does not necessarily imply that everything remains unchanged over time. The assumption of equilibrium may be confined to certain variables of the model considered, or to the relationship between certain variables. For example, we may assume constant relative prices without necessarily having constant absolute prices; the model will then be in equilibrium in the relative prices, but not necessarily in the absolute prices (Chapter 10). Alternatively, we may assume constant relative quantities and yet permit all quantities to change continuously over time. The basic assumption of equilibrium growth is that there is equilibrium in the relative quantities (Chapters 15 to 18). To analyze a dynamic process, and to simplify the analysis, it may be necessary to "tie" or "lock" the process in certain respects. One way to accomplish that is to introduce equilibrium assumptions similar to those just mentioned, thereby enabling us to study dynamic equilibrium processes. Whether such simplifications are useful is an empirical question that can only be answered by testing the model against those phenomena it sets out to describe. It is important to understand only that evolution does not *a priori* rule out equilibrium assumptions.

Early dynamic theory worked with the notion of "moving equilibrium" (Moore, 1929). Moving equilibrium models assume that exogenous forces (population growth, for example) cause demand and supply functions to change over time, but that demand and supply are nevertheless continuously equal in size. This is tantamount to assuming instantaneous adaptation of prices and quantities in case of exogenous disturbances, and for certain markets this may be a reasonable approximation. Modern equilibrium growth theory has to a large extent worked with such instantaneous adaptation (see Chapter 18). In this respect we may also mention "stochastic models," which are subject to random shocks. Econometric models, formulated for empirical testing, are of this type. Random shocks are also important in purely theoretical problems, as in the theory of cyclical fluctuations (Frisch, 1933). Random shocks may be introduced in both dynamic and static models. A static equilibrium model extended with random variables is an example of a moving equilibrium model. It has been shown by Yule and Slutsky (1937) that under certain conditions the random shocks may make the variables of such a model describe cyclical variations over time.

A third important reason for the preoccupation of economic theory with economic equilibrium is that economic policy targets are very often formulated in terms of equilibrium (politicians ask for "balance" or "stabilization"), and optimum solutions are very often found to be identical to equilibrium solutions. The great example, of course, is the coincidence of competitive equilibrium and the conditions for optimum Paretoan welfare. This circumstance even led J. R. Hicks (1965) to define equilibrium as a state where everybody produces and consumes what they prefer. This definition seems to be equivalent to Lindahl's (see above), however, and calls for explicit dynamization.

3 / The existence of equilibrium

When we ask whether an equilibrium "exists," we may have two entirely different problems in mind. Equilibrium may exist either in an empirical or in a logical sense. That equilibrium exists in an empirical sense can only be asserted by testing empirically the equilibrium model concerned. Before we study the empirical problem of whether equilibrium exists, we should be certain that our model does have an equilibrium solution. Typically this will involve a logical, mathematical problem of solving a set of equations and showing that the equations (the model) have an economically meaningful solution.

For years economists were content to count equations and unknowns when discussing the existence of a solution to general equilibrium models. Although in general equality of equations and unknowns is neither a necessary nor sufficient condition for the existence of a unique, economically acceptable solution, counting equations and unknowns is by no means a futile exercise. For the sake of empirical application, we must keep open the possibility that the model is linear; for linear models, to count (independent) equations and unknowns certainly makes sense. For that reason it would be rather unpleasant to find that a general equilibrium system had fewer or more independent equations than unknowns. Generally, of course, more is needed than the counting of equations and unknowns. The problem has been explored by modern mathematical economics, and it has been shown that with certain specifications the neoclassical general equilibrium system will in fact have a unique, economically meaningful solution (A. Wald, 1935; K. J. Arrow and G. Debreu, 1954; see also, Dorfman, Samuelson, and Solow, 1958, Chapter 13). The proofs require mathematics that go beyond those used in this book. The reader is referred to the exposition of J. Quirk and R. Saposnik (1968), or Kuenne (1963). We shall return to the problem in Chapter 4.

References

ARROW, K. J., and G. DEBREU: "Existence of an Equilibrium for a Competitive Economy," *Econometrica*, vol. 22, no. 3, July, 1954.

DORFMAN, R., P. A. SAMUELSON, and R. SOLOW: *Linear Programming and Economic Analysis*, McGraw-Hill, New York, 1958.

FRISCH, R.: "Propagation Problems and Impulse Problems in Dynamic Economics," in *Economic Essays in Honor of Gustav Cassel*, George Allen and Unwin, London, 1933. Reprinted in R. A. Gordon and L. R. Klein (eds.), *Readings in Business Cycles*, A.E.A. Series, George Allen and Unwin, London, 1966.

—: "On the Notion of Equilibrium and Disequilibrium," *Review of Economic Studies*, vol. 3, 1935–36.

HICKS, J. R.: *Value and Capital*, Clarendon Press, Oxford, 1939; 2d ed., 1946.

—: *Capital and Growth*, Clarendon Press, Oxford, 1965.

KUENNE, R. E.: *The Theory of General Economic Equilibrium*, Princeton University Press, 1963. Second printing with corrections, 1967.

LINDAHL, E.: *Studies in the Theory of Money and Capital*, Part I, George Allen and Unwin, London, 1939.

MOORE, H. L.: *Synthetic Economics*, Macmillan, New York, 1929.

QUIRK, J., and R. SAPOSNIK: *Introduction to General Equilibrium Theory and Welfare Economics*, McGraw-Hill, New York, 1968.

RUTHERFORD, D. C.: *Classical Mechanics*, 2d ed., University Mathematical Texts, Oliver and Boyd, Edinburgh and London, 1957.

SAMUELSON, P. A.: "The Stability of Equilibrium: Comparative Statics and Dynamics," *Econometrica*, vol. 9, no. 1, January, 1941.

—: *Foundations of Economic Analysis*, Harvard University Press, Cambridge, Mass., 1947.

SLUTSKY, E.: "The Summation of Random Causes as the Source of Cyclic Processes," *Econometrica*, vol. 5, no. 2, April, 1937.

WALD, A.: "Some Systems of Equations of Mathematical Economics," *Econometrica*, vol. 19, no. 4, October, 1951. Originally published as "Über einige Gleichungssysteme der mathematischen Ökonomie," *Zeitschrift für Nationalökonomie*, vol. 7, 1936.

Statics and dynamics of some simple models

2

To inject some life into the concepts introduced in Chapter 1, we shall discuss briefly the theory of equilibrium for isolated competitive markets and for a simple Keynesian macro model. The purpose of the discussion is to demonstrate the close relationship between statics and dynamics, and the dynamic nature of the concept of equilibrium. Only the most elementary and basic economic theory is involved, but this serves to emphasize the importance of the results. General equilibrium systems consist of agglomerations of interdependent markets. What is relevant to the individual markets will usually be important to the system as a whole. In Chapter 4, Sections 4 and 5, we shall see how considerations for the individual market do, in fact, extend to a system of markets.

The exposition follows rather closely Samuelson's own presentation (1947) of the "correspondence principle," albeit at a lower level of rigor.

1 / Static equilibrium model for isolated markets

The standard model for the isolated competitive market consists of a demand function and a supply function, which together determine the equilibrium quantity and price of the commodity or service traded in that particular market. Comparative statics for the isolated market study the effects on the equilibrium price and quantity of shifts in the demand and supply functions, and various kinds of intervention in the market. We shall consider four standard problems.

In a given initial equilibrium situation, we assume that an increase in demand occurs. Two problems then arise:

(1) What will happen to the equilibrium price?
(2) What will happen to the equilibrium quantity?

Alternatively, we may assume that the government intervenes in the market and levies a specific tax on production. Several problems are encountered then. Among them are:

(3) What will happen to the equilibrium price, including tax?

(4) How will the tax incidence be distributed among consumers and producers?

Experimentation with graphs should make it clear that the answers depend upon the slopes of the demand and supply curves. It should also reveal that the formulation of the first two questions is ambiguous. An increase in demand may mean either that (1) more is purchased at any given price, or (2) a higher price will be paid at any given quantity purchased. In the traditional demand and supply diagram, with the price along the ordinate, the first interpretation implies a horizontal, and the second a vertical shift of the demand curve. With a "normally" sloped demand curve, these two interpretations would make no difference; but we cannot exclude cases with "abnormal" slopes. Here it matters exactly how the demand curve is shifted.

Moreover, we have two static models for the isolated, competitive market, differing with respect to the treatment of price and quantity as dependent and independent variables in the demand and supply functions. For purposes of comparative statics the two models are equivalent. As soon as we turn to the dynamics of the models and their stability properties, however, they prove to be very different. To formulate our four problems precisely, we shall work on both models concurrently. In Model I the price p is the independent variable and, at any given price, a distinction must be made between quantity in demand q^d and quantity in supply q^s. In Model II, where the quantity q is an independent variable, we distinguish, at any given quantity, between demand price p^d and supply price p^s. Finally, we let T denote the tax in terms of dollars per unit of production (supply).

The two models are then:

	Model I	Model II
[2.1]	$q^d = a_1 p + b_1$	$p^d = \alpha_1 q + \beta_1$
[2.2]	$q^s = a_2(p - T) + b_2$	$p^s = \alpha_2 q + \beta_2$
[2.3]	$q^d = q^s$	$p^d = p^s + T$

In both models, the first equation is the demand function, the second is the supply function, and the third is the equilibrium condition. The solutions, indicated by a bar over the variable, are:

[2.4]
$$\bar{p} = \frac{b_1 - b_2 + a_2 T}{a_2 - a_1} \qquad \bar{p}^d = \frac{\beta_1 \alpha_2 - \beta_2 \alpha_1 - \alpha_1 T}{\alpha_2 - \alpha_1}$$

[2.5]
$$\bar{q}^d = \bar{q}^s = \frac{a_2 b_1 - a_1 b_2 + a_1 a_2 T}{a_2 - a_1} \qquad \bar{q} = \frac{\beta_1 - \beta_2 - T}{\alpha_2 - \alpha_1}$$

In Model I, p includes tax and corresponds to p^d in Model II; $\bar{p}^s$ is equal to $\bar{p}^d - T$. If we assume that $\alpha_1 = 1/a_1$, $\beta_1 = -b_1/a_1$, $\alpha_2 = 1/a_2$, and $\beta_2 = -b_2/a_2$, the two models have the same equilibrium solution with

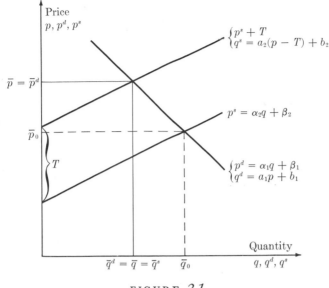

FIGURE 2.1

$\bar{q} = \bar{q}^d = \bar{q}^s$ and $\bar{p} = \bar{p}^d$. This is easily seen by inserting the values of α_1, β_1, α_2, and β_2 in the solutions for Model II. We follow this assumption throughout this chapter. The geometrical picture of the two models is shown in Figure 2.1.

To depict the models in the same figure, Model I has the independent variable measured along the ordinate and the dependent variable along the abscissa; Model II is represented in the opposite way.

We turn, then, to our four problems. First we wish to determine the effects of an increase in demand. In Model I it is taken to mean that b_1 increases; in Model II, that β_1 increases. An increase in b_1 implies a horizontal shift of the demand curve in Figure 2.1; an increase in β_1 implies a vertical shift. The displacements of the equilibrium called forth by these shifts are:

[2.6]
$$\frac{d\bar{p}}{db_1} = \frac{1}{a_2 - a_1} \qquad \frac{d\bar{p}^d}{d\beta_1} = \frac{\alpha_2}{\alpha_2 - \alpha_1}\left(= \frac{-a_1}{a_2 - a_1}\right)$$

[2.7]
$$\frac{d\bar{q}^s}{db_1} = \frac{d\bar{q}^d}{db_1} = \frac{a_2}{a_2 - a_1} \qquad \frac{d\bar{q}}{d\beta_1} = \frac{1}{\alpha_2 - \alpha_1}\left(= \frac{-a_1 a_2}{a_2 - a_1}\right)$$

The effects of a change in b_1 in Model I are different from those for β_1 in Model II. The displacements $d\bar{p}/db_1$ and $d\bar{p}^d/d\beta_1$ may even have different signs; similarly for $d\bar{q}^s/db_1 = d\bar{q}^d/db_1$ and $d\bar{q}/d\beta_1$.[1] Note, also, that in this linear model the effects are independent of the level of taxation.

[1] This is not to deny that the same shift of the demand curve can be described by both models. With $d\beta_1 = -(db_1)/a_1$ we obtain the same effects in both models.

With respect to the effects of taxation, it does not matter which model we use. Let $\bar{p}_0$ denote the equilibrium price when there is no taxation; that is, $T = 0$. The change in the equilibrium price that follows from imposing the tax is:

[2.8] $$\bar{p} - \bar{p}_0 = \frac{a_2 T}{a_2 - a_1} \quad \bigg| \quad \bar{p}^d - \bar{p}_0 = \frac{-\alpha_1 T}{\alpha_2 - \alpha_1} \left(= \frac{a_2 T}{a_2 - a_1} \right)$$

With our assumptions concerning the coefficients, the effects of a certain production tax on price are identical. The last problem concerned the incidence of the tax. Let $T_d = \bar{p} - \bar{p}_0$ be the incidence of tax on the purchasers, and $T_s = \bar{p}_0 - \bar{p}^s$ the incidence of tax on the producers $T_d + T_s = T$. We have then:

[2.9] $$T_d = \frac{a_2 T}{a_2 - a_1} \quad \bigg| \quad T_d = \frac{-\alpha_1 T}{\alpha_2 - \alpha_1} \left(= \frac{a_2 T}{a_2 - a_1} \right)$$

[2.10] $$T_s = \frac{-a_1 T}{a_2 - a_1} \quad \bigg| \quad T_s = \frac{\alpha_2 T}{\alpha_2 - \alpha_1} \left(= \frac{-a_1 T}{a_2 - a_1} \right)$$

and

[2.11] $$T_d - T_s = \frac{a_2 + a_1}{a_2 - a_1} = \frac{-\alpha_2 - \alpha_1}{\alpha_2 - \alpha_1}$$

from which it follows that:

[2.12] $T_d < T_s$ if $-1 < \dfrac{a_2}{a_1} = \dfrac{\alpha_1}{\alpha_2} < 1$ or $\left| \dfrac{a_2}{a_1} \right| = \left| \dfrac{\alpha_1}{\alpha_2} \right| < 1$

Equations 2.6, 2.7, 2.8, and 2.12 contain the precise answers to the four problems posed at the beginning of this section. The four answers depend upon the slopes of the demand and supply curves; that is, on a_1 and a_2, or α_1 and α_2, but in different ways. If we knew the values of the coefficients, we could calculate the values of Equations 2.6, 2.7, 2.8, and 2.12. Without having the necessary quantitative information about the slopes (which is the rule rather than the exception, unfortunately) we may have to be satisfied with merely obtaining some idea about the signs of 2.6, 2.7, 2.8 (that is, the direction of the effects) and knowing whether 2.12 is fulfilled. It is here that the "correspondence principle" enters the picture. We find we can draw conclusions about some of the signs of the expressions from the presence of stability in dynamic models corresponding to the static models. For that purpose we shall discuss two dynamic models corresponding to Model I and one corresponding to Model II.

2 / Walras' excess demand hypothesis

We first consider a dynamic law of motion for prices, which is ascribed to Walras, and which we meet time and again in economic theory. It states simply that the rate of change of the price of a particular commodity is determined by the difference between demand and supply for that commodity; that is, by the excess demand. If demand and supply are equal, the price will be constant. If demand exceeds supply, the price will increase. The more demand exceeds supply, the faster the price increases. Whether explicit or implicit, Walras' law of motion, sometimes called "the law of supply and demand," is probably one of the most generally accepted hypotheses in economics, and may be traced far back in the history of doctrine. Formally, it may be written as:

[2.13] $$\frac{dp}{dt} = f(q^d - q^s) = f(q^x) \qquad f(0) = 0 \qquad f' > 0$$

where dp/dt is the time rate of the change of price, and $q^x = q^d - q^s$ is the excess demand.

Dynamic Equation 2.13, with the demand and supply functions from Model I, that is, Equations 2.1.I and 2.2.I, is a dynamic model corresponding to Model I. It contains the static model, Equations 2.1.I, 2.2.I, and 2.3.I as a special case. To see this, put $dp/dt = 0$. It follows from Equation 2.13 that $q^d - q^s = 0$, which is the equilibrium condition shown in Equation 2.3.I. Figure 2.2 indicates how this dynamic model works. In the NE quadrant we have drawn the demand and supply curves. In the NW quadrant we have price on the ordinate and time measured to the left along the abscissa. Point of time zero is at the origin. Assume that at time zero, the price is $p(0)$. At this price the excess demand is $q^x(0) = q^d(0) - q^s(0)$, which is negative. The price is therefore falling, and from the curve $p(t)$ in the NW quadrant we can read that at time 1 the price will have fallen to $p(1)$. At

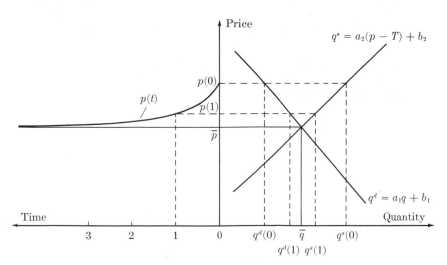

FIGURE 2.2

this price the excess demand has fallen to $q^x(1) = q^d(1) - q^s(1)$, which is still negative but numerically smaller than $q^x(0)$. At time 1 the price thus continues to fall, but at a slower rate than at time zero; hence, the convexity of the curve $p(t)$. In this way the price will continue to fall, albeit more and more slowly, and will finally approach $\bar{p}$, the equilibrium value of the static Model I. The stationary solution for the dynamic model thus coincides with the equilibrium solution for Model I. It is in this sense that the dynamic model corresponds to Model I.

As we have drawn the curves in Figure 2.2, the dynamic model is stable: No matter what the price is at time zero, eventually we shall have the price $\bar{p}$. If the slopes of the demand or supply curves are "abnormal," however, the model may be unstable, so that it does not move toward the equilibrium price. It can be proved[1] that the market will be stable if $a_2 - a_1$ is positive; that is, if the slope of the supply curve against the price axis is larger than the slope of the demand curve. But $a_2 - a_1 > 0$ is nothing but the condition for $d\bar{p}/db_1$ to be positive. (See Equation 2.6.I.) Hence, we conclude that an increase in demand in Model I will lead to an increase in the equilibrium price if the system is stable, given Walras' excess demand hypothesis, in Equation 2.13.

This conclusion can also be understood from a study of Figure 2.3, where we have shown all possibilities with respect to the positions and slopes of the (linear) demand and supply curves. In all eight cases we consider a horizontal shift of the demand curve from D to D_1 at a given supply curve S. The stability of the market is checked by imagining a price change away from the equilibrium level (upward or downward). If after this change in price, demand exceeds supply, then the price will increase; if supply exceeds demand, the price will fall. The direction of the price changes around the equilibrium price is indicated by arrows. If both arrows point toward the equilibrium price, the market is stable; if both point away from that price, it is unstable.

We first dispose of the two cases G and H where the demand and supply curves are parallel and there is either no solution, or an infinite number of solutions. If there is no solution, the system cannot be stable, since there is no equilibrium point toward which the system can move. If the curves coincide and there are an infinite number of equilibrium solutions, any price is an

---

[1] Assuming Equation 2.13 to be linear, $dp/dt = k(q^d - q^s), k > 0$, and inserting Equations 2.1.I and 2.2.I, we obtain a first-order differential equation in p,

$$\frac{dp}{dt} + k(a_2 - a_1)p = k(b_1 - b_2 + a_2 T)$$

which has the solution (Allen, 1956, Chapter 5)

$$p(t) = \bar{p} - [\bar{p} - p(0)]e^{-k(a_2-a_1)t}$$

where e is the base of the natural logarithms and $\bar{p}$ is the solution of Model I, Equation 2.4.I. For $a_2 - a_1 > 0$, $p(t) = \bar{p}$ in the limit for $t \to \infty$.

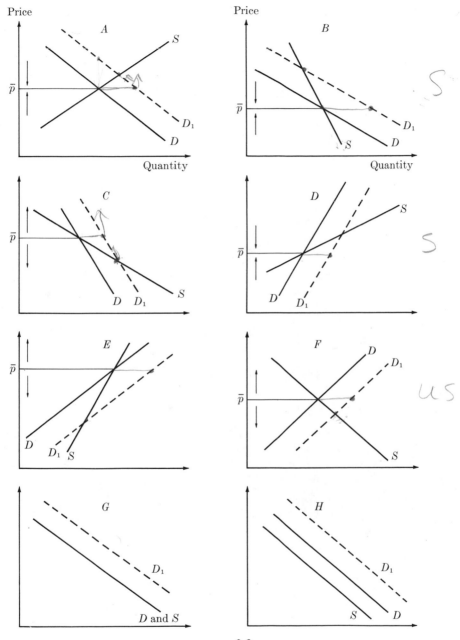

FIGURE 2.3

equilibrium price; and at any price, the system will remain where it is. In such cases, we might speak about a "neutral equilibrium"; that is, a system that is neither stable nor unstable. Therefore, in both cases *G* and *H* our problems make no sense and have no answers.

Of the other six cases, *A*, *B*, and *D* are stable. In these cases a shift in demand to the right leads to an increase in the equilibrium price. It will also be seen that in cases *A*, *B*, and *D* the absolute slope of the supply curves against the price axis is larger than that of the demand curve (notice being taken of the sign of the slope).

In the unstable cases *C*, *E*, and *F* the price will fall. In this simple model we are thus able to infer its static equilibrium properties from the presence of instability in the system, but generally this is not possible.

3 / Marshall's excess price hypothesis

With this dynamic law of motion it is assumed that the market price always adjusts to clear the market. The demand price is therefore the market price. If the supply price is lower than the market (demand) price, minus tax, so that there is a net profit over and above taxation at the margin of production, producers are supposed to expand production and supply. The larger the excess of demand price over supply price, plus tax, the faster production will expand. Formally, this hypothesis can be written as:

[2.14] $$\frac{dq}{dt} = g(p^d - T - p^s) = g(p^x) \qquad g(0) = 0 \qquad g' > 0$$

where $p^x = p^d - T - p^s$ is the excess price; that is, the marginal net profit.

The law of motion, Equation 2.14, with the demand and supply functions from Model II (that is, Equations 2.1.II and 2.2.II) is a dynamic model corresponding to the static Model II. The equation $dq/dt = 0$ implies $p^d - T - p^s = 0$, which is the equilibrium condition in Equation 2.3.II. Figure 2.4 shows how this dynamic model works. The NE quadrant contains the demand and supply functions of Model II. In the SE quadrant, the time path of q from $q(0)$ is shown. Eventually it will approach the static equilibrium quantity $\bar{q}$. The stationary solution for the dynamic model is identical to the static equilibrium solution for Model II. Moreover, the dynamic model is stable as we have drawn the figure.

More generally, it can be proved[1] that with this dynamic hypothesis the market will be stable if $\alpha_2 - \alpha_1 > 0$; that is, $(1/a_2) - (1/a_1) > 0$. Stability thus requires that the slope of the supply curve against the quantity axis be larger than the slope of the demand curve. Thus, at identical demand and supply curves the market could very well be stable with Walras' excess

[1] The proof is the same as in the previous model, Note 1, p. 12, *mutatis mutandis*.

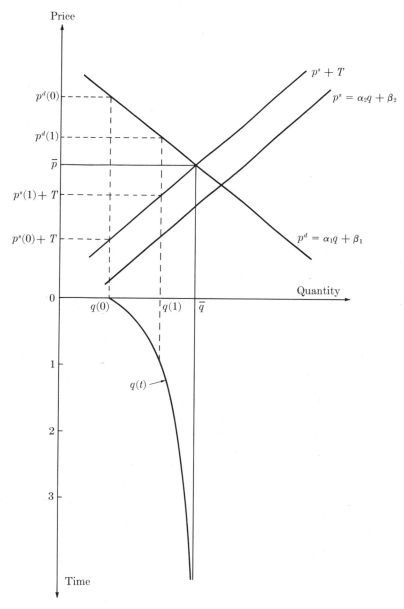

FIGURE 2.4

demand hypothesis, and unstable with Marshall's excess price hypothesis, and vice versa. The inequality $\alpha_2 - \alpha_1 > 0$ is simply the condition for $d\bar{q}/d\beta_1$ to be positive; that is, for a vertical shift of demand to lead to an increase in the quantity produced (Equation 2.7.II). Hence the conclusion: An increase in demand in Model II will lead to an increase in the equi-

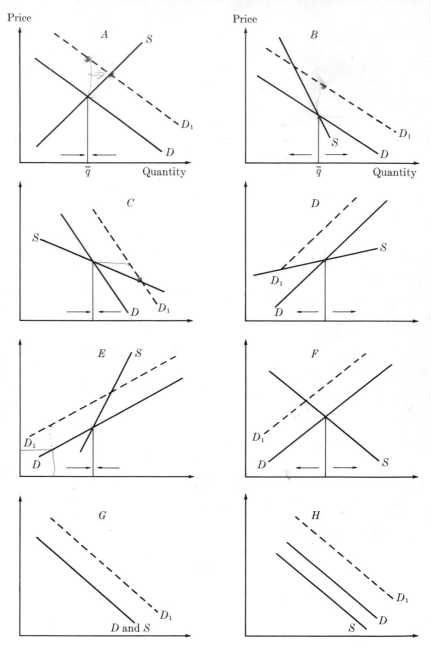

FIGURE 2.5

librium quantity if the system is stable, given Marshall's excess price hypothesis (Equation 2.14).

Figure 2.5 shows all the possible positions and slopes of the demand and supply curves. The cases are lettered as in Figure 2.3 for ease of comparison. The demand curve is shifted vertically from D to D_1 at a given supply curve S. Taxation is not shown, but S may be interpreted as including tax $p^s + T$. Stability is asserted through changing the quantity away from equilibrium. If the demand price exceeds (falls short of) the supply price, the quantity supplied increases (falls). The arrows show the tendency for the quantity supplied to change. If both arrows point toward the equilibrium quantity, the market is stable.

As before, we can dispose of cases G and H, where there is either no equilibrium or an infinite number of equilibria.

The cases A, C, and E are now stable. These are also the cases where a (vertical) shift in demand leads to an increase in the equilibrium quantity, and where the slope of the supply curve against the quantity axis is larger than the slope of the demand curve. Note that in this case stability does not permit any conclusions as to the effect of a vertical demand shift on the equilibrium price. Nor does it help us predict the effects of a horizontal demand shift, either on price or on quantity.

4 / The cobweb mechanism

Finally, we shall consider a second dynamic model corresponding to the static Model I. The mechanism in this model was suggested independently by Hanau, Ricci, and Tinbergen in 1930 to explain empirically observed, short-term cycles in agricultural markets. In the simplest case, producers are assumed to have static expectations; that is, they expect current prices to remain unchanged in the future. Production is thus planned on the assumption that sales will be made at last period's prices, and it reacts to price changes with a lag of one period. Therefore, we replace the supply equation in Model I, 2.2.I with:

[2.2']
$$q^s(t) = a_2[p(t-1) - T] + b_2$$

In the other two equations of Model I we date the variables but make no other changes.

[2.3']
$$q^d(t) = q^s(t)$$

[2.1']
$$q^d(t) = a_1 p(t) + b_1$$

The model works as follows: Given the price in period $t-1$, the quantity supplied in period t is determined by 2.2'. With the supply given, the demand is given, too, by Equation 2.3', and the market price adjusts according to Equation 2.1' to clear the market. The new market price determines next year's supply according to Equation 2.2'.

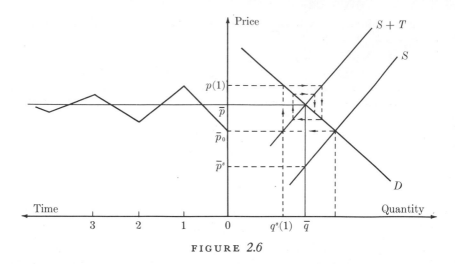

FIGURE 2.6

Turning now to the tax problem, we begin with the tax at zero and the market in equilibrium. Thus, we shall initially have $T = 0$ and

$$p(t) = p(t - 1) = \bar{p}(0)$$

as shown by the curves D and S in Figure 2.6. A tax T is then imposed on production, which causes a drop in next year's supply to $q^s(1)$, with the result that the price increases to $p(1)$. The process will continue (as the figure is drawn) until the new equilibrium point $(\bar{p}, \bar{q})$ is reached. However, given different slopes of the demand and supply curves, the new equilibrium may not be reached.

It can be proved[1] that the model consisting of Equations 2.1′, 2.2′, and 2.3′ is stable if the ratio between the slope against the price axis of the supply and the demand curves is numerically smaller than 1; that is, $|a_2/a_1| < 1$. But this was also the condition that caused the tax to fall more heavily on producers than consumers (Equation 2.12). We conclude, then, that the incidence of a specific tax on production will fall mainly on the producers if Model I is stable and is subject to the "cobweb mechanism."

In Figure 2.7, we demonstrate all possible cases except those without a solution or with an infinite number of solutions. The lettering of the cases

[1] Eliminating q^d and q^s from Equations 2.2′, 2.3′, and 2.1′, we obtain the first-order, linear difference equation $p(t) = (a_2/a_1)p(t - 1) + (b_2 - b_1 - a_2T)/a_1$, which has the solution (Allen, 1956, Chapter I)

$$p(t) = \bar{p} - [\bar{p} - p(0)]\left(\frac{a_2}{a_1}\right)^t$$

where $\bar{p}$ is the equilibrium solution of Model I, Equation 2.4.I, and $p(0)$ is the initial price. If $|a_2/a_1| < 1$, we have in the limit $p(t) = \bar{p}$ for $t \to \infty$.

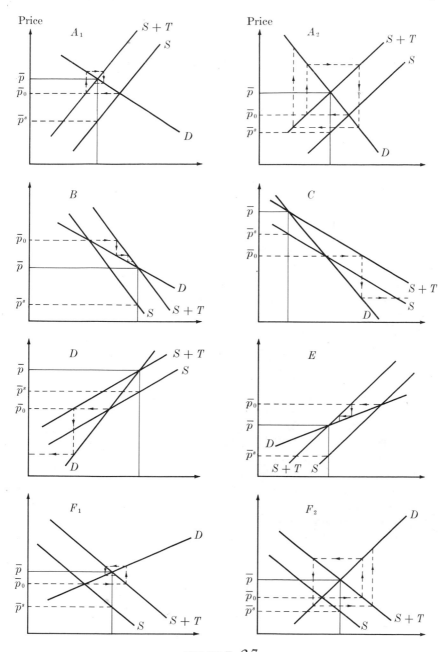

FIGURE 2.7

corresponds to those in Figures 2.3 and 2.5, except that cases A and F are now divided into subcases 1 and 2. In all cases we have indicated the path of adjustment following introduction of the production tax; this path shows whether the case is stable.

Of the eight cases, A_1, B, E, and F_1 are stable. It is obvious that these are the cases where the tax incidence is mainly on the producers; in cases B and E the new market price is even lower than the initial price. The figures also reveal that in these cases the slopes of the supply curves are numerically smaller (against the price axes) than the slopes of the demand curves.

Note that two borderline cases between A_1 and A_2 on the one side, and F_1 and F_2 on the other, are not included in Figure 2.7. If the slopes of the demand and supply curves have opposite signs, but are numerically equal, the model will exhibit steady fluctuations around the static equilibrium point, and thus neither converge nor diverge. These are also the limiting cases where the tax incidence on consumers and producers is equal.

5 / Some conclusions about the isolated, competitive market

We can conclude that the establishment of corresponding dynamic models helped us determine the signs of $d\bar{p}/db_1$, $d\bar{q}/d\beta_1$, and $T_d - T_s$. They did not enlighten us with regard to the signs of $d\bar{q}^d/db_1 = d\bar{q}^s/db_1$, $d\bar{p}^d/d\beta_1$, and $\bar{p} - p_0$. It may be that corresponding dynamic models will be discovered that will help us with these signs, as well. It should be remembered, however, that all these corresponding dynamic models cannot exist concurrently and simultaneously. If, for instance, we believe that Walras' excess demand hypothesis is relevant, and the market is stable, then we know the sign of $d\bar{p}/db_1$, but nothing more. Moreover, to be sure that a market really is stable, we must make certain that the stability conditions are fulfilled. Therefore we need knowledge about the slopes of the demand and supply functions, but if we had had this knowledge it would not have been necessary to introduce the dynamic considerations, since we could have calculated the effects directly. Despite its great theoretical importance, the practical usefulness of the correspondence principle is very limited.

It should be noted also that all our results are dependent upon the linearity assumptions made. The results may thus hold only in the small, that is, in an infinitesimal neighborhood of the static equilibrium position, which is another reason why their practical importance may not be too great.

Finally, we note that when we leave the realm of the simplest linear models the very concept of stability becomes more complicated. We shall not embark upon these problems here. A general treatment of them can be found in Samuelson (1947, Chapter X).

6 / Statics and dynamics of Keynesian systems

As the final example we shall consider a simple static Keynesian system where Y denotes national income (product), C consumption, and I investments. We have then:

[2.15]
$$C = c_1 Y + c_2$$
[2.16]
$$I = i_1 Y + i_2$$
[2.17]
$$Y = C + I$$

where Equation 2.15 is the consumption function, Equation 2.16 the investment function, and Equation 2.17 the equilibrium condition that the total supply of goods for final use Y be equal to the total demand for such goods $C + I$.

A standard problem in static Keynesian theory is to find the effect on equilibrium income of an increase in autonomous investment, i_2. Solving the equations, we obtain:

[2.18]
$$\bar{Y} = \frac{1}{1 - (i_1 + c_1)} (i_2 + c_2)$$

from which we obtain

[2.19]
$$\Delta \bar{Y} = \frac{1}{1 - (i_1 + c_1)} \Delta i_2$$

For the effect on income to be positive, the multiplier $1/[1 - (i_1 + c_1)]$ must be positive; that is,

[2.20]
$$1 - (i_1 + c_1) > 0 \quad \text{or} \quad i_1 + c_1 < 1$$

in other words, the sum of the marginal propensities to invest and consume must be smaller than 1. *A priori* there is nothing to guarantee that this requirement is fulfilled.

Let us then consider a corresponding dynamic model. We shall assume that producers have static expectations so that they always expect the sales of the next period to be equal to those of the current period. Production reacts thus to demand with a lag of one period. We have

[2.21]
$$Y(t) = C(t - 1) + I(t - 1)$$

or, inserting Equations 2.15 and 2.16,

[2.22]
$$Y(t) = (i_1 + c_1)Y(t - 1) + (i_2 + c_2)$$

That this is a dynamic model corresponding to the static model is seen immediately by considering the stationary state where $Y(t) = Y(t - 1)$. Equation 2.22 here reduces to Equation 2.18, which is the equilibrium solution to the static model. It can be proved[1] that this dynamic model is stable if

---

[1] The mathematical proof is the same as in the case of the cobweb mechanism. See Note 1, p. 18, *mutatis mutandis*.

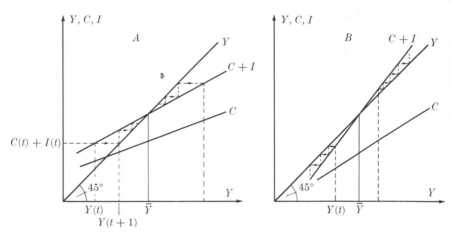

FIGURE 2.8

$i_1 + c_1 < 1$. This is the condition for the multiplier to be positive, however. It follows that the static multiplier is positive if the Keynesian system is stable, given Equation 2.21.

This result is also easily understood from Figure 2.8. In A we have a stable case. The income $Y(t)$ generates demand equal to $C(t) + I(t)$, which in the next period calls forth production $Y(t + 1) = C(t) + I(t)$ until, finally, income is equal to $\bar{Y}$, the static equilibrium solution. In this case, the slope of the demand curve $C + I$ is smaller than 1. In B we have the unstable case, where the slope of the demand curve exceeds 1: If any $Y(t)$ is different from the equilibrium income $\bar{Y}$ there will begin a movement away from the equilibrium. In A a vertical, upward shift of $C + I$ leads to an increase of the equilibrium income; that is, the multiplier is positive. In B the effect is the opposite.

References

ALLEN, R. G. D.: *Mathematical Economics*, Macmillan, London, 1956.

SAMUELSON, P. A.: *Foundations of Economic Analysis*, Harvard University Press, Cambridge, Mass., 1947.

The Walrasian system

3

Léon Walras was the founder of modern general equilibrium theory. He presented his first equation system in 1874 in *Éléments d'économie politique pure;* the final version appeared in the *Édition définitive* (1926; English translation, 1954). A similar equation system was presented by G. Cassel (1918). Here we shall consider the system set forth by Walras in Lesson 20 of the *Édition définitive* (1926, 1954). After the discussion of the original Walrasian system, we shall proceed to its more modern version.

1 / The demand for goods equations

We assume that the number of goods produced in the economy is n, with π_i and q_i being price and quantity, respectively, of the ith good. The number of productive services, labor, land, and so forth, is m, with Π_j and Q_j being the price and quantity, respectively, of the jth productive service. Following Walras, we assume that produced goods are not used as inputs in the production process. All the n goods produced are thus (consumer) goods for final use.

For each of the n goods we have a demand equation

[3.1] $\qquad q_i = q_i(\pi_1, \ldots, \pi_n; \Pi_1, \ldots, \Pi_m) \qquad i = 1, \ldots, n$

The demand for final use is thus supposed to depend upon all the prices for produced goods as well as upon the prices for factor services. Such demand equations may either be derived on the basis of consumers' utility maximization, assuming that all income from productive services accrue to consumers (which was Walras' method), or they may be postulated directly, which was Cassel's method. We could, without difficulty, allow produced goods to be used as intermediary inputs in the production process. Formally we could also include produced capital goods and allow some of prices π_i to represent prices of capital goods, and some of prices Π_j to represent prices for capital services. For the purpose of discussing some of the problems dealt with in the following chapters, we will suppose that all kinds of produced commodities are included in the system. Of course, simply to postulate that some of the outputs are capital goods and some of the inputs capital services does not constitute a real treatment of capital accumulation and the role of capital in production and price formation. Those problems will be taken up in Chapters 15 to 18; see in particular Chapter 17.

2 / The cost equations

For the system to be in equilibrium, the price of each produced good must be equal to its costs. To express the costs, we define the technical coefficients a_{ij} as the quantity of productive service i necessary for producing one unit of good number j. We can then write the n cost equations

$$[3.2] \qquad \pi_i = \sum_{j=1}^{m} a_{ji}\Pi_j \qquad i = 1, \ldots, n$$

which say that price must be equal to total average costs, including payments for entrepreneurial and capital services. Equation 3.2 is nothing but a set of long-term equilibrium conditions for produced goods; in equilibrium, demand price must be equal to supply price.

3 / Technical substitution

Cassel considered the technical coefficients defined in the previous section as constants, but Walras was fully aware that they depend on the choice of technique, which, assuming profit maximization, must depend upon the prices of productive services. We have thus mn equations expressing the possibilities of technical substitution

$$[3.3] \qquad a_{ij} = a_{ij}(\Pi_1, \ldots, \Pi_m) \qquad \begin{matrix} i = 1, \ldots, n \\ j = 1, \ldots, m \end{matrix}$$

The prices for produced goods do not enter into these functions. Since we have assumed that produced goods are not used as inputs, their prices do not play the same role as other input prices; they do not enter into the costs and thus do not directly affect the choice of technique. They may nonetheless do that, however; namely, via the demand for produced commodities. If the choice of technique were dependent upon the scale of production, the prices of produced goods might in this way appear as determinants of the technical coefficients. In line with neoclassical thinking, however, we have assumed constant returns to scale. Hence the form of Equation 3.3.

4 / The supply of productive services

It is natural to assume that the m supply equations for productive services have the same form as the demand equations for produced goods

[3.4] $Q_j = Q_j(\pi_1, \ldots, \pi_n; \Pi_1, \ldots, \Pi_m)$ $j = 1, \ldots, n$

Cassel postulated the equations to have this form, whereas Walras derived them through the same utility maximization that leads to the demand equations for consumer goods, Equation 3.1.

5 / Equilibrium conditions for productive services

Equilibrium is assumed to require that all productive services be exhausted in production, with no excess and no shortage, which means that demand and supply of services are equal. We have thus m equilibrium conditions

[3.5] $$Q_j = \sum_{i=1}^{n} a_{ji}q_i \qquad j = 1, \ldots, m$$

where on the left we have the supply of service j, and on the right the demand, or requirement, for this service, $a_{ji}q_i$ being the amount of service j required for production of the actual demand for commodity i.

Note the interesting difference between the equilibrium conditions for produced goods and those for productive services. For the former Walras used the condition of demand price equal to supply price (Marshall's condition), whereas for the service markets the condition is that the demand quantity be equal to the supply quantity. In competitive equilibrium (at the point where the demand and supply curves cross each other) it does not matter which condition we use. If one is fulfilled, the other is also fulfilled. When we study the forces that work upon the system, however, the way we view the equilibrium conditions makes all the difference. It appears that the under-lying dynamic assumptions are that in the markets for productive services the law of motion is Walras' excess demand hypothesis, while in the markets for produced goods Marshall's excess price hypothesis rules (Dorfman, Samuelson, and Solow, 1958, p. 369). This is obviously a rather special assumption, which deprives the general equilibrium system of some of its alleged generality.

6 / The *numéraire*

Walras chose to measure prices in a special way that is important to the interpretation of the demand and supply equations as written above. Gen-erally, a "price" can be defined as an exchange relationship between two goods, one of which is chosen as a standard of value, a *numéraire*. Usually this standard of value is money, and the price of a commodity or service is simply the number of units of money exchanged for one unit of the commodity or service in question. Walras, however, expressed the prices in terms of an arbitrarily chosen commodity; let us say commodity n. The price of a particular commodity or service (for example commodity i), is then defined as the number of units of commodity n exchanged for one unit of commodity i. Commodity n is then the *numéraire*. The price of the *numéraire* commodity in terms of itself is, of course, equal to 1, so that we have:

[3.6] $$\pi_n = 1$$

All the prices entering the demand Equations 3.1, the supply Equations 3.4, and the expressions for technical substitution in Equations 3.3 (that is, π_i and Π_j) are thus prices in terms of the *numéraire*, *not* in terms of money. The relationship between *numéraire* prices and money prices is very simple. Let $p_i, i = 1, \ldots , n$, and $P_j, j = 1, \ldots , m$ be the money prices of produced commodities and productive services, respectively. Let us then assume that iron has been chosen as the *numéraire* commodity and that the money price of wheat is p_w, and that of iron is p_n. It follows that the number of units of iron that can be obtained on the market for one unit of wheat must be p_w/p_n, so that $\pi_w = p_w/p_n$. In other words, the *numéraire* prices entering the demand and supply functions are relative money prices; the assumption is that demand and supply and the choice of technique depend on relative money prices. This, of course, is in accord with ordinary demand and supply theory. We shall return to this point in Chapter 6.

7 / Number of unknowns and equations

Walras' basic general equilibrium system consists of Equations 3.1 to 3.6. We have here n prices π_i of produced goods, n quantities q_i of produced goods, m prices Π_j, and m quantities Q_j of productive services, and nm technical coefficients a_{ij}, or altogether $2n + 2m + nm$ unknowns. We have n Equations 3.1, n Equations 3.2, nm Equations 3.3, m Equations 3.4, m Equations 3.5, and 1 Equation 3.6, or altogether $2n + 2m + nm + 1$ equations. We have so far one more equation than we have unknowns.

Walras solved this problem by showing that one of the equations, arbitrarily chosen, can be deduced from the rest of the system. This means that one of the equations contains no information that is not contained in the rest of the system, and that the number of *independent* equations is only $2n + 2m + nm$. Awareness of the dependency of one of the equations upon the others is crucial to understanding certain problems in macroeconomics. It permits us, for instance, to express certain macro relations in alternative, but equivalent, ways.

To prove the dependency, it can be shown that for the system as a whole total planned expenditure for produced goods must be equal to total income from planned sales of productive services

[3.7] $$\sum_{i=1}^{n} q_i \pi_i \equiv \sum_{j=i}^{m} Q_j \Pi_j$$

identically in all prices of goods and services.[1] Why does this expression hold true? Behind it we find the budget restrictions under which economic subjects are assumed to act. Equation 3.7 is arrived at through a summation of all individual budget restrictions. Assume that there are K individual economic subjects in the economy, and that the quantities related to individual subject h are indicated by a prefix. If for individual h we have the budget restriction

[3.8] $$\sum_{i=1}^{n} {}_h q_i \pi_i \equiv \sum_{j=1}^{m} {}_h Q_j \Pi_j$$

summation over all K individuals should give us Equation 3.7. Equation 3.8 shows that the total value of an individual's purchases of produced goods, no matter what the prices, is always equal to the total value of his sales of productive services. The aggregated budget restriction is called *Walras' law*. But for Equation 3.7 to be true we must not only assume that all individuals respect their budget restriction (that is, that Walras' law holds true); we must also assume that the individual does not change his cash holdings. Hoarding and dishoarding of money are thus ruled out by assumption. When this additional assumption is made the aggregated budget restriction is called Say's law.[2] Here we disregard credit. Note that we assume that all individuals are faced with the same set of prices, not necessarily the equilibrium prices.

Given Equation 3.7 it follows, for example, that

[3.9] $$q_n \equiv \sum_{j=1}^{m} Q_j \Pi_j - \sum_{i=1}^{n-1} q_i \pi_i$$

In other words, if we know the supply functions Q_j, $j = 1, \ldots, m$, and the demand functions q_i, $i = 1, \ldots, n - 1$, then we know also the demand

---

[1] Note the difference between an identity ($\equiv$) and an equality ($=$).

$$(a + b)^2 \equiv a^2 + 2ab + b^2$$

is an identity; it holds true for all possible values of a and b. On the other hand, $a = 3 + 2b$ is an equality (equation). It holds true only for certain values of a and b; namely, those corresponding to the coordinates of all the points on a certain straight line. Accordingly, when we use an identity sign in Equation 3.7 and add the words "identically in all prices of goods and services," it means that Equation 3.7 holds true not only for the set of equilibrium prices, but for any set of (non-negative) prices of goods and services.

[2] The terms "Walras' law" and "Say's law" appear in the literature with many different meanings. There exist no generally accepted standard definitions. With the definitions adopted here, Say's law is simply a special case of Walras' law.

function q_n. We can disregard equation $q_n = q_n(\pi_1, \ldots, \pi_n; \Pi_1, \ldots, \Pi_m)$ and yet solve the system. The same reasoning applies to any other demand or supply function in the system.

It goes without saying that in equilibrium, also, total expenditures for produced goods must equal the total income from sales of productive services. To assert this, multiply both sides of Equation 3.2 by q_i and sum all the n expressions thus obtained. Multiply thereafter Equation 3.5 on both sides by Π_j and add all these m expressions. In this way we obtain two equations, both of which have the nm terms $q_i a_{ji} \Pi_j$ on the right, and on the left have the same expressions that we find on the left and right, respectively, of Equation 3.7. This operation does not prove the *identity* of Equation 3.7, however; it only reassures us that the equilibrium system actually fulfills this specification.

8 / Money prices, the price level, and the quantity theory of money

Hitherto we have expressed all prices in terms of the *numéraire*. In solving the system of Equations 3.1 to 3.6, which is often called the "real part" of the general equilibrium system, we can, at most, obtain information about the equilibrium prices in terms of the *numéraire;* that is, the relative money prices. We derive no information about the prices in terms of money. As Cassel (1938, p. 171) very ably stated: The general equilibrium system determines the relative money prices, while the absolute money prices are determined "only up to a multiplicative factor." To determine the absolute money prices we need an additional equation, the exchange equation for money; for the neoclassicists an important task of the theory of money was to determine the multiplicative factor.

The money price of the *numéraire* commodity is p_n. The other money prices may be expressed as $p_n\pi_1, \ldots, p_n\pi_{n-1}$, and $p_n\Pi_1, \ldots, p_n\Pi_m$. In other words, the multiplicative factor is p_n. Our problem is to determine p_n. For this purpose we can use either Fisher's equation of exchange $MV = PT$, where M stands for quantity of money, V velocity, P price level, and T turnover, or the Cambridge equation $M = kY$, where Y is the total money income and k is a constant, the Cambridge k, being the inverted value of the income velocity of money (Fisher, 1918, Chapter II; Keynes, 1923, Chapter III).

Fisher's equation of exchange may be written

$$[3.10] \qquad MV = \sum_{i=1}^{n} p_i q_i + \sum_{j=1}^{m} P_j Q_j = p_n \left(\sum_{i=1}^{n} \pi_i q_i + \sum_{j=1}^{m} \Pi_j Q_j \right)$$

which, given M and V, and, from the "real part" of the general equilibrium system, π_i, q_i, Π_j, and Q_j, suffices to determine p_n. Given the *numéraire* prices, all other money prices can then be calculated.

The Cambridge equation leads to

[3.11] $$M = kY = kp_n \sum_{j=1}^{m} \Pi_j Q_j$$

which, given M, k, Π_j, and Q_j, also suffices to determine p_n.

Whether we use the Fisher equation or the Cambridge equation, the same result follows. A change in the quantity of money implies a proportional change in p_n and, hence, in all money prices; but all "real" prices (that is, the prices in terms of the *numéraire*) and all quantities in demand and supply are unchanged. This result is sometimes considered the essence of the quantity theory of money.

There are some problems inherent in this way of handling the determination of the price level. The reader may have already asked himself how it is possible for the quantity of money to change if there is no hoarding or dishoarding. We shall return to these problems in Chapter 5.

9 / Walras' equations, free goods, and goods not produced

The Walrasian system, as presented now, is deficient in several respects. We have already mentioned that it does not discuss problems related to capital and credit, and its way of handling money is dubious, as we shall see later. Here we shall deal with one other shortcoming of the system; namely, that it works with scarce goods and services, the number of which is given *a priori*. The system cannot tell us which services are scarce and have a price, and which services are free. Neither does it tell us which goods will actually be taken up for production and which goods will not be produced. Free services and goods not produced do not appear anywhere. It is certainly an important economic problem to determine which services will be free and which goods will be produced. Consider such questions as whether there is surplus labor in an underdeveloped country, or whether such a country should produce capital goods. Or, is water a free service of nature? If not, will it be produced? This point was first made by Zeuthen (1932) and has become a central problem in modern programming analysis. From a purely formal point of view it is easy to remedy this deficiency (see, for instance, Dorfman, Samuelson, and Solow, 1958, Chapter 13-2).

We assume that n goods are known, which may or may not actually be produced and that there exist m productive services, which may or may not prove to be scarce. Demand Equations 3.1, supply Equations 3.4, and the equations for technical substitution are not affected by this. But the equilibrium conditions must be stated differently.

Cost Equations 3.2 must now be written

[3.2'] $$\pi_i \leqq \sum_{j=1}^{m} a_{ji} \Pi_j \qquad i = 1, \ldots, n$$

We are thus allowing for the possibility that in equilibrium there may be goods for which the demand price will not be sufficient to cover the costs. Such goods can only be produced at a loss, and will therefore not be produced at all. In all cases where the inequality sign holds, the quantity produced will be zero.

Similarly, the equilibrium conditions for productive services must be written

$$[3.5'] \qquad Q_j \geqq \sum_{i=1}^{n} a_{ji} q_i \qquad j = 1, \ldots, m$$

Here we allow for the possibility that a productive service may not be used up entirely. In that case it cannot have a positive price and it will be a free good. The inequality sign will then hold and the price of the service will be zero.

References

CASSEL, G.: *Theoretische Sozialökonomie*, Winter, Leipzig, 1918. English Edition, *The Theory of Social Economy*, Harcourt, Brace, New York, 1924. Final, second Swedish Edition, *Teoretisk Socialekonomi*, Kooperativa Förbundets Bokförlag, Stockholm, 1938.

DORFMAN, R., P. A. SAMUELSON, and R. SOLOW: *Linear Programming and Economic Analysis*, McGraw-Hill, New York, 1958.

FISHER, I.: *The Purchasing Power of Money*, Macmillan, New York, 1918.

KEYNES, J. M.: *A Tract on Monetary Reform*, Macmillan, London, 1923.

WALRAS, L.: *Éléments d'économie politique pure*, Édition définitive, R. Pichon, Paris, 1926. English Edition, *Elements of Pure Economics*, George Allen and Unwin, London, 1954.

ZEUTHEN, F.: "Das Prinzip der Knappheit, technische Kombination und ökonomische Qualität," *Zeitschrift für Nationalökonomie*, vol. 4, October, 1932.

A simplified
Walrasian system

4

The original Walrasian system of general equilibrium presented in the last chapter has helped modern economic theory to expand in several directions. Discussions of the existence of solutions to general equilibrium systems began with Walras' formulation of the system. Input-output analysis is closely connected to the Walrasian technical coefficients, and modern, so-called "neoclassical" capital and growth theories are working along the same line. For certain problems another, simplified version of the general equilibrium system has proved more useful. The difference between the two versions of the system is mainly that in the latter the production process is not explicitly analyzed. Supplies of goods may even be considered given exogenously; in the latter case we have a "pure exchange system." The simplified, or generalized, system was first suggested by J. R. Hicks (1939, Mathematical Appendix, Chapters 13 and 21), and has proved particularly useful in discussions of stability and matters related to money and credit.

1 / The simplified demand and supply system

We assume here that there are n goods in the economy. We do not specify the nature of these goods; they may be produced goods or nonproduced factor services. Prices are assumed to be expressed in terms of a *numéraire*. Again, let the *numéraire* be good number n. We then have $n - 1$ prices π_1 to π_{n-1}, the *numéraire* price of the *numéraire* itself being 1. The quantities of the goods are denoted q_1 to q_n, and we distinguish explicitly between quantity in demand q_i^d and quantity in supply q_i^s.

Then we simply write n demand equations

[4.1] $$q_i^d = q_i^d(\pi_1, \ldots, \pi_{n-1}) \qquad i = 1, \ldots, n$$

n supply equations

[4.2] $$q_i{}^s = q_i{}^s(\pi_1, \ldots, \pi_{n-1}) \qquad i = 1, \ldots, n$$

and n equilibrium conditions

[4.3] $$q_i{}^d = q_i{}^s \qquad i = 1, \ldots, n$$

This is the simplified Walrasian system.

2 / The excess demand system

Our simplified system may be simplified even further. Define the excess demand $q_i{}^x$ for good number i as the difference between the quantity in demand and the quantity in supply at given prices; that is, $q_i{}^x = q_i{}^d - q_i{}^s$. The excess demand for a good may, of course, be negative; in that case it is convenient to refer to excess supply. Since both demand and supply are functions of all prices, the same must hold true for excess demand. The condition for equilibrium in a particular market is obviously that the excess demand be zero. We arrive at the excess demand system as follows:

[4.4] $$q_i{}^x(\pi_1, \ldots, \pi_{n-1}) = 0 \qquad i = 1, \ldots, n$$

3 / Number of unknowns and equations

In the system shown in Equations 4.1, 4.2, and 4.3 we find $3n - 1$ unknowns; namely, n quantities in demand, n quantities in supply, $n - 1$ *numéraire* prices, and $3n$ equations. The excess demand system set forth in Equation 3.4 has $n - 1$ unknowns, the prices, and n equations. The situation is the same, then, as in the original Walrasian system, and we must show that one of the equations follows from the rest. To do that it is necessary to return again to the individual budget restrictions and form from them the aggregate budget restriction; that is, Walras' law. We maintain also the special assumption, Say's law, referred to in Chapter 3, which holds that whatever people earn through sales of commodities and services they are assumed to spend on commodities and services, no matter what the prices are. This means that for each individual economic subject, the total value of all his supplies of commodities and services equals the value of his total demand for commodities and services. We have then, identically in the prices, and, recalling that $\pi_n = 1$,

[4.5] $$\sum_{i=1}^{n} \pi_i q_i{}^s \equiv \sum_{i=1}^{n} \pi_i q_i{}^d$$

which implies that if we know all demand and supply functions except one, we are able to write the last one, too. Moreover, we have

[4.6]
$$\sum_{i=1}^{n} \pi_i q_i^x \equiv 0$$

One excess demand function can thus be calculated from the rest. We have, for instance,

[4.7]
$$q_n^x(\pi_1, \ldots, \pi_{n-1}) \equiv \sum_{i=1}^{n-1} \pi_i q_i^x(\pi_1, \ldots, \pi_{n-1})$$

It follows also that if all markets except one are in equilibrium, the last one must also be in equilibrium. From Equation 4.6 it is seen that if $q_i^x = 0$ for, say, $i = 1, \ldots, n - 1$, then $q_n^x = 0$. In other words, we can select $n - 1$ markets and use their equilibrium conditions to solve the equilibrium prices. We do not need to specify the last market.

The systems set forth in Equations 4.1, 4.2, 4.3, and 4.4 can, at best, be solved for the prices expressed in terms of the *numéraire;* that is, in terms of the relative money prices. To determine the absolute money prices, we must proceed the way we did with the original Walrasian system.

4 / A fundamental problem in general equilibrium theory

Increasing generality must be paid for by increasing abstraction and decreasing concreteness. Looking at a system such as shown in Equation 4.4, we are justified in asking if the generality has not been paid for by an almost complete emptiness. Can any meaningful conclusions be deduced from such a general system? The system states that in equilibrium all excess demands are zero. If this were the only feature of the system that could be verified or refuted empirically, it would be rather uninteresting. With the addition of further specification, however, important questions can be asked and answered. What is needed, for instance, is a specification of the dynamic forces behind the state of equilibrium. Samuelson has shown, as an application of his correspondence principle, that such a specification will enable us to say something about the effects on the equilibrium of a change in demand or supply.

Consider the simplified excess demand system set forth in Equation 4.4, which for the sake of the dynamization we shall write in terms of relative money prices rather than *numéraire* prices:

[4.4']
$$q_i^x\left(\frac{p_1}{p_n}, \ldots, \frac{p_{n-1}}{p_n}\right) = 0 \qquad i = 1, \ldots, n$$

By virtue of Say's law, one of the equations follows from the rest and could be deleted. We shall assume, then, that Walras' excess demand hypothesis for money-price changes[1] (Chapter 2, Section 2) holds for all markets.

[4.8] $\dfrac{dp_i}{dt} = f_i(q_i{}^x)$ $f_i(0) = 0$ $f_i' > 0$ $i = 1, \ldots, n$

Since $q_i{}^x$ is a function of all prices, we have in 4.8 a system of n differential equations in p_1 to p_n. If we set $dp_i/dt = 0$, then 4.8 reduces to 4.4. This means that 4.8 is a dynamic model corresponding to the static model 4.4. P. A. Samuelson (1941, 1947) and Lange (1944) showed that the conditions required for the system in Equation 4.8 to be stable (in the small) implies fulfillment of the conditions for an increase in the excess demand (that is, an increase in demand or a fall in supply) for a particular good to result in an increase in the equilibrium price of that good. This is an extension of the results obtained for the isolated market (Chapter 2, Section 2). It proves that if the general equilibrium system is governed by Walras' excess demand hypothesis for price changes, we can also be sure that an increase in demand for (or a decrease in supply of) a commodity, even considering all indirect repercussions throughout the system, will be followed by an increase in the price of that commodity. Elementary though it is, this proposition is fundamental to economic analysis.

To make this proposition really useful we will go one step further. It is fine to know that *if* the general equilibrium system is stable in this sense, then an increase in demand will lead to an increase in price. We would also like to know, however, whether the system actually *is* stable, which requires an answer to the problem of whether solutions to the system exist. If an equilibrium solution does not exist, we cannot reasonably ask for the effects of a change in demand on the equilibrium prices. Moreover, the system is only stable if it tends to move toward an equilibrium.

The problem of the existence of a solution and stability has been studied in detail by a number of authors, and various conditions sufficient for existence and stability have been discovered. Thus it has been proved that if, *inter alia*, all individual excess demand functions are continuous and no individual is saturated (so that his marginal utility for all goods is zero), a competitive equilibrium solution will exist (Wald, 1951; Arrow and Debreu, 1954;

---

[1] We could also have worked on the following specification of Walras' excess demand hypothesis

$$\frac{d\pi_i}{dt} = g_i(q_i{}^x) \qquad g(0) = 0 \qquad g_i' > 0 \qquad i = 1, \ldots, n-1$$

$d\pi_n/dt = 0$. This is a different hypothesis, unless we add the assumption that $q_n{}^x = 0$ identically in the *numéraire* prices. To add such an assumption, however, would impose a kind of "super Say's law" upon the system, and we can find no economic justification for doing that. Fortunately, for our purpose it does not matter which specification we use. See K. Arrow, H. Block, and L. Hurwicz (1959).

Debreu, 1959; et al.). In relation to processes of adaptation it may also be necessary to assume single-valued functions. There is probably little reason to quarrel with the assumptions about nonsaturation. But continuity is not an obvious assumption, and single-valued excess demand functions may rule out such phenomena as backward-bending supply curves for labor. Moreover, the existence of a solution does not imply stability. The assumption of so-called "gross substitutability" is, however, sufficient to accomplish this. We say that commodities i and j are (strong) gross substitutes if an increase in the price of commodity i leads to an increase in the demand for commodity j. (Note that gross substitution is different from Hicks' income-compensated substitution effect.) Gross substitutability is said to prevail in the system if all $\partial q_i^x / \partial p_j > 0$ for all $i \neq j$. Under this assumption our excess demand system will actually have a unique equilibrium solution around which the system is stable in the large (F. Hahn, 1958). This condition is not very likely to be fulfilled in reality, however. It conflicts with complementarities, which we know are quite frequent. Other sufficient conditions have been presented, but from an empirical viewpoint they do not appear more convincing than those just discussed. For a general survey of the contributions in this field, see T. Negishi (1962).

No set of reasonably realistic, sufficient conditions for stability of the general equilibrium system has ever been presented; nonetheless, some economists are content to assume that the system is stable on the basis of casual observations of the behavior of modern economies, asserting that since they appear stable, we can safely assume that the general equilibrium system is stable. Such observations do not prove anything, of course, and there is reason to warn against this kind of reasoning. Not only do modern economies actually explode occasionally, in hyperinflations, for example, but the definitions of stability say nothing about how quickly an economic system is supposed to approach equilibrium or move away from it, assuming that an equilibrium does exist. An economy that appears to be stable may be slowly on its way toward the abyss. After all, our sun is exploding! Moreover, such arguments may not be altogether free from wishful thinking. Political conviction about the superiority or inferiority of the capitalist economies may color judgments of the possible stability or instability of the general equilibrium system and the relevance of this system to capitalist economies.

5 / A two-commodity illustration

It may be useful to demonstrate how the above conditions imply a unique solution and lead to stability, and how repercussions work their way through a general equilibrium system in the case of a simple two-commodity world.

We consider thus an economy with two commodities and two markets.

The demand equations are

[4.9] $$q_1{}^d = a_{11} + a_{12}\frac{p_2}{p_1}$$

[4.10] $$q_2{}^d = a_{21} + a_{22}\frac{p_1}{p_2}$$

The supply equations are

[4.11] $$q_1{}^s = \bar{q}_1$$
[4.12] $$q_2{}^s = \bar{q}_2$$

which means that the supplies are given constants $\bar{q}_i$. The equilibrium conditions, finally, are

[4.13] $$q_1{}^d = q_1{}^s$$
[4.14] $$q_2{}^d = q_2{}^s$$

We have written the demand functions as dependent upon the relative money prices. If we had used commodity 2 as the *numéraire*, the *numéraire* price of commodity 1 would have been $\pi_1 = p_1/p_2$; for the other commodity we would, of course, have $\pi_2 = p_2/p_2 = 1$. Counting the relative price as one unknown, the system has six equations and five unknowns. Consequently, if we consider the first market and solve Equations 4.9, 4.11, and 4.13 for the relative price, we find

[4.15] $$\frac{p_1}{p_2} = \frac{a_{12}}{\bar{q}_1 - a_{11}}$$

If we look at Equations 4.10, 4.12, and 4.14, however, we find

[4.16] $$\frac{p_1}{p_2} = \frac{\bar{q}_2 - a_{21}}{a_{22}}$$

For a unique, positive solution to exist we must therefore have not only $\bar{q}_1 - a_{11} \neq 0$ and $a_{22} \neq 0$, but also

[4.17] $$\frac{\bar{q}_2 - a_{21}}{a_{22}} = \frac{a_{12}}{\bar{q}_1 - a_{11}} > 0$$

The equality in Equation 4.17, however, is fulfilled by virtue of Walras' law,

[4.18] $$p_1q_1{}^d + p_2q_2{}^d \equiv p_1\bar{q}_1 + p_2\bar{q}_2$$

from which we obtain (inserting Equation 4.10)

[4.19] $$q_1{}^d \equiv (\bar{q}_1 - a_{22}) + (\bar{q}_2 - a_{21})\frac{p_2}{p_1}$$

Comparison with Equation 4.9 shows that we must have $a_{11} = \bar{q}_1 - a_{22}$, that is, $a_{22} = \bar{q}_1 - a_{11}$, and $a_{12} = \bar{q}_2 - a_{21}$. This means, however, that the equality in Equation 4.17 is satisfied. If in addition we assume (strong)

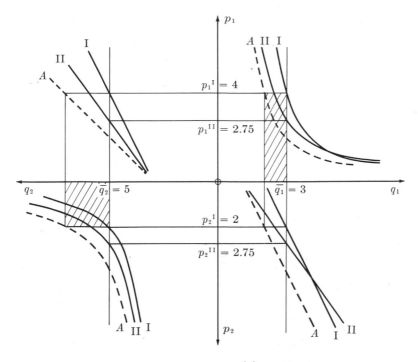

FIGURE *4.1*

gross substitutability (that is, $a_{12} > 0$ and $a_{22} > 0$) it is obvious that the inequality is also fulfilled. Walras' law and gross substitutability thus secure a unique, positive solution to our system.

Let us then consider a change in demand for commodity 1, which necessarily implies a corresponding change in demand for commodity 2 (at given supplies). The implication follows because we have assumed that Say's law holds. It is instructive to follow the process in geometrical terms instead of proceeding algebraically.

In Figure 4.1 we measure p_1 along the ordinate in the positive direction, and p_2 in the negative direction. Along the abscissa we measure q_1 in the positive direction and q_2 in the negative direction. The two vertical lines $q_1 = \bar{q}_1 = 3$ and $q_2 = \bar{q}_2 = 5$ are the supply curves, supply being independent of the prices. In the initial situation we assume that the constants of the system have the values $a_{21} = 3$ and $a_{22} = 1$. We are forced (by Say's law) to assume that $a_{11} = 2$ and $a_{12} = 2$. The relative equilibrium price is $p_1/p_2 = 2$. Assuming further that $MV = 22$ (the Fisher equation), it follows that in the initial equilibrium $p_1 = 4$ and $p_2 = 2$. In the NE quadrant we have shown the demand curve for commodity 1, assuming the price of commodity 2 to be fixed at its equilibrium value $p_2 = 2$. In the SW quadrant we have drawn the corresponding demand curve for commodity 2, assuming the price of commodity 1 to be fixed at its equilibrium value $p_1 = 4$. In the SE and NW quadrants we have drawn what could be called the cross-demand curves (recall the concept of cross-elasticity). In the SE quadrant we find demand for commodity 1 as a function of the price of commodity 2, the price of commodity 1 being fixed at its equilibrium level $p_1 = 4$. In the NW quadrant, finally, we have the cross-demand curve for commodity 2; that is, the demand for commodity 2 as a function of the price of commodity 1, the price of commodity 2 being fixed at its equilibrium level $p_2 = 2$. The assumption of gross substitutability means that the two cross-demand curves must have positive slopes toward the price axes; that is, positive cross-elasticities. The implication is that the ordinary demand curves must have negative slopes. The four demand curves belonging to the initial situation are marked "I." Inspection shows that at the equilibrium prices, demand equals supply in all four quadrants. The equilibrium price of commodity 1, $p_1 = 4$, secures equality between demand and supply for both commodities 1 and 2, given that the price of commodity 2 is at its equilibrium level $p_2 = 2$ (see the NE and NW quadrants). The equilibrium price of commodity 2 secures equality of demand and supply of both commodities 1 and 2, given that the price of commodity 1 is at its equilibrium level (see the SE and SW quadrants).

We assume, then, that there is a shift in demand so that the demand for commodity 2 increases and the demand for commodity 1 falls. This shift can occur in many different ways. We shall assume that a_{22} changes value from 1 to 2, implying that a_{11} changes from 2 to 1. With $MV = 22$ unchanged, the new equilibrium prices become $p_1 = p_2 = 2.75$. The price of commodity 1 has thus fallen in relation to the price of commodity 2. Moreover, because we keep the value of MV unchanged, the absolute price of commodity 1 falls and the absolute money price of commodity 2 increases. This is exactly what we expect from a system with gross substitutability. The four curves marked "II" are the demand curves after the shift in demand, with "the other price" fixed at its new equilibrium level.

We are also interested in how the change from situation I to II takes place. For that purpose we consider situation A, wherein the change in the demand relations has occurred, but the prices are unchanged at the initial equilibrium values. We are led then to the four demand curves marked "A." We note that both demand curves A for commodity 1 are to the left of the demand curves II (the NE and SE quadrants), and that both demand curves A for commodity 2 (the NW and SW quadrants) are to the right of demand curves II (seen from the price axes). At the old equilibrium prices $p_1 = 4$ and $p_2 = 2$, then, we have excess supply for commodity 1 and excess demand for commodity 2. By Say's law their values are equal in size (see the shaded areas in Figure 4.1).

This is the starting point for the dynamic process. According to Walras' excess demand hypothesis for price changes, p_1 will now begin to fall and p_2

will begin to rise. Since p_2 tends to rise, the A curve in the NE quadrant must tend to move to the right, a shift that follows from the assumption of gross substitutability. An increase in p_2 leads to a larger demand for commodity 1 at any given price p_1. Moreover, p_1 tends to fall. We are certain, therefore, that the excess supply for commodity 1 must be falling; the same is true for the value of the excess supply. Similar reasoning applies to the demand curve A for commodity 2 in the SW quadrant. Since p_1 is falling, the assumption of gross substitutability guarantees us that the curve A there, seen from the price axis, is moving to the left. In addition, the price p_2 is higher; therefore, the excess demand for commodity 2 must be falling. Because the value of the excess supply for commodity 1 is falling, the value of the excess demand for commodity 2 must also be falling. Since there remains an excess supply for commodity 1, p_1 will continue to fall, but more slowly, because the excess supply is smaller. Similarly, p_2 will continue to increase, albeit more slowly. In this way p_1 and p_2 will move toward the new equilibrium position as all the A curves move toward II. The fact that the value of the excess supply for commodity 1 must always be equal to the value of the excess demand for commodity 2 ensures that excess supply and excess demand must vanish together, and that the two markets will thus reach their equilibrium at the same time.

References

ARROW, K. J., H. D. BLOCK, and L. HURWICZ: "On the Stability of the Competitive Equilibrium, II," *Econometrica*, vol. 27, no. 1, January, 1959.

ARROW, K. J., and G. DEBREU: "Existence of an Equilibrium for a Competitive Economy," *Econometrica*, vol. 22, no. 3, July, 1954.

DEBREU, G.: *Theory of Value*, Cowles Foundation Monograph No. 17, John Wiley & Sons, New York, 1959.

HAHN, F. H.: "Gross Substitutes and the Dynamic Stability of General Equilibrium," *Econometrica*, vol. 26, no. 1, January, 1958.

HICKS, J. R.: *Value and Capital*, Clarendon Press, Oxford, 1939.

LANGE, O.: *Price Flexibility and Employment*, appendix, Principia Press, Bloomington, Ind., 1944.

NEGISHI, T.: "A Note on the Stability of an Economy Where All Goods Are Gross Substitutes," *Econometrica*, vol. 26, no. 3, July, 1958.

—: "The Stability of a Competitive Economy: A Survey Article," *Econometrica*, vol. 30, no. 4, October, 1962.

SAMUELSON, P. A.: "The Stability of Equilibrium: Comparative Statics and Dynamics," *Econometrica*, vol. 9, no. 1, January, 1941.

—: *Foundations of Economic Analysis*, Harvard University Press, Cambridge, Mass., 1947.

WALD, A.: "On Some Systems of Equations of Mathematical Economics," *Econometrica*, vol. 19, no. 4, October, 1951.

Money and
the Walrasian system

5

Money was introduced in the original Walrasian system to permit us to work with and determine money prices. The introduction of money took place through appending an exchange equation to the system. No other changes were thought necessary. In connection with the simplified Walrasian systems we constructed a numerical example which, among other things, illustrated how money prices are determined in such a system by assuming a given quantity and velocity of money. In so doing we encountered no logical problems. Nevertheless, the system has been under heavy criticism for the way it treats money. J. R. Hicks (1935) was probably the first critic who blamed neoclassical theory for not integrating money properly into the general equilibrium system. Hicks' attack started a long debate about the role of money and the so-called "dichotomy" of neoclassical theory. In this chapter we shall briefly consider the main issues.

1 / The dichotomy of the Walrasian system
and the neutrality of money

We have already noticed the peculiar logical or mathematical structure of the Walrasian system. It consists of two parts of which the "real part," the demand and supply equations and equilibrium conditions for commodities and services, suffices to determine the *numéraire* prices and the quantities bought and sold. The "monetary part," the equation of exchange, serves to determine a multiplicative factor, the money price of the *numéraire* commodity, by means of which the absolute money prices thereafter can be calculated. This decomposition of the system is called the "dichotomy." Money does not appear at all in the real part of the system, which is invariant to changes in the quantity of money. In this sense money is neutral with respect to relative prices and quantities bought and sold.

The notion of neutrality of money was deeply rooted in neoclassical thinking. Money was considered a "veil" which had to be removed before the real economy, relative prices and quantities in demand and supply, could be studied and explained. The dichotomization of the general equilibrium system reflects this basic philosophy. The modern criticism argues that money is more than a "veil," that it has a direct influence on demand and supply of commodities and services, and that the neoclassical dichotomy cannot be upheld; the neutrality of money is thereby also brought in doubt.

There are several problems involved here, and they should not be confused. That the system "suffers" from a dichotomy is not by itself a deficiency. Formally, the existence of a dichotomy simply means that the system is recursive, or decomposable. From various points of view this is actually an advantage; it facilitates both analysis and computation. Some critics seem to have felt that it contradicts one of the basic ideas of economic theory: the general interdependence of all economic phenomena, the idea that "everything depends upon everything else." This idea, however, is little more than an aesthetic viewpoint on the verge of metaphysics, and cannot be considered an argument of any weight. There is no ultimate philosophical or economic principle which says that everything must depend upon everything else. Rather than being taken as a dictum, this well-known phrase should only be considered a practical reminder to the student that he should expect economic phenomena to be fairly complex.

Moreover, the invariance of the real part of the system with respect to changes in the quantity of money should not be taken to mean that money has no importance whatsoever for relative prices and quantities in demand and supply. The neoclassicists were fully aware of the fundamental difference between barter economies, where money does not exist, and monetized exchange economies (Samuelson, 1968). The real part of the system, taken by itself, may of course be conceived of as the model for a barter economy in which commodities and services are exchanged directly, possibly with a *numéraire* commodity as a measure of value. It would be entirely ridiculous, however, to assume that the very same system, expanded only by the exchange equation, would describe a monetized exchange economy, and that thus money historically should have been neutral in the sense that relative prices and quantities bought and sold should be the same before and after the invention and introduction of money.

Economic history tells us that money has been an important vehicle of economic progress and a *conditio sine qua non* for extensive specialization. Money greatly facilitates the exchange of commodities and services. To be sure, a certain amount of resources is inevitably used up in producing and using money (even fiat money has to be printed, check deposits need accounting and office work, not to mention gold coins), but much larger amounts of resources must have been saved through the rationalization of trade which money makes possible. The redundant resources have been used for expanding the production of commodities and services. Money has thus helped to increase physical productivity and must therefore have modified the demand and supply functions of producers profoundly. Concurrently with the increase of real income in society it has served directly to make life more comfortable through saving time in trading and adding to convenience and security. Hence, the households' demand and supply functions must have changed. See, for instance, H. G. Johnson, (1969). With the changes in the demand and supply functions, the equilibrium values of relative prices and quantities produced, bought, and sold must change, too. In this sense money is certainly not neutral; nobody has probably ever maintained that, either. Even though the abstract systems for a barter economy and for the real part of a monetized exchange economy perhaps might turn out to be indistinguishable, both containing relative prices as the only arguments in the demand and supply functions, their concrete solutions must be very different. In this way the importance of the introduction of money for the real economy could be acknowledged, and yet it could be maintained that a change in the actual size of the quantity of money does not matter for the real economy in the long run—granted the existence of money and the monetization of the economy.

The point is, however, as we shall see later, that the introduction of money makes new arguments appear in the demand and supply functions. Whereas the demand and supply functions of the Walrasian system may perhaps describe a barter economy adequately, they are inadequate for describing a monetized economy. The system does not fully reflect all the basic functions of money. Money may serve as a standard of value, as a means of exchange, and as a store of value. The first function is clearly considered by the Walrasian system when it talks about money prices. It is true that the *numéraire* was introduced to make it possible to discuss the real part of the system without taking up problems related to money, but when money subsequently is introduced there is no doubt that it serves as a standard of value. Concerning the other functions, matters are less clear. The neoclassicists were not very explicit about the process of exchange,[1] and with respect to the store of value function they even appear to be confused. Say's law rules out, by assumption, the possibility that sales proceeds are used to increase cash holdings, or that cash holdings are spent to finance purchases. On the other hand, in establishing the exchange equation, we did assume that money actually exists. And its existence must imply that people keep cash. But the

---

[1] In an attempt to analyze the process through which market equilibrium is established, Walras (1954, Lessons 12, 20, etc.) discussed at some length how exchange takes place during the period when the market is "groping," *par tatonnement*, for the equilibrium prices. But this is a problem of when contracts are made and not of the role played by money in the process of exchange and its impact on productivity and so forth.

system does not explain how these individuals obtain the cash, or why they hold it. And it remains a small mystery how changes in the quantity of money take place.

2 / The dynamics of the price level

It is tempting at this point to quote K. Wicksell at some length because he saw so clearly the shortcomings of this kind of monetary theory. In a celebrated passage directed toward the quantity theory of money (1935, pp. 159, 160, italics in the original) he said:

> That a large and a small quantity of money *can* serve the same purposes of turnover if commodity prices rise or fall proportionately to the quantity is one thing. It is another thing to show why such a change of price must always follow a change in the quantity of money and to describe what happens.
>
> Every rise and fall in the price of a particular commodity presupposes a disturbance of the equilibrium between the supply of and the demand for that commodity, whether the disturbance has actually taken place or is merely prospective. What is true *in this respect* of each commodity separately must doubtless be true of all commodities collectively. A general rise in prices is therefore only conceivable on the supposition that the general demand has for some reason become, or is expected to become, greater than the supply. This may sound paradoxical, because we have accustomed ourselves, with J. B. Say, to regard goods themselves as reciprocally constituting and limiting the demand for each other. And indeed *ultimately* they do so; here, however, we are concerned with precisely what occurs, *in the first place*, with the middle link in the final exchange of one good against another, which is formed by the demand of money for goods and the supply of goods against money. Any theory of money worthy of the name must be able to show how and why the monetary or pecuniary demand for goods exceeds or falls short of the supply of goods in given conditions.

The general equilibrium systems presented in Chapters 3 and 4 are obviously failing on all points, and their monetary theories are not "worthy of the name." Not only are these systems based on Say's law, which precludes a general excess of demand over supply, but they are without any mechanism through which changes in the quantity of money can influence the individual money prices of goods. Moreover, it would seem that because of their structure, the stability of the systems does not extend to the price level.

With the rate of change of money prices governed by Walras' excess demand hypothesis as formulated in Equation 4.8, a change in the quantity of money can only cause changes in the money prices if it is accompanied by excess demand or supply in the individual commodity and service markets. With all money prices still at their initial equilibrium values, excess demands will continue to be zero everywhere, despite the change in the quantity of money; there are no forces in the system that can cause money prices to begin moving. This is a simple consequence of the fact that money does not appear in the real part of the system.

Assume, on the other hand, that the system is in equilibrium at the level of money prices indicated by the exchange equation. Imagine that for some reason, by mistake, for instance, all money prices in the markets for commodities and services are suddenly quoted 10 per cent higher than the levels determined by the exchange equation. What will happen? Nothing! All relative money prices will remain unchanged. Hence, all excess demands remain at zero, and there are no forces in the system that can serve to bring the money prices down to their initial levels. This example demonstrates that the neoclassical systems are not stable at the price level as determined by the exchange equation.

A final question concerns the exchange equation itself. What is the exchange equation? From whence did it come? Some neoclassical authors have conceived of this equation as a national accounting identity which states only that the value of total turnover is equal to itself, and that this value is expressed in two different ways on the two sides of the identity. There can be no objection to this approach from a purely logical viewpoint. On the other hand, it has the unpleasant implication that demand for and supply of money do not appear in the system. And why should there be no demand and supply functions for money? We might reply that we have ruled this out by assumption with the adoption of Say's law; but since there actually does exist a quantity of money that is held by someone as cash, the answer is not very satisfactory. As a matter of fact, many neoclassical authors did interpret the exchange equation in terms of demand for and supply of money at the same time that they, in their monetary theory at least, rejected Say's law. Wicksell is a good example. This interpretation, unfortunately, only leads to new problems, as we shall now see.

3 / The notion of homogeneity

Before we proceed, however, we must define the concept of homogeneity. A function

[5.1] $$y = f(x_1, \ldots, x_n, x_{n+1}, \ldots, x_m)$$

is said to be homogeneous of degree k in the arguments x_1 to x_n if

[5.2] $$f(\lambda x_1, \ldots, \lambda x_n, x_{n+1}, \ldots, x_m) = \lambda^k f(x_1, \ldots, x_n, x_{n+1}, \ldots, x_m)$$

where λ is an arbitrary number. In economic theory we meet in particular functions that are homogeneous of degree 1 and degree zero.

Homogeneity of zero degree, $k = 0$ in the arguments x_1 to x_n, means that if in Equation 5.1 all arguments x_1 to x_n inside the function f are multiplied by a certain number, the value of y will be unchanged. As an example of a function homogeneous of degree zero in x_1 and x_2, we have $y = a + b(x_1/x_2)$, where a and b are constants. Thus the neoclassical assumption that demand and supply depend on relative money prices amounts to an assumption that demand and supply functions are homogeneous of zero degree in all money prices. We call this "price homogeneity." Note that if a demand function is homogeneous of degree zero in the money prices, the corresponding expenditure function $p_i q_i^d$, which is the value of demand, will be homogeneous of degree 1 in the money prices.[1]

4 / Demand for and supply of money

Let us try, then, to introduce demand for and supply of money explicitly in the Walrasian system by interpreting the exchange equation in terms of demand and supply. We shall limit ourselves to consideration of the simplified systems in Chapter 4 and Fisher's equation of exchange. For this purpose we shall write the Fisher equation as

[5.3]
$$M = \frac{1}{V} \Sigma p_i q_i$$

where the summation extends over the n commodities and services, and q_i is the actual turnover of commodity i. This equation gives rise to no ambiguities in equilibrium where $q_i = q_i^d = q_i^s$. If the system is not in equilibrium we shall assume that the actual turnover q_i is equal to the smallest of q_i^d and q_i^s. This is to assume that outside equilibrium the actual turnover is equal to demand when supply exceeds demand, and equal to supply when demand exceeds supply.[2] The assumption is an arbitrary one, but quite usual. We interpret the left side of Equation 5.3 as the supply of money

[5.4]
$$M^s = M$$

---

[1] Homogeneity of degree 1 (that is, $k = 1$) also plays an important role in the theory of production, and means here that there are constant returns to scale. Production functions are then assumed to be homogeneous of degree 1 in all factors of production. The Cobb-Douglas function $q = aL^\alpha K^\beta$, $\alpha + \beta = 1$, where q is the quantity of output, L labor input, and K capital input, and a, α, and β are constants, is the standard example. The zero-degree homogeneity of demand and supply functions has nothing to do with the first-degree homogeneity of production functions.

[2] We assume, accordingly, that transactions take place also when the system is in disequilibrium, which contradicts the assumptions usually made in discussions of the *tatonnement* process.

The supply of money M^s is exogenously given. In the same way, we identify the right side as the demand for money M^d.

[5.5] $$M^d = \frac{1}{V} \Sigma p_i q_i$$

We assume, further, that demand for and supply of money may differ; we define the excess demand for money M^x as

[5.6] $$M^x = M^d - M^s = \frac{1}{V} \Sigma p_i q_i - M$$

Considering velocity V as an institutionally given constant, the excess demand for money is dependent upon all money prices and the quantity of money. Indeed, it is a function homogeneous of degree 1 in all money prices and in the quantity of money, it being recalled that q_i is a function of the relative money prices (that is, homogeneous of zero degree in all money prices), and that the expenditure function $p_i q_i$ is homogeneous of degree 1 in the prices.

In assuming that a positive or negative excess demand for money may occur, we have discarded Say's law. An excess demand for money can only exist if someone tries to increase his cash holdings. With the supply of money equal to the actual cash holdings, the demand can only exceed or fall short of the supply if someone desires more or less cash than he actually has. But an individual can only increase or decrease his cash holdings if he is willing to let his receipts exceed or fall short of his expenditures, a consideration that has obvious consequences for the formulation of the aggregated budget restriction.

Let us imagine that in their planning the individual economic subjects are concerned with a short period. They enter the period with certain cash holdings; this is the supply of money. During the period they expect certain receipts from the sales of commodities and services, and plan certain expenditures or purchases of commodities and services. Finally, they plan to carry over certain cash balances to the following period; this is the demand for money. Adding all the individual budget restrictions, it is easily understood that Walras' law must now become

[5.7] $$M + \Sigma p_i q_i^s \equiv \Sigma p_i q_i^d + M^d$$

(compare with Equation 4.5), which states that the sum of all ingoing cash holdings, plus expected receipts from sales, must be equal to planned expenditures, plus planned, outgoing cash balances, no matter what the prices are. Recalling the definitions of M^x and q_i^x Equation 5.7 may be written

[5.8] $$M^x \equiv -\Sigma p_i q_i^x$$

that is, the excess demand for money is (identically) equal to the total value of all excess demands for commodities and services (with opposite sign).

Say's law assumed that $M^x \equiv 0$. Equation 5.8 is the implicit excess demand function for money, and we thus find ourselves confronted with two excess demand functions for money, Equations 5.6 and 5.8. This would be no catastrophe if the two excess demand functions for money were identical; but, unfortunately, they are not. Equation 5.6 is homogeneous of degree 1 in all money prices *and* the quantity of money; Equation 5.8 is homogeneous of degree 1 in all money prices alone. This can be stated another way: According to Equation 5.6, the excess demand function for money contains M as an argument, which is not the case with Equation 5.8. We have thus derived two different excess demand functions for money, and economically this is clearly unsatisfactory.

It can be shown, in addition, that we cannot discard Say's law here without encountering other difficulties. In the simplified excess demand system, Say's law helped us show that one of the excess demand equations for commodities and services is dependent upon the rest. When we discard Say's law this no longer holds true. We still have an aggregated budget restriction, of course, but it only helps us eliminate the excess demand equation for money (Equation 5.8). We cannot prove that one of the n excess demand equations for commodities and services (in $n - 1$ relative money prices) is dependent upon the rest of the equations. This circumstance does not preclude a solution to the system (Encarnacion, 1958), but it causes difficulty because it rules out linearity in the system.

These were the difficulties that led O. Lange (1942) and D. Patinkin (1948, 1949, 1951) to criticize the neoclassical system and even attack it for inconsistencies and overdeterminedness. There can be no doubt that if the systems we discussed in Chapters 3 and 4 accurately present the theories of the neoclassicists, then charges of inconsistencies and overdeterminedness are unjustified. On the other hand, it is certainly true that the theory of money contained in these systems is very poor and, as Wicksell would state, hardly "worthy of the name." It excludes a discussion of demand for and supply of money, and it is unable to handle the problems of price-level dynamics. The reasoning in this section, which contains Patinkin's main criticism of the neoclassical system, shows, moreover, that if we wish to incorporate money into the system so as to consider all three functions of money, we cannot simply discard Say's law and interpret the exchange equation in terms of demand for and supply of money. A more extensive overhaul of the system is needed. It was left to Patinkin to show how money can be integrated into the general equilibrium system.

We shall review Patinkin's system in Chapter 8. First we must discuss in some detail the problem of the form of the demand and supply functions and the budget restrictions that led to Say's law. We find that there is a close relationship here in that the choice of budget restriction has implications for the form of the demand and supply functions.

References

ENCARNACION, J.: "Consistency between Say's Law and the Cambridge Equation," *Economic Journal*, vol. 68, no. 1, March, 1958.

HICKS, J. R.: "A Suggestion for Simplifying the Theory of Money," *Economica*, N.S. vol. 2, no. 1, February, 1935. Reprinted in F. A. Lutz and L. W. Mints (eds.), *Readings in Monetary Theory*, George Allen and Unwin, London, 1951.

JOHNSON, H. G.: "Inside Money, Outside Money, Income, Wealth and Welfare in Monetary Theory," *Journal of Money, Credit and Banking*, vol. 1, no. 1, February, 1969.

LANGE, O.: "Say's Law: A Restatement and Criticism," in O. Lange, et al. (eds.), *Studies in Mathematical Economics and Econometrics*, University of Chicago Press, 1942.

PATINKIN, D.: "Relative Prices, Say's Law, and the Demand for Money," *Econometrica*, vol. 16, no. 2, 1948.

—: "The Indeterminacy of Absolute Prices in Classical Economic Theory," *Econometrica*, vol. 17, no. 1, 1949.

—: "The Invalidity of Classical Monetary Theory," *Econometrica*, vol. 19, no. 2, 1951.

—: *Money, Interest, and Prices*, 2d ed., Harper and Row, New York, 1966.

SAMUELSON, P. A.: "What Classical and Neo-Classical Theory Really Was," *Canadian Journal of Economics*, vol. 1, no. 1, February, 1968.

WALRAS, L.: *Elements of Pure Economics*, George Allen and Unwin, London, 1954.

WICKSELL, K.: *Föreläsningar i Nationalekonomi*, Glerup, Lund, 1906. Final, fourth edition, Lund, 1929. English translation, *Lectures on Political Economy*, vols. 1 and 2, Routledge and Kegan Paul, London, 1934 and 1935.

Budget restrictions, homogeneity, and demand for money

6

In the previous chapters we took for granted that demand and supply functions for commodities and services are characterized by homogeneity of degree zero in the money prices. In this respect there has been general agreement among the neoclassicists, from Walras to Hicks. Now we shall examine the economic reasons for giving demand and supply functions this particular mathematical form. We shall see how the neoclassical specification depends on very special assumptions, of which the neoclassicists may not always have been fully aware. We shall see, also, how a relaxation of these assumptions leads to radically different demand and supply functions.

1 / A common-sense argument

It is, quite common to argue that the absolute level of prices cannot affect demand and supply, because the absolute level of money prices is, among other things, determined by the unit of currency. A change in the unit of currency changes the absolute money prices accordingly. Such a change is a matter of the formal standard of measurement and cannot possibly have any impact on real demand and supply, just as a change from the British measure of pounds, pints, yards to the metric system is a formality that leaves the actual physical weights, volumes, and lengths unchanged. Cassel (1938, p. 170) postulated price homogeneity in this way, but generally, the neoclassicists were more sophisticated. They usually derived the price homogeneity from theories of utility maximization by the households and profit maximization by the enterprises.

2 / Utility maximization and price homogeneity

Let us consider a household that derives its income from sales of labor services, and spends that income on consumer goods. In all circumstances it spends exactly in line with what it earns; we disregard explicitly savings and changes in assets, including cash. In other words, Say's law is assumed to apply. Consumer goods are designated 1 to h, and labor is designated L. With the usual notation, we then have the following budget restriction, identically in the prices,

[6.1]
$$\sum_{i=1}^{h} p_i q_i^d \equiv p_L q_L^s$$

The household is presumed to have a utility function, with expected utility as a function of planned purchases of consumer goods and sales of labor

[6.2] $\qquad U(q_1^d, \ldots, q_h^d, q_L^s) \qquad \dfrac{\partial U}{\partial q_i^d} > 0 \qquad$ and $\qquad \dfrac{\partial U}{\partial q_L^s} < 0$

Form the expression

[6.3] $\qquad U(q_1^d, \ldots, q_h^d, q_L^s) - \lambda \left(\sum_{i=1}^{h} p_i q_i^d - p_L q_L^s \right)$

where λ is a Lagrangian multiplier. (R. G. D. Allen, 1938, Chapter XIV, pp. 264 et seq.) The necessary conditions for utility maximization are

[6.4]
$$\frac{\partial U}{\partial q_i^d} - \lambda p_i = 0 \qquad i = 1, \ldots, h$$
$$\frac{\partial U}{\partial q_L^s} + \lambda p_L = 0$$

from which we derive, after eliminating λ,

[6.5] $\qquad \dfrac{\partial U/\partial q_i^d}{\partial U/\partial q_L^s} = -\dfrac{p_i}{p_L} \qquad i = 1, \ldots, h$

Equations 6.5 and 6.1, written as

[6.1'] $$\sum_{i=1}^{h} \frac{p_i}{p_L} q_i^d - q_L^s \equiv 0$$

furnish us with $h + 1$ equations in the unknowns $q_1^d, \ldots, q_h^d, q_L^s$. In Equations 6.5 and 6.1' the prices appear only as price ratios; that is, in the form p_i/p_L. The solution must therefore have the form

[6.6]
$$q_i^d = q_i^d \left(\frac{p_1}{p_L}, \ldots, \frac{p_h}{p_L} \right) \qquad i = 1, \ldots, h$$
$$q_L^s = q_L^s \left(\frac{p_1}{p_L}, \ldots, \frac{p_h}{p_L} \right)$$

We have now shown that the household's demand for consumer goods and supply of labor services depend only upon the relative prices of consumer goods and labor. The household's demand and supply functions are thus homogeneous of degree zero in the money prices.

3 / Profit maximization and price homogeneity

The demand and supply from productive enterprises can be treated similarly. Here price homogeneity may be derived from the assumption of profit maximization. Consider a firm producing only one commodity q_1^s and using only one factor of production, labor q_L^d. The production function of the firm is

[6.7] $$q_1^s = \phi(q_L^d) \qquad \phi' > 0 \qquad \phi'' < 0$$

Total profits v are then defined as

[6.8] $$v = p_1 q_1^s - p_L q_L^d$$

Profit maximization is reached when

[6.9] $$\frac{dv}{dq_L^d} = p_1 \phi'(q_L^d) - p_L = 0$$

or

[6.10] $$\phi'(q_L^d) = \frac{p_L}{p_1}$$

Solve Equation 6.10 for q_L^d and obtain

[6.11] $$q_L^d = \phi'^{-1}\left(\frac{p_L}{p_1}\right) = f\left(\frac{p_L}{p_1}\right)$$

which shows that the demand for labor depends on the relationship between product price and labor price. The supply of commodity 1 is determined by inserting Equation 6.11 into Equation 6.7 to obtain

[6.12] $$q_1^s = \phi\left[f\left(\frac{p_L}{p_1}\right)\right]$$

proving that the supply of the output commodity as well depends only on the relative prices. The results extend to firms producing any number of commodities with any number of inputs. We have thus shown that the demand and supply functions of the firm also are homogeneous of degree zero in the money prices of outputs and inputs.

4 / Say's law and price homogeneity in the neoclassical systems

The derivation of the neoclassical household's demand and supply functions (Equation 6.6) was explicitly based on Say's law and on the utility function set forth in Equation 6.2. If any of these assumptions is relaxed, we may not have price homogeneity in the demand and supply functions. Here we are particularly interested in Say's law. Given the utility function, Equation 6.2, Say's law is obviously a sufficient condition for price homogeneity. That it is also a necessary condition is not so obvious. If, for instance, Equation 6.1 contained an additional constant term, the homogeneity would break down because Equation 6.1' could no longer be expressed in terms of relative prices. On the other hand, if we assume that only a constant fraction of the wage income, say $kp_Lq_L{}^s$, is spent on consumer goods, then the demand function for consumer goods and the supply function for labor services would remain homogeneous of zero degree in the money prices. We would then be left with savings to be accounted for, however, or our theory would not be complete. Disregarding money and credit, the savings could only be used for purchasing capital goods and, unless we excluded by definition such purchases by households, we would have to establish explicit demand functions for capital goods. Inasmuch as this problem really belongs to the theory of capital, and will therefore be discussed in a later chapter, we shall merely mention that if all savings were spent on capital goods and we assumed utility or profit maximization, we would once again arrive at demand functions homogeneous in the money prices.

We encounter a similar problem when we turn to the demand and supply functions of the enterprise. All we need here to obtain price homogeneity, apparently, is the assumption of profit maximization. There is still the problem of disposing of the profits v earned by the firm, however. It might be argued that if we are considering a long-run equilibrium, profits are in any case zero. This is the assumption made by the original Walrasian system (Equations 3.2); but in deriving the demand and supply functions of the system we cannot assume *a priori* that the system is in equilibrium. Therefore, neither can we exclude positive or negative profits at this stage of the analysis. Two possibilities are open, disregarding money and credit. We may assume that the firm uses the profits exclusively for purchasing capital goods, which brings us back to the problem just mentioned. Otherwise, all profits must be transferred as dividends to the households, which increase or decrease their spending by the same amount. In this way Say's law applies to the enterprises, as well. This circumstance does not have any consequences for the price homogeneity of the households' demand and supply functions, because the profits v are themselves homogeneous of degree 1 in the money prices. From Equations 6.8, 6.11, and 6.12 we obtain

$$[6.13] \qquad v = p_1\phi\left[f\left(\frac{p_L}{p_1}\right)\right] - p_Lf\left(\frac{p_L}{p_1}\right)$$

Adding this expression to the right side of Equation 6.1, we are still able to write Equation 6.1' as an expression in the relative prices, and the price homogeneity of the households' demand and supply functions is intact. We must obviously assume that the households know the profit expectations of their firms.

In the cases discussed, we assumed that the proceeds from the sales of commodities and services were spent in purchasing commodities and services, identically in the prices, so that Say's law applies. Say's law, and utility and profit maximization, are conditions sufficient for price homogeneity in the system. It seems to be a necessary condition, as well. If money exists, the cash holdings of the individual must appear to the left of Equation 6.1; the only way to eliminate this constant is to assume that there is a demand for cash appearing on the right that is identically equal to the existing cash holdings on the left. But this assumption is merely a restatement of Say's law.

It would seem, then, that in assuming price homogeneity the neoclassicists had to assume, explicitly or implicitly, that Say's law did hold (W. Leontief, 1950). To assume price homogeneity but deny the existence of Say's law (and many neoclassicists undoubtedly did just that) is illogical.

The interesting problem that the neoclassicists never encountered is: what happens to the homogeneity when Say's law is abandoned? It was Patinkin (see Chapter 8) who first asked and answered this question. In the remainder of this chapter we will assume that Say's law does not hold, and we therefore must consider the individual's cash holdings explicitly.

5 / The payments technical approach

The Cambridge version of the quantity theory of money was based on a simple hypothesis concerning transactions demand for money.[1] It held that for payments technical reasons individuals try to keep their cash holdings in certain fixed proportions k to their incomes. The example of a household's demand and supply for commodities and services presented in Section 2 can easily be extended to include this hypothesis (Henderson and Quandt, 1958, pp. 142 et seq.). Since the expected income of a household is equal to its expected sales of labor (we disregard sales of other services and profits carried over from enterprises) the Cambridge approach, in effect, postulates the demand function for money,

[6.14] $$M^d = kp_L q_L{}^s$$

We assume, moreover, that the household enters its planning period with certain cash holdings M carried over from the previous period; the budget restriction, therefore, becomes

[6.15] $$M + p_L q_L{}^s \equiv \sum_{i=1}^{h} p_i q_i{}^d + M^d$$

---

[1] The analysis of this section can easily be repeated on the basis of the Fisher equation.

The utility function U is assumed to be the same as before (Equation 6.2), so that utilizing Equations 6.15 and 6.14, we can form

[6.16]
$$U - \lambda \left[\sum_{i=1}^{h} p_i q_i^d - (1 - k) p_L q_L^s - M \right]$$

Utility maximization now yields, after elimination of λ,

[6.17]
$$\frac{\partial U / \partial q_i^d}{\partial U / \partial q_L^s} = - \frac{p_i}{(1 - k) p_L} \qquad i = 1, \ldots, h$$

which, with the budget restriction, written as

[6.18]
$$\sum_{i=1}^{h} \frac{p_i}{p_L} q_i^d - (1 - k) q_L^s \equiv \frac{M}{p_L}$$

furnishes us with $h + 1$ equations to determine the $h + 1$ unknowns q_i^d and q_L^s. But the solution differs from Equation 6.6. Inspection of Equations 6.17 and 6.18 shows us that the solution now has the form

[6.19]
$$q_i^d = q_i^d \left(\frac{p_1}{p_L}, \ldots, \frac{p_h}{p_L}, \frac{M}{p_L} \right) \qquad i = 1, \ldots, h$$

$$q_L^s = q_L^s \left(\frac{p_1}{p_L}, \ldots, \frac{p_h}{p_L}, \frac{M}{p_L} \right)$$

The demand and supply functions of the household for commodities and services are no longer homogeneous in the prices alone. Money has entered the functions. The demand and supply functions are now homogeneous of zero degree in all money prices *and* in the quantity of money; that is, in the given cash holdings at the beginning of the period. From Equations 6.14 and 6.19 we find the demand function for money to be

[6.20]
$$M^d = k p_L q_L^s \left(\frac{p_1}{p_L}, \ldots, \frac{p_h}{p_L}, \frac{M}{p_L} \right)$$

a function that is homogeneous of degree 1 in all money prices and the quantity of money. Equation 6.20 shows the demand for money in money terms. We may also ask for the demand for money in real terms. Dividing through in Equation 6.20 on both sides by p_L we obtain

[6.20']
$$\frac{M^d}{p_L} = k q_L^s \left(\frac{p_1}{p_L}, \ldots, \frac{p_h}{p_L}, \frac{M}{p_L} \right)$$

It is important to distinguish clearly between demand for money *in money terms* as shown in Equation 6.20, and *in real terms* as shown in Equation 6.20'. Whereas the demand for money in money terms is homogeneous of degree 1 in the prices and the quantity of money, like any expenditure function $p_i q_i^d$ for commodities and services, the demand for money in real terms is homogeneous of zero degree in the same variables, as is any demand function q_i^d for commodities or services. Note also the slightly confusing terminology:

the quantity of money is a value sum (namely, a number of dollars), and the (economic) analogue to the physical quantity of a commodity or service is the real amount of money, which is the quantity of money deflated by some suitable price (or price index).

It is now easy to understand why we encountered difficulty in Chapter 5 when we dropped Say's law, interpreted the right side of the exchange equation as a demand function for money (in money terms), but left the rest of the general equilibrium system unchanged. Granted that household behavior can be described by utility maximization, and business behavior by profit maximization, this procedure is illogical. The Cambridge hypothesis of demand for money implies that household demand and supply functions for commodities and services are homogeneous of degree zero in money prices and the quantity of money. We can also express this implication by saying that demand and supply for commodities and services become functions of the relative prices *and* real cash balances. The same applies, by hypothesis, to the real demand for money.

Wicksell (1935, pp. 83–84; 1936, pp. 66–68) suggested a somewhat different demand for money hypothesis. Whereas the Cambridge theory postulates proportionality between money income and demand for money (in money terms), Wicksell argued that the demand for money might rather tend to grow in proportion to the square root of the amount of the transactions. If cash is kept only for the purpose of bridging gaps between payments and receipts, and if the timing of payments and receipts within a given period may be considered erratic, then by virtue of the law of large numbers, the cash holdings necessary to keep the risk below a certain level should, under certain further assumptions, tend to increase in proportion to the square root of the transactions. Assume, for instance, that the probability of a \$1 payment being accompanied by a \$1 receipt is a; the standard deviation then, under certain conditions, is equal to $\sqrt{a(1-a)N}$ where N is the number of dollars transacted. To keep the risk of default below a given level, a household or firm[1] should, in terms of the analysis presented here, have a demand for cash $M^d = k\sqrt{a(1-a)}p_L q_L{}^s$. The homogeneity properties of this demand function, however, are different from those derived in Equation 6.20. The problem will be solved if we assume that probability a is attached to a unit of real transactions rather than to a unit of transactions in terms of money; this change in our assumption leads us to a demand function of the form $M^d = kp_L\sqrt{a(1-a)q_L{}^s}$, which has the same homogeneity properties as the demand function for money in Equation 6.20. Patinkin (1966, pp. 82–88) reached similar conclusions in a probabilistic approach based on different assumptions.

A square root law for the demand for cash through a so-called "inventory theoretical approach" was derived by W. J. Baumol (1952; see also

[1] Wicksell was actually discussing the liquidity of banks.

Tobin, 1956). Baumol's analysis does not fit too well into the kind of period analysis applied here. Yet his results are interesting because he obtains a demand function for money that has the same homogeneity properties as those of Equation 6.20. He assumes that the value of transactions during a specific period is given and equal to T. Payments are made steadily and continuously. To make a steady stream of payments the individual may borrow a sum C at regular intervals. His average cash holdings will then be $C/2$ and his interest cost for the period $rC/2$, r being the rate of interest per period. In addition to the interest cost there is a fixed fee b per loan. The number of loans per period is T/C, and the total fees bT/C. The individual's total costs per period will thus amount to $bT/C + rC/2$. Cost minimization (differentiate with respect to C and set the result equal to zero) leads to $-bT/C^2 + r/2 = 0$, or $C = \sqrt{2bT/r}$. Cash holdings are proportional to the square root of the total value of the transactions. Baumol (1952, p. 547, Note 5), however, notes that with a proportional change in all prices in the economy, both T and the fee b (b being nothing but the price of the bank's service) will increase proportionately. Therefore, if we write $T = tp_t$ and $b = \beta p_\beta$, the cash holdings, at minimum costs, become $C = \sqrt{2\beta p_\beta t p_t/r}$, which is homogeneous of degree 1 in the prices, and inversely related to the rate of interest.

6 / Money and utility

In the previous section we retained the traditional utility function; that is, utility was assumed to depend only upon quantities consumed and worked. Money was introduced through certain prior considerations about the determinants of the household's demand for money for purposes of transactions. Logically, this method does not give rise to objections, and economically it seems quite reasonable. The fact that money is kept in cash because it is useful, however, leads naturally to the notion that money should somehow appear directly in the utility function, alongside commodities and services consumed or delivered. Utility maximization would then simultaneously determine quantities to be consumed and worked and the amount of cash to be held.

Neoclassical theory tended to exclude money from the utility function. A common argument was that money had no direct utility since its utility was derived from the commodities purchased. It would be double counting, then, to include in the utility function both the money and the commodities purchased for money. Other arguments concerned a possible circularity in the theory, because the utility of money depends upon the prices of commodities, which are determined by a system whereby the utility of money belongs to the data. It was thus thought impossible to ascribe utility to money. This does not follow logically, however. If utility is attached to money, it must be the *real* value of money, *real* cash balances that give utility. Moreover, money in real terms is useful not only because it can be exchanged for useful commodities, but because it facilitates the process of transactions, bridges gaps between payments and receipts, makes unexpected purchases possible, and so forth. These latter kinds of usefulness are what justify the incorporation of money into the utility function.

Instead of writing the household's utility function as $U(q_1, q_2, \ldots, q_h)$, Patinkin suggested (1951, for instance), that we write

[6.21]
$$U\left(q_1, q_2, \ldots, q_h, \frac{M}{P}\right)$$

where P is a price index, and M/P the real cash balance of the household. It is questionable which of the many possible price indexes would be relevant in this context. Samuelson (1947, p. 119; see also 1968) suggested earlier that the utility function, apart from the quantities consumed and worked, should generally be written as a function homogeneous of degree zero in the quantity of money and in all individual prices. Provided that P is a linear combination of all prices, that is, $P = \Sigma\alpha p_i$, Equation 6.21 fulfills this specification.

How to treat money in the context of general equilibrium depends partly upon the axiomatic level on which we prefer to work. The simplest approach is to postulate demand and supply functions for money. Cassel adopted this approach in general, and it was applied in Section 5 in connection with the payments technical approach when we postulated a demand function for money based on the Cambridge equation. A somewhat more sophisticated method is to postulate that real balances yield utility. Utility maximization then helps us derive a demand function for money together with other demand and supply functions. We may, however, want to go even "deeper" and ask why money yields utility. Indeed, when money is included in the utility function, it is usually justified, as we did above, by more or less vague references to uncertainty, convenience, and so forth. The need then arises to establish what could be called a rational theory of the utility of money.

Uncertainty does not by itself necessarily imply a need for holding cash. Models have been presented (Arrow, 1964; Debreu, 1959) in which there is uncertainty about future events but where markets are so perfect that future disbursements and receipts can be planned and fixed today through contracts about forward delivery and payment; with perfect futures markets everywhere there can be no incentive to keep money. The same holds true in the case of differences in information (Radner, 1968). Models which explain the utility and demand for money on the basis of uncertainty (Tobin, 1958) assume, explicitly or implicitly, that markets are not perfect in this sense, and it has been argued that only imperfections of the markets can really explain why individuals and enterprises hold cash (Marschak, 1950; Hahn, 1965; Radner, 1968). Since general equilibrium theory largely has been based on the assumption of perfect markets and absence of uncertainty within the economic horizon it is thus brought in doubt whether a satisfactory theory of money can at all be established within the frame of neoclassical theory. To assume that money is held because of uncertainty with respect to that part of the future which lies beyond the economic horizon is, of course, tantamount to postulate utility of money.

7 / Simple case with money in the utility function

Without loss of generality we can assume that the household only demands one consumer good, of the quantity q_c^d and the price p_c, and supplies labor with the quantity q_L^s and the price p_L. The actual cash holding is M, and M^d is the desired cash holding. The budget restriction is then

[6.22] $$M + q_L^s p_L \equiv q_c^d p_c + M^d$$

which can also be written as

[6.22'] $$\frac{M}{p_c} + \frac{p_L q_L^s}{p_c} - q_c^d - \frac{M^d}{p_c} \equiv 0$$

We assume now that the utility function has this form

[6.23] $$U\left(q_c^d, q_L^s, \frac{M^d}{p_c}\right) \qquad \frac{\partial U}{\partial q_c^d} > 0 \qquad \frac{\partial U}{\partial q_L^s} < 0 \qquad \frac{\partial U}{\partial (M^d/p_c)} > 0$$

Utility is thus assumed to increase with the quantity consumed, to fall with the amount of labor supplied, and to increase with the amount of real cash balances held. Note that it is the *future*, planned cash balances that are assumed to give utility, not the *actual* cash holdings. The theory is that households plan for current consumption and labor, and for cash holdings to meet future contingencies.

Form, then, the expression

[6.24] $$U - \lambda\left(\frac{M}{p_c} + \frac{p_L}{p_c}q_L^s - q_c^d - \frac{M^d}{p_c}\right)$$

where λ is a Lagrangian multiplier. The necessary conditions for utility maximum are now

[6.25]
$$\frac{\partial U}{\partial q_c^d} + \lambda = 0$$
$$\frac{\partial U}{\partial q_L^s} - \lambda\frac{p_L}{p_c} = 0$$
$$\frac{\partial U}{\partial (M^d/p_c)} + \lambda = 0$$

Eliminating λ we obtain

[6.26]
$$\frac{\partial U/\partial q_L^s}{\partial U/\partial q_c^d} = -\frac{p_L}{p_c}$$
$$\frac{\partial U/\partial (M^d/p_c)}{\partial U/\partial q_c^d} = 1$$

which with Equation 6.22' may be solved for $q_c{}^d$, $q_L{}^s$ and M^d/p_c. A study of Equations 6.22' and 6.26 shows that the solutions must have the form

$$q_c{}^d = q_c{}^d \left(\frac{p_L}{p_c}, \frac{M}{p_c} \right)$$

[6.27]
$$q_L{}^s = q_L{}^s \left(\frac{p_L}{p_c}, \frac{M}{p_c} \right)$$

$$\frac{M^d}{p_c} = m^d = m^d \left(\frac{p_L}{p_c}, \frac{M}{p_c} \right)$$

where m^d is the demand for money in real terms.

Once again we find that household demand and supply are dependent upon relative prices *and* existing real cash balances; that is, homogeneous of degree zero in money prices and in the quantity of money. This applies also to the demand for real cash balances; the demand for cash in money terms M^d is, of course, homogeneous of degree 1 in the same variables.

The payments technical approach and the utility-of-money approach thus lead to the same form of demand and supply equations, which are different from the form assumed by the neoclassicists. Patinkin (1966, pp. 82 et seq.) showed that the same result may be reached through a revealed-preferences approach, but we do not need to consider that here.

References

ALLEN, R. G. D.: *Mathematical Analysis for Economists*, Macmillan, London, 1938.

ARROW, K. J.: "The Role of Securities in the Optimal Allocation of Risk Bearing," *Review of Economic Studies*, vol. 31, no. 86, April, 1964. Originally published in French, 1953.

BAUMOL, W. J.: "The Transactions Demand for Cash: An Inventory Theoretic Approach," *Quarterly Journal of Economics*, vol. 66, no. 4, November, 1952.

CASSEL, G.: *Teoretisk Socialekonomi*, Kooperativa Förbundets Bokförlag, Stockholm, 1938.

DEBREU, G.: *Theory of Value*, John Wiley & Sons, New York, 1959.

HAHN, F. H.: "On Some Problems of Proving the Existence of an Equilibrium in a Monetary Economy," in F. H. Hahn and F. P. R. Brechling (eds.), *The Theory of Interest Rates*, St. Martin's Press, New York, 1965.

HENDERSON, J. M., and R. E. QUANDT: *Microeconomic Theory*, McGraw-Hill, New York, 1958.

LEONTIEF, W. W.: "The Consistency of the Classical Theory of Money and Prices," *Econometrica*, vol. 18, no. 1, January, 1950.

MARSCHAK, J.: "The Rationale of Money Demand and of 'Money Illusion,'" *Metroeconomica*, vol. 2, no. 2, August, 1950.

MILLER, M., and D. ORR: "A Model of the Demand for Money by Firms," *Quarterly Journal of Economics*, vol. 80, no. 3, August, 1966.

PATINKIN, D.: "A Reconsideration of the General Equilibrium Theory of Money," *Review of Economic Studies*, vol. 18, no. 45, 1951.

—: *Money, Interest, and Prices*, 2d ed., Harper and Row, New York, 1966.

RADNER, R.: "Competitive Equilibrium under Uncertainty," *Econometrica*, vol. 36, no. 1, January, 1968.

SAMUELSON, P. A.: *Foundations in Economic Analysis*, Harvard University Press, Cambridge, Mass., 1947.

—: "What Classical and Neoclassical Monetary Theory Really Was," *Canadian Journal of Economics*, vol. 1, no. 1, February, 1968.

TOBIN, J.: "Liquidity Preference as Behaviour Towards Risk," *The Review of Economic Studies*, vol. 25, no. 67, February, 1958. Reprinted in H. R. Williams and J. D. Huffnagle, *Macroeconomic Theory: Selected Readings*, Appleton-Century-Crofts, New York, 1969.

WICKSELL, K.: *Lectures on Political Economy*, vol. 2, Routledge and Kegan Paul, London, 1935.

—: *Interest and Prices*, Macmillan, London, 1936. Originally published in German as *Geldzins und Güterpreise*, Göttingen, 1898.

Assets and debts, intertemporal theory

7

In the previous chapter we began to discuss the demand for money explicitly. Money is clearly a stock entity; demand for and supply of money is demand for and supply of a stock. Demand for and supply of commodities has thus far only been conceived of as flow entities. Flows are defined per unit of time or, if defined at a point of time, as time rates; stocks are defined at a point of time and do not have a time dimension. The discussion of money led us necessarily to consideration of both existing and desired stocks of money; since a change in stocks implies a flow, we were led to introduce a unit period; that is, two points of time and the interval between them. But why only one period? And why only *money* assets? To generalize we ought to consider household and enterprise planning of purchases, sales, and stocks for all unit periods simultaneously within the economic horizon and, including all assets, financial as well as real. This is the logical extension of the theory, and leads us to the so-called "intertemporal theory" of demand and supply. It also leads us to consideration of another phenomenon; namely, the rate of interest. Money is then considered an asset among many others and demand for money arises as a result of substitution between assets rather than from transaction needs. We shall not attempt to present a general intertemporal theory of household and enterprise planning here. For our purpose it suffices to consider a few simplified, but characteristic examples. A general treatment of the theory can be found in Irving Fisher (1907, 1930), and K. Wicksell (1935), the founders of modern intertemporal theory. Authors who have contributed to its further development are Ramsey (1928), J. R. Hicks (1939), J. Mosak (1944), E. Schneider (1951), Malinvaud (1953, 1961), Debreu (1959), A. Lindbeck (1963), and others.

1 / Demand for interest-bearing deposits

Let us consider a simple intertemporal household model where the house-hold may have interest-bearing bank deposits. We shall assume that the deposits can be used to make payments, in which case the household has no reason to keep cash. As a matter of fact, during periods of very high interest rates check deposits have carried interest in some countries.

Only two periods are considered here. It is assumed that the economic horizon is at the end of the second period. This simplification permits us to discuss both the present (the first period) and the future (the second period). The household is presumed to plan for both period 1 and 2 at the beginning of period 1, and is presumed to have single-valued, but not necessarily correct, expectations about all relevant matters within the horizon. The expected income from labor for periods 1 and 2, Y_1 and Y_2, is assumed to be given. There is only one consumer good, and its expected price p is assumed to be the same during both periods. At the beginning of period 1 (that is, the time of planning), the household has bank deposits in the amount of D_0 (carried over from period 0) on which a rate of interest of r is obtained. The rate of interest r is assumed to remain constant. Money is deposited at the beginning of each period; interest is paid at the end of the period and is available to the household at the beginning of the next period. Interest earned during period 0 is included in Y_1.

For period 1 we have the following budget restriction

[7.1] $$Y_1 + D_0 = q_1{}^d p + D_1{}^d$$

where $q_1{}^d$ is the quantity of consumer goods to be purchased in period 1 and $D_1{}^d$ represents the deposits the household plans to carry into the next period. Planned savings are thus equal to $D_1{}^d - D_0$.

For period 2 we have

[7.2] $$Y_2 + (1 + r)D_1{}^d = q_2{}^d p + D_2{}^d$$

where $q_2{}^d$ is the planned quantity of consumer goods to be purchased in period 2, and $D_2{}^d$ is the amount of deposits planned at the end of period 2; that is, at the horizon. Savings in period 2 equal $D_2{}^d - D_1{}^d$. Entities like $D_2{}^d$ are called "final stocks." They are supposed to be carried beyond the horizon although there is no explicit planning for periods beyond the horizon.

Finally, we need a utility function. We shall assume that it is

[7.3] $$U = U\left(q_1{}^d,\ q_2{}^d,\ \frac{D_0}{p},\ \frac{D_1{}^d}{p},\ \frac{D_2{}^d}{p}\right)$$

which means that the expected utility of the household is dependent upon planned consumption during both periods, and upon the real value of its deposits at the three points of registration at the beginning and end of the two periods. The deposits carried over from period 0, D_0 are given, of course, and are no longer subject to planning. The other four real quantities entering the utility function must be planned so that utility maximization is achieved, given the two budget restrictions.

Form, then, the expression

$$[7.4] \quad U - \lambda_1 \left(\frac{Y_1}{p} + \frac{D_0}{p} - q_1{}^d - \frac{D_1{}^d}{p} \right)$$
$$- \lambda_2 \left[\frac{Y_2}{p} + (1 + r) \frac{D_1{}^d}{p} - q_2{}^d - \frac{D_2{}^d}{p} \right]$$

The necessary conditions for utility maximum are

$$\frac{\partial U}{\partial q_1{}^d} + \lambda_1 = 0$$

$$\frac{\partial U}{\partial q_2{}^d} + \lambda_2 = 0$$

$$[7.5]$$

$$\frac{\partial U}{\partial (D_1{}^d/p)} + \lambda_1 - (1 + r)\lambda_2 = 0$$

$$\frac{\partial U}{\partial (D_2{}^d/p)} + \lambda_2 = 0$$

Eliminating the λ's, which are of no special interest for our purpose, we obtain:

$$[7.6] \quad \frac{\partial U/\partial q_1{}^d}{\partial U/(\partial D_1{}^d/p) + (1 + r)\partial U/\partial q_2{}^d} = 1$$

$$\frac{\partial U/\partial q_2{}^d}{\partial U/\partial (D_2{}^d/p)} = 1$$

Interpretation of these marginal conditions for utility maximum is simple. The marginal rate of substitution between consumption during period 1 and deposits carried over to period 2 and (together with interests) consumed in period 2 is equal to 1. The same interpretation applies to consumption during period 2 and to deposits carried beyond the horizon. The possible use of deposits and interest earned beyond the horizon is not specified in the model. Here we are more interested in the implicit demand functions, however. Equations 7.6 and the two budget restrictions, set forth in Equations 7.1 and 7.2, written as

$$[7.1'] \quad \frac{Y_1}{p} + \frac{D_0}{p} = q_1{}^d + \frac{D_1{}^d}{p}$$

$$[7.2'] \quad \frac{Y_2}{p} + (1 + r) \frac{D_1{}^d}{p} = q_2{}^d + \frac{D_2{}^d}{p}$$

furnish us with four equations to determine the four unknowns q_1^d, q_2^d, D_1^d/p, and D_2^d/p. A study of Equations 7.6, 7.1', and 7.2' immediately shows that the four demand functions must all have the form

[7.7]
$$f\left(\frac{Y_1}{p}, \frac{Y_2}{p}, \frac{D_0}{p}, 1 + r\right)$$

Since the predetermined incomes for periods 1 and 2, Y_1 and Y_2, both may be written as the product of a quantity and a price of labor, Equation 7.7 shows that all real demands are functions of relative prices (or real income), initial real deposits, and the interest factor, $1 + r$. Three points should be stressed. Demand functions for consumer goods and for interest-bearing financial assets in real terms have the same form. Existing holdings of financial assets in real terms enter the demand functions as determinants the same way that real cash balances enter demand functions (Chapter 6, Sections 5 and 7). The rate of interest, or the interest factor, appears unde-flated in the demand functions. In other words, the demand functions are homogeneous of degree zero in income, prices, and financial assets, but not in the rate of interest. This special position of the rate of interest calls for comment.

2 / The rate of interest as a price

It is very common to speak about the rate of interest as a price, but the literature on the subject is surprisingly confused as to exactly what it is the price *of*. We are sometimes told that it is the price of credit or loanable funds. We have also been told that it is the price of liquidity. It has also been called the price of capital, or "waiting." It is odd that this should be a problem. Nobody doubts that the price of butter is the price of butter. Why, then, the ambiguity about the rate of interest?

As we shall see, the ambiguity arises from attempts to identify the rate of interest as a price. From our previous analysis we see that the rate of interest cannot be a price like the price of butter or the money price of any other commodity or service. We have seen that in contradistinction to the absolute money prices, demand functions are not homogeneous in the rate of interest. It would be a great mistake, to assume, for instance, that the simplified Walrasian system discussed in Chapter 4 could be interpreted as though one of the absolute prices were the rate of interest, and one of the markets were the market for that "something" for which the interest rate were the price.

Closer scrutiny of the concepts of money price and interest rate would have told us in advance that the rate of interest is not merely another money price. By definition, a money price is the number of units of money (dollars, francs, and so forth) given in exchange for a unit of the goods in question.

The rate of interest has a different dimensionality—a time dimension. The rate of interest may be 6 per cent per annum; that is, six-hundreths per year.

The rate of interest is actually a relative price (Makower and Marschak, 1938). To fully comprehend the relation between money prices and interest rates we need to introduce the concepts of "spot" and "forward" prices. In certain well-organized competitive commodity and financial markets (bourses), and in foreign-exchange markets, for instance, it is possible to purchase commodities or claims either for immediate delivery or for delivery at a fixed future date. In both cases the price is determined at the time the contract is made. The spot price is to be paid upon "immediate delivery," which usually means within a few days. The forward price is the price agreed to be paid upon delivery at a predetermined future date. Forward contracts may be for any period of time, although for business reasons delivery is usually set at certain dates, such as the last days of the month. In well-organized markets there will be quotations of both spot prices and a series of forward prices, depending upon the length of the forward contract; that is, the date of delivery and payment.

Consider, for example, a promissory note for a certain amount of money, which is due for payment at a fixed time T in the future. There is no debt service; that is, interest payments and amortizations do not occur currently. Assume that the amount owed at time T is \$1. The promissary note may then be sold or bought, spot or forward. At a given time t the market will thus quote a series of prices

$$n_t^t, n_t^{t+1}, n_t^{t+2}, \ldots, n_t^T$$

for this claim. The subscript denotes the time of the quotation (contract), and the superscript the time of delivery and payment. Obviously, $n_t^T = 1$. The other prices will generally be lower; otherwise the rate of return is negative. A typical risk-free investment may be to buy the claim spot at price n_t^t and simultaneously sell it forward for delivery after one period of time at price n_t^{t+1}. Such transactions are very common in foreign-exchange markets and are called "swaps." The rate of return on this financial investment is $(n_t^{t+1} - n_t^t)/n_t^t$. We are now in a position to *define* the money rate of interest r_t^t at the time t for the period t to $t+1$, as

$$[7.8] \qquad r_t^t = \frac{n_t^{t+1} - n_t^t}{n_t^t} = \frac{n_t^{t+1}}{n_t^t} - 1$$

and the money-interest factor for the same period as

$$[7.9] \qquad 1 + r_t^t = \frac{n_t^{t+1}}{n_t^t}$$

By definition the money rate of interest for a certain period is thus equal to the ratio between the relevant forward price and the spot price of a money claim. Both the forward price and the spot price are money prices, a dollar amount to be paid for one unit of claim. The money-interest factor is simply the ratio of forward to spot price of the money claim.

Note that we have been careful in specifying the period to which the interest rate applies, t to $t + 1$. Given the series of forward prices above, we can also define the money rate of interest for any future period $t + \tau$ to $t + \tau + 1$ as

$$[7.10] \qquad r_t^{t+\tau} = \frac{n_t^{t+\tau+1} - n_t^{t+\tau}}{n_t^{t+\tau}}$$

This is the money rate of interest for period $t + \tau$ to $t + \tau + 1$ at point of time t, which means that this is the interest rate that can be obtained for money invested risk-free during period $t + \tau$ to $t + \tau + 1$ if the investment is arranged today through a simultaneous forward purchase for delivery at $t + \tau$, with forward sale for delivery at $t + \tau + 1$. Note that for the last period $T - 1$ to T we have $r_t^{T-1} = (1 - n_t^{T-1})/n_t^{T-1} = 1/n_t^{T-1} - 1$. The long-term rate of interest may be defined as the geometrical average of all the one-period rates.

We have also been careful in speaking about the *money* rates of interest. In commodity markets with spot and forward prices for commodities it is possible to define so-called "commodity rates of interest." The theory of forward markets and commodity rates of interest was founded by J. M. Keynes (1923, pp. 122–132; 1930, pp. 142 et seq.; 1936, Chapter 17; see also, Kaldor, 1939).

For bank and other institutionalized loans and deposits we do not find market quotations of spot and forward prices, but such transactions can easily be described in this terminology. Depositing $100 at an interest rate of 3 per cent per annum can be seen as a purchase by the depositor of a claim on the bank for $103 to be paid after one year, with a promise from the bank to repurchase the claim at that price after one year. The spot price paid by the depositor, then, is $100, and the forward price to be paid by the bank $103; the interest factor is $103/100 = 1.03$.

Being a relative price, the rate of interest is in one sense a derived variable, and the theory could be expressed entirely in terms of absolute money prices without explicitly introducing the interest rate. We shall demonstrate this in the following model where some other complications will be introduced. On the other hand, since forward markets only exist for a limited number of commodities and claims, there are certainly good reasons for expressing the theory in terms of the interest rate.

3 / Model with money claims and money

We shall again consider a household, planning for two periods, with given, expected money incomes Y_1 and Y_2. The quantities of consumer goods demanded for the two periods are q_1^d and q_2^d, respectively. The prices of the consumer goods are expected to be different during the two periods p_1 and p_2, respectively. The household carries over cash holdings M_0 from period 0. There is a stock market where the household can buy and sell money claims of one period, that is, claims of \$1 that have just been issued (by the government, for instance), and will be redeemed at the beginning of the next period. The spot price for these promissory notes at the time of planning (that is, at the beginning of period 1) is n_1^1; at the same point of time the forward price for delivery at the beginning of period 2 is equal to 1. The household carries over N_0 such claims from period 0. It purchases N_1 claims at the beginning of period 1, and purchases at forward price n_2^2, N_2 claims to be delivered at the beginning of period 2 and carried beyond the horizon.

The budget restriction for period 1, dividing through by p_1, is now:

[7.11] $$\frac{Y_1}{p_1} + \frac{N_0}{p_1} + \frac{M_0}{p_1} = q_1^d + \frac{n_1^1 N_1}{p_1} + \frac{M_1^d}{p_1}$$

and for period 2, dividing through by p_2,

[7.12] $$\frac{Y_2}{p_2} + \frac{N_1}{p_2} + \frac{M_1^d}{p_2} = q_2^d + \frac{n_2^2 N_2}{p_2} + \frac{M_2^d}{p_2}$$

We will assume the utility function to be

[7.13] $$U = U\left(q_1^d, q_2^d, \frac{M_0}{p_1}, \frac{M_1^d}{p_1}, \frac{M_2^d}{p_2}, \frac{N_0}{p_1}, \frac{n_1^1 N_1}{p_1}, \frac{n_2^2 N_2}{p_2}\right)$$

The utility function is based on the hypothesis that both real cash holdings and real money-claim holdings give the owner some kind of utility. The methods of deflation are far from obvious, but are not significant for the main results as long as we do deflate cash and money claims.

By introducing the two Lagrangian multipliers λ_1 and λ_2, we obtain the necessary conditions for utility maximum:

[7.14]
$$\frac{\partial U}{\partial q_1^d} + \lambda_1 = 0$$
$$\frac{\partial U}{\partial q_2^d} + \lambda_2 = 0$$
$$\frac{\partial U}{\partial (M_1^d/p_1)} + \lambda_1 - \lambda_2 \frac{p_1}{p_2} = 0$$
$$\frac{\partial U}{\partial (M_2^d/p_2)} + \lambda_2 = 0$$
$$\frac{\partial U}{\partial (n_1^1 N_1/p_1)} + \lambda_1 - \lambda_2 \frac{p_1}{p_2 n_1^1} = 0$$
$$\frac{\partial U}{\partial (n_2^2 N_2/p_2)} + \lambda_2 = 0$$

Elimination of λ_1 and λ_2 leads to the marginal conditions for utility maximum:

$$\frac{\partial U/\partial q_1{}^d}{\partial U/\partial (M_1{}^d/p_1) + \dfrac{p_1}{p_2}\,\partial U/\partial q_2{}^d} = 1$$

$$\frac{\partial U/\partial q_1{}^d}{\partial U/\partial (n_1{}^1 N_1/p_1) + \dfrac{p_1}{p_2 n_1{}^1}\,\partial U/\partial q_2{}^d} = 1$$

[7.15]

$$\frac{\partial U/\partial q_2{}^d}{\partial U/\partial (M_2{}^d/p_2)} = 1$$

$$\frac{\partial U/\partial (n_2{}^2 N_2/p_2)}{\partial U/\partial (M_2{}^d/p_2)} = 1$$

Interpretation of these marginal conditions is quite simple. With the two budget restrictions, they furnish us with six equations for determining the six unknowns, the demands for consumer goods $q_1{}^d$ and $q_2{}^d$, the demands for real cash holdings $M_1{}^d/p_1$ and $M_2{}^d/p_2$, and the demands for money-claim holdings in real terms $n_1{}^1 N_1/p_1$ and $n_2{}^2 N_2/p_2$.[1] The solutions give us the six demand functions; Equations 7.1, 7.2, and 7.15 show that they must all have the general form

[7.16]
$$f\left(\frac{Y_1}{p_1}, \frac{Y_2}{p_2}, \frac{M_0}{p_1}, \frac{N_0}{p_1}, \frac{p_1}{p_2}, \frac{p_1}{p_2 n_1{}^1}\right)$$

Thus we find that all real demand functions contain the relative prices of consumer goods, initial real cash holdings, and initial real money-claim holdings as arguments. In other words, the demand functions are homogeneous of degree zero in all money prices for consumer goods, in the initial quantity of money, and in the initial value of money claims. Note, however, that the homogeneity does not extend to the price for claims $n_1{}^1$. Neither does the rate of interest appear. Recalling, however, that the interest factor for the first period $1 + r_1{}^1 = 1/n_1{}^1$, the last argument under the function sign in Equation 7.16 can obviously be written as:

[7.17]
$$\frac{p_1}{p_2 n_1{}^1} = \frac{p_1}{p_2}(1 + r_1{}^1) = 1 + R_1{}^1$$

where $R_1{}^1$ is Fisher's "real rate of interest" (at period 1); that is, the money rate of interest adjusted for changes in the real value of a money claim of \$1 induced by changes in the price level between periods 1 and 2.[2]

---

[1] The fact that we do not specify what happens beyond the horizon affects the last two marginal conditions and, accordingly, Equation 7.16. This is why $n_2{}^2$ does not appear in that expression.

[2] Since $p_2 = p_1 + \Delta p$ we have $p_2/p_1 = 1 + \Delta p/p_1 = 1 + i$, where i is the expected rate of inflation. It follows from Equation 7.17 that

$$1 + R_1{}^1 = \frac{1 + r_1{}^1}{1 + i}$$

4 / Intertemporal production models

Intertemporal consumption models are also savings models. Similarly, intertemporal production models are investment models. Taken together they constitute the theory of capital. The entrepreneur plans to buy inputs and sell outputs during a number of periods, and arranges inputs and outputs in such a way that he maximizes his profits. The concept of profits is not well defined in this context, however. Each period will show a net surplus or deficit, and it is these surpluses and deficits that somehow add up to the total profit of the intertemporal production process. Fisher (1930, Part III) showed that if the net incomes accrue to utility-maximizing households, the utility maximization requires maximization of the present value of all the expected surpluses and deficits in the production process. Maximization of the present value of production processes implies demand functions for inputs and supply functions for outputs that are homogeneous of degree zero in all output and input prices, and are dependent upon the rate of interest. Assume that the rate of interest per period is constant and equal to r. The quantities of inputs purchased in period t are denoted q_{it}^d and the quantities of outputs sold q_{it}^s. There are n commodities and services, but they may not all be used or produced. The expected (spot) prices are p_{it}. The expected surplus for period t, then, is $\Sigma p_{it}(q_{it}^s - q_{it}^d)$, and its present value is $(1 + r)^{-t}\Sigma p_{it}(q_{it}^s - q_{it}^d)$.[1] The process extends over $T + 1$ periods, and the present value V of the process is

[7.18] $$V = \sum_{t=0}^{T} (1 + r)^{-t} \sum_{i=1}^{n} p_{it}(q_{it}^s - q_{it}^d)$$

The production possibilities are described by the transformation function

[7.19] $$Q(q_{it}^s, q_{it}^d) = 0$$

where q_{it}^s and q_{it}^d should be understood as vectors, each one containing $n(T + 1)$ elements $i = 1, \ldots, n$ and $t = 0, 1, \ldots, T$. Form $V - \lambda Q$.

---

or, approximately, for small values of i and $r_1{}^1$,

$$R_1{}^1 = r_1{}^1 - i$$

that is, the real rate of interest is equal to the money rate of interest *minus* the rate of the expected price increase (inflation). In continuous terms this relation holds exactly. In this particular sense it could be said that the rate of interest appears in deflated form in the demand and supply functions.

[1] If the rate of interest is expected to vary and r_t is the expected rate of interest for period t, then we have to replace $(1 + r)^{-t}$ by the product $\prod_{\tau=0}^{t} (1 + r_\tau)^{-1}$.

Maximization then yields the $2n(T+1)$ necessary conditions

[7.20]
$$(1+r)^{-t}p_{it} - \lambda\delta Q/\delta q_{it}^s = 0 \qquad i = 1, \ldots, n$$
$$-(1+r)^{-t}p_{it} - \lambda\delta Q/\delta q_{it}^d = 0 \qquad t = 0, \ldots, T$$

Elimination of λ furnishes us with $2n(T+1) - 1$ equations, which together with Equation 7.19 may be solved for the $2n(T+1)$ unknown quantities of inputs demanded and outputs supplied. Examination shows that all demands and supplies are functions of the relative present and expected future (spot) prices of inputs and outputs, and of the interest factor.

This model includes the possibility that inputs are kept for a number of periods and thus appear as stocks (fixed capital or inventories), or that outputs are undergoing processing during several periods and thus appear as inventories (goods in process). It does not explicitly discuss financial transactions. Since the expected surpluses and deficits of the individual periods represent gaps between receipts and payments, however, they must be bridged somehow via the credit market. Indeed, it is for this reason that the rate of interest appears in the equation for present value. The model, therefore, implies demand (supply) functions for credit for each single period. This is easily seen when we write the budget restrictions for the individual periods. For period t we have net (new) lending (disregarding dividends)

[7.21]
$$L_t = \Sigma p_{it}(q_{it}^s - q_{it}^d)$$

Since all demands for inputs and supplies of outputs are homogeneous of degree zero in the input and output prices, and dependent upon the rate of interest, it follows that demand (supply) for new loans in money terms are homogeneous of degree 1 in output and input prices, and dependent upon the interest rate. It is in this way that Walras' law applies in this model. Deflating the loans in money terms by some price index, we find that the demand and supply for new loans in real terms have the same homogeneity properties as the demand and supply functions for commodities and services. Finally, we note that by summing all the new loans (positive or negative) from period 0 to period t we find the stock of loans held at point of time t. It will obviously be a function of the same variables as the demand (supply) of new loans and have the same homogeneity properties.

Thus far, the theory does not explain the demand for cash from enterprises. Demand for cash may be introduced in various ways and for the same reasons that the households' demand for cash was introduced. One way is to let real cash holdings enter the production, or transformation function (Equation 7.19) (Uzawa, 1966). The concept of production would thus be extended to include trade and payments, which in one sense would be very reasonable (see Chapter 5, Section 1). We would in this way obtain demand functions for inputs and cash holdings and supply functions for outputs, which are homogeneous of zero degree in all output and input prices and in the quantity of money, and dependent upon the interest rate. The loan-demand functions derived from the budget restrictions would have similar properties, of course.

A simple example suffices to show what happens when real cash holdings enter the production function. Let the production function be $q(L,K,m)$, where L denotes quantity of labor, K quantity of productive equipment, and m real cash holdings, $m = M/p$. All first derivatives are positive. Profits are then determined by the expression $pq - wL - kK - rmp$, where w is the wage rate, k the rental per physical unit of equipment, and r the interest rate. The necessary conditions for profit maximum are then $q'_L = w/p$, $q'_K = k/p$, and $q'_m = r$. From these three equations we can obtain the demand functions for input of labor and equipment, and for real cash holdings. The demand functions are homogeneous of zero degree in the output price and the input prices, and dependent upon the rate of interest. Notice that in this formulation of the problem there are no initial cash holdings which accordingly do not appear as a determinant in the demand functions either.

Another, more general approach to intertemporal production theory would be to establish special utility functions for enterprises where both profits and various kinds of stocks give utility to the enterprise. The enterprise is then considered a self-contained organism, such as a modern corporation, which has objectives other than merely to help the owners maximize their utility. The theory thus developed differs from the type originated by I. Fisher. For a detailed analysis based on this approach, see A. Lindbeck (1963).

5 / Hicks' futures economy: Intertemporal equilibrium

In *Value and Capital* (1939, Chapter X) J. R. Hicks discussed a kind of science-fiction economy wherein perfect forward markets for all commodities, services, and financial claims existed, and where equilibrium was established simultaneously in all spot and forward markets.

In each market for commodities, services, and claims there is a spot price and one forward price for each future period within the horizon. The number of prices quoted on a certain day is accordingly equal to the product of the number of periods within the horizon and the number of commodities, services, and claims traded. Each individual household and enterprise plans purchases and sales for all periods within the horizon (all individuals and enterprises having the same horizon) and tries to obtain spot and forward contracts corresponding to those plans. Spot and forward prices must therefore adjust themselves until all markets, spot and forward, are cleared. The economy is then in equilibrium, not only for the current period, but for all future periods within the horizon. All future trading consists of merely making deliveries and payments in accordance with the forward contracts. Such models have been discussed by Debreu (1959) and Malinvaud (1953, 1965).

Imperfect foresight with respect to external disturbances may disrupt future periods and necessitate renewed planning, new contracts, and new prices. Forward contracts remaining to be fulfilled at some future date must nevertheless be honored and belong to the data for the new equilibrium. In this way, the futures economy would proceed.

6 / Flow and stock equilibrium

Assets and liabilities are *stock* concepts. They constitute the balance sheets of enterprises, households, and public authorities, and are defined and measured per a certain point of time. On the other hand, output, input, production, sales, purchases, income, investments, savings, and so forth, are *flow* concepts and are defined and measured per a certain unit of time (a day, week, year). Having a time dimension, they are time rates. We are not prevented, however, from discussing the size of a flow at a certain point of time. In continuous analysis we may, for instance, at the end of the year, ask for the rate of income per year. In discrete analysis we may speak about the annual rate of the GNP for the last quarter of the year, or for the last day of the year. The fundamental time dimension of the flow concepts remains unchanged, however. When both concepts appear simultaneously in analysis, it is important not to confuse their dimensionalities (Patinkin, 1966, pp. 518–523).

Stocks and flows are closely related. Each stock has a corresponding flow which is equal to the change in the stock between two specific points of time divided by the length of the period. If the stock of capital at time 0 is K_0 and at time t is K_t, then the net investment during the period 0 to t is $\Delta K = K_t - K_0$, and the net investments per unit of time is $\Delta K/t$. When there are continuous changes, the flow, that is the rate of net investment, will be dK/dt. Conversely, a flow concept will be accompanied by a corresponding stock concept, whose rate of change is the flow in question. In the case of labor services this correspondence tends to break down, because man has no marketable capital value, except in slave economies. Nevertheless, modern economics has found the concept of human-capital value useful, as in discussions of educational problems. It is then a pure bookkeeping concept, however.

The concepts of supply and demand apply to flow as well as to stock entities. Demand for and supply of labor services are clearly concerned with a flow entity. In the case of money, land, buildings, and so forth, demand for and supply of a stock are involved. In the analysis of demand for and supply of stocks, it is common to identify a *supply* of stocks with stocks actually existing at a given time; stock *demand* is identified with the stocks desired at a given time. It is also customary to speak about stock equilibrium at a given time if actual stocks are equal to desired stocks, the reason being that if desired stocks deviate from actual stocks, the stockholders will act to adjust them.

A commodity may appear in the economy as both a flow and a stock. Indeed, apart from all services it *must* appear as both. A capital good may be produced and invested at certain amounts per year, which is the supply and demand for that good in the flow sense. But the same capital good may be kept as a stock by enterprises and used in production. The stock will usually be much larger than the current flows (at least for fixed capital), and the actual stock may be larger or smaller than what the producer would prefer, considering expected future production, prices, and so forth. Thus we have supply and demand for this good in the stock sense. What do we mean, then, when we say that there is equilibrium for this capital good? Is it the flows or the stocks that we have in mind? Or both? The problem was originally posed by L. R. Klein (1950). We shall see, however, that with a complete specification of the demand and supply situation there is no real problem involved here, simply because flow and stock planning are interrelated.

We note first that in models with instantaneous adaptation of stocks we do not need to concern ourselves with the distinction between stock and flow equilibrium (Fellner and Somers, 1950), because on this assumption stock and flow equilibrium coincide. Assume, for instance, that enterprises need 1,000 machines more than they actually have. The desired number of machines minus the actual number of machines on hand thus equals 1,000. Assume also that the enterprises plan to fill the gap immediately by purchasing 1,000 machines, and that the manufacturers of the machines deliver 1,000 machines immediately. There will then be both stock and flow equilibrium. If flow equilibrium is not established (that is, if the manufacturers produce more or fewer than 1,000 machines) there will be no stock equilibrium either. If production exceeds 1,000, some machines will remain unsold and undesired stocks will accumulate with the seller. If machine production does not reach 1,000, the enterprises will be unable to adjust the gap between the desired number of machines and the number of machines on hand. With instantaneous adaptation the two kinds of equilibria are identical.

The assumption of instantaneous adaptation of stocks is quite common in the analysis of money and financial assets and, in this field, may be a sensible assumption. In relation to real capital, however, it is highly unrealistic and must be abandoned (compare old and modern formulations of the acceleration principle). What, then, is the relationship between stock and flow equilibrium and market equilibrium? The available literature on the subject is not clear.

To fix these ideas, assume that enterprises at a given time $t = 0$, keep a certain stock K_0 of a specific type of machine, and that *ceteris paribus* K_0 is considered optimal. K is measured in physical units. Assume, then, that at $t = 0$ the price of this machine falls. The enterprises calculate now that a stock $K^d > K_0$ will be optimal, but decide that the increase in the stock is to take place over a certain period of time so that the new optimal stocks will not be built up until $t = T$. To simplify, let us assume that between $t = 0$ and $t = T$ there are T unit periods, and that the enterprises plan to increase the stock by $(K^d - K_0)/T = I$ per period.

The flow demand (investment) is then I units per period. If at the given price the current supply (production) of machines S per period is equal to I, then there is flow equilibrium; if $S \neq I$, there is flow disequilibrium.

To discuss stock equilibrium in this setting we must distinguish between optimal or desired stock in the short run and desired stock in the long run. This distinction clears up all problems. In our example, the long-run desired stock is K^d. The short-run desired stock at $t = 0$ is $K_0 + I$; that is, the stock that the enterprises plan to build up and hold at $t = 1$. Indeed, if the enterprises have a plan for subsequent adjustment to the long-run level, they have by implication also planned short-term stock developments. We have no reason not to assume that this is also the path of optimal stock development. The short-run stock supply consists of the total stock available at the end of the first period; that is, at $t = 1$. Stocks available at $t = 1$ are K_0 *plus* what the enterprises have accumulated for sale during the period S. It now becomes obvious that flow equilibrium is identical with short-run stock equilibrium. If $I = S$ then, of course, $K_0 + I = K_0 + S$, and if $I \neq S$ then $K_0 + I \neq K_0 + S$. Flow equilibrium and short-run stock equilibrium are equivalent. Instantaneous flow equilibrium and short-run stock equilibrium for the first period do not imply long-run stock equilibrium, however.[1]

In a long-run stationary stock equilibrium $I = 0$. The actual stock is equal to the long-run desired stock K^d, and there is no further need for investments. The demand for stock is therefore K^d. The supply of stock is $K^d + S$, and if there is to be stock equilibrium, S must be equal to zero; that is, $I = S$. Long-run stationary stock equilibrium thus implies flow equilibrium. The conclusion is not altered if we discard the assumption of a stationary long-run stock equilibrium, and assume instead that the long-run optimal stock K^d is increasing by ΔK per unit of time. Stock demand is then $K^d + \Delta K$. For a stock equilibrium to exist, the stock supply must be $K + S = K + \Delta K$; since $K^d = K$, $S = \Delta K$, which means that there is flow equilibrium. It would seem, then, that both stationary and dynamic long-run stock equilibria imply flow equilibrium.

Recalling that we defined price equilibrium as a state wherein the forces affecting the prices cancel each other out (that is, where the prices are constant) we must now be more explicit and ask ourselves what law governs the motion of prices in a market with stocks? Is the rate of the price change determined by flow excess demand, implying that equality of flow demand and supply means zero price change, or does stock excess demand influence

[1] We are disregarding the situation where $T = 1$. There we have instantaneous stock adaptation (*ex-ante*), and flow equilibrium is identical with (short-run and/or long-run) stock equilibrium. See above.

the price change? What is the condition for the price to be constant? To answer this question, posed by Klein (1950), we must first make clear what is meant by stock excess demand. If it means short-run stock excess demand, the question is easily answered. Flow excess demand and short-run stock excess demand are identical. If long-run stock excess demand is meant (that is, the difference between long-run desired and present, actual stocks) the answer is less simple; it depends partly on the market behavior of the stock-building enterprises.

Assume, as we did above, that enterprises have for technical reasons, or because of limited managerial capabilities, decided in advance upon a rigid path of adaptation, which determines their investments per period. If the supplying industries have sufficient capacities, and prices are given, there is no apparent reason why the long-run stock excess demand (that is, the long-run desired stock minus the existing stock) should in any way manifest itself in the market, except, perhaps, as an expectation of the suppliers. Hence, it would seem that nothing but the flow demand should appear in the market and affect prices, except perhaps through expectations of suppliers. On the other hand, if the investment per period is a fixed proportion of the total stock change to be accomplished, it is really a matter of semantics whether we say that prices are affected by flow or long-run stock demand.

The next question we ask is: what determines the planned path of adaptation of stocks? Here we must consider the relationship between the market prices and the stock-adjustment path. It is clear, for instance, that the faster the deliveries are requested, the higher the price will tend to be. On the other hand, the higher the price the longer the enterprises are presumably prepared to wait for delivery. If all enterprises go to the market to obtain contracts for immediate or future delivery, and meet the suppliers, we may assume that an intertemporal equilibrium may be reached where the price for each period is such that flow supply (production) and flow demand (desired investments) tally. Since all the subsequent investments add up to the long-run desired stock, there is, in this sense, both short- and long-run stock equilibrium. The long-run desired stock, the path of investments (the subsequent flow demands and short-run desired stocks), and the adjustment time are not determined in advance, but are influenced by the prices arrived at. The market will actually consist of a spot market and a series of forward markets where equilibrium is reached simultaneously, and where spot and forward prices may differ.[1] In such a market the flow equilibria and the long-run stock equilibrium mutually govern each other. It is clear that for each single period the (spot or forward) price must be such that, *ceteris paribus* with respect to the other prices, production and investment will tally. This means we assume that for the *single* period flow excess demand is decisive for the movement of

---

[1] For an intertemporal market price equilibrium to exist we do not require that spot and forward prices be equal, only that the price of each period does not tend to change.

the forward price. There seems to be no reason or need to adopt any other hypothesis. For the single period flow excess demand and short-term stock excess demand coincide. On the other hand, since both production and investment in each single period are affected by the prices for the other periods, and all prices are determined simultaneously, it makes little sense to ask whether equilibrium prices are determined by stocks or flows. Against the background of Hicks' futures economy, described in Section 5, the problem simply evaporates.

Finally, we consider a third market form where the stock builders place all their orders for subsequent additions at one time, but where no inter-temporal equilibrium is reached (prices may be sticky, or suppliers may be unwilling or unable to commit themselves to fixed delivery dates). The waiting stock builders may have expectations about the delivery times, and thus have an *ex ante* adaptation path, but must accept the deliveries whenever they arrive. Although the market here is imperfect in the sense that spot and forward equilibrium prices are not formed instantaneously, price tendencies may, nevertheless, be influenced by both the total increase in the orders and the anxiety of the stock builders to obtain quick deliveries. In this sense both the long-run stock excess demand and the flow excess demand influence price formation.

Other market forms and mechanisms may be envisaged, but it seems clear that the question of the relationship between long-run stock equilibrium and flow equilibrium cannot be answered without precise assumptions about the market mechanisms in an intertemporal setting. It is also clear that with competitive, perfect spot and forward markets, stock and flow equilibria are determined simultaneously in a general equilibrium system where there is no reason to single out a particular market as determining a particular price.

References

DEBREU, G.: *Theory of Value*, John Wiley & Sons, New York, 1959.

FELLNER, W., and H. SOMERS: "Stock and Flow Analysis: Comment," *Econometrica*, vol. 18, no. 3, July, 1950.

FISHER, IRVING: *The Theory of Interest*, 1930. Reprinted by Augustus M. Kelley, New York, 1965.

HICKS, J. R.: *Value and Capital*, Clarendon Press, Oxford, 1939.

KALDOR, N.: "Speculation and Economic Stability," *The Review of Economic Studies*, vol. 7, no. 1, October, 1939. Reprinted in N. Kaldor, *Essays on Economic Growth and Stability*, Duckworth, London, 1960.

KEYNES, J. M.: *A Tract on Monetary Reform*, Macmillan, London, 1923.

—: *A Treatise on Money*, vol. 2, Macmillan, London, 1930.

—: *The General Theory of Employment, Interest, and Money*, Harcourt, Brace, New York.

KLEIN, L. R.: "Stock and Flow Analysis in Economics," *Econometrica*, vol. 18, no. 3, July, 1950.

—: "Stocks and Flows in the Theory of Interest," in F. H. Hahn and F. P. R. Brechling (eds.), *The Theory of Interest Rates*, Macmillan, London, 1965.

LINDBECK, A.: *A Study in Monetary Analysis*, Almqvist and Wiksell, Stockholm, 1963.

MAKOWER, HELEN, AND JACOB MARSCHAK: "Assets, Prices, and Monetary Theory," *Economica*, N.S., vol. 5, no. 19, August, 1938.

MALINVAUD, E.: "Capital Accumulation and Efficient Allocation of Resources," *Econometrica*, vol. 21, no. 2, April, 1953.

—: "Interest Rates in the Allocation of Resources," in F. H. Hahn and F. P. R. Brechling (eds.), *The Theory of Interest Rates*, Macmillan, London, 1965.

—: "The Analogy between Atemporal and Intertemporal Theories of Resource Allocation," *Review of Economic Studies*, vol. 28, no. 77, June, 1961.

MOSAK, J.: *General Equilibrium Theory in International Trade*, Principia Press, Bloomington, Ind., 1944.

PATINKIN, D.: *Money, Interest, and Prices*, 2d ed., Harper and Row, New York, 1966.

RAMSEY, F.P.: "A Mathematical Theory of Saving," *Economic Journal*, vol. 38, no. 152, December, 1928.

SCHNEIDER, E.: *Wirtschaftlichkeitsrechnung*, Mohr, Tübingen, 1951.

UZAWA, H.: "On a Neoclassical Model of Economic Growth," *Economic Studies Quarterly*, vol. 17, September, 1966.

WICKSELL, K.: *Value, Capital, and Rent*, George Allen and Unwin, London, 1954. First published in German, 1893.

—: *Lectures on Political Economy*, vols. 1 and 2, Routledge and Kegan Paul, London, 1934 and 1935.

Patinkin's system

8

Neither Hicks nor Lange, who initiated criticism of the role of money in neoclassical systems, made any positive contributions to the theory of money in a general equilibrium setting. This was left to Patinkin, who, in addition to sharpening the critique, suggested a solution to the neoclassical dichotomy much in line with the earlier suggestions of T. Scitovsky (1940) and A. C. Pigou (1947, 1948). Patinkin presented the first versions of his system in various articles *circa* 1950 (1949, 1949/1950, 1951); a more elaborate exposition, discussing both disaggregated and aggregated systems, appeared in his book *Money, Interest, and Prices* (1956). An extensive debate arose in response to Patinkin's contributions. Part of it concerned logical problems in Patinkin's own system, and part of it concerned the more nebulous problem of what "the neoclassicists really meant." Most of the debate has been reviewed by Patinkin in the second edition of his book (1966). In this chapter we shall discuss only Patinkin's disaggregated general equilibrium system. Whether this is what "the neoclassicists really meant" is not very important. What matters is Patinkin's positive suggestion for integrating money into the real part of the system, a contribution that resulted in the general equilibrium theory taking a great step forward.

1 / Patinkin's system without credit markets

In the previous chapters we did the groundwork for the introduction of the Patinkin system, particularly by discussing the role of assets in relation to demand and supply. Therefore, we do not need to explain the logics underlying the form of the demand and supply functions with which Patinkin works.

Using the same notation as earlier, we shall first define the general price level P as a weighted average of all prices of commodities and services

[8.1]
$$P = \sum_{i=1}^{n} w_i p_i \qquad \sum_{i=1}^{n} w_i = 1$$

where the w_i are the given weights. The choice of weights is arbitrary. What matters in the following analysis is that the general price index be a linear combination of the individual prices. All we have to assume about P is that it is homogeneous of degree 1 in the individual prices.[1]

With the quantity of money given and equal to M, we let the demand and supply in real terms be homogeneous of zero degree in all money prices and in the quantity of money. We thus have $n + 1$ demand functions

[8.2]
$$q_i^d = q_i^d \left(\frac{p_1}{P}, \ldots, \frac{p_n}{P}, \frac{M}{P} \right) \qquad i = 1, \ldots, n$$

$$m^d = m^d \left(\frac{p_1}{P}, \ldots, \frac{p_n}{P}, \frac{M}{P} \right)$$

$n + 1$ supply functions

[8.3]
$$q_i^s = q_i^s \left(\frac{p_1}{P}, \ldots, \frac{p_n}{P}, \frac{M}{P} \right) \qquad i = 1, \ldots, n$$

$$m^s = \frac{M}{P}$$

and $n + 1$ equilibrium conditions

[8.4]
$$q_i^d = q_i^s \qquad i = 1, \ldots, n$$

$$m^d = m^s$$

In this system, m^d is the demand for money in real terms, that is, M^d/P, and m^s the supply of money in real terms, or the supply of money deflated by P.

Thus we have $3n + 4$ equations to determine $3n + 3$ unknowns, namely, $P, p_1, \ldots, p_n, q_1^d, \ldots, q_n^d, m^d, q_1^s, \ldots, q_n^s, m^s$. The form of the demand and supply functions implies, and presumes that we have dropped Say's law; but Walras' law holds, of course. Therefore, we can be sure that one equation follows from the rest, so that the number of independent equations is equal to the number of unknowns. We could also simply disregard the whole "money market," thereby reducing both the number of equations and the number of unknowns to $3n + 1$. We have no problem, then, with the number of equa-

---

[1] If we specified the demand and supply functions of all individuals, we could actually work with a special index for each individual.

tions and unknowns. (See Chapter 5, Section 4.) We assume that it has a unique, meaningful solution.[1]

The system directly determines the money prices p_i and the price level P and all real demands and supplies. We do not need the exchange equation to determine the level of absolute prices. Money is actually integrated into the system of demand and supply relations. It is remarkable, however, that the system nevertheless shares a characteristic feature of the Walrasian system and the quantity theory of money: an increase in the quantity of money will increase all equilibrium prices and the price level proportionately, and leave all relative prices and real quantities unchanged. This property of the system is easily proved. Assume that the set of numbers $\bar{p}_i$, $\bar{P}$ is a solution to the system when $M = \bar{M}$. If M is then increased to $k\bar{M}$, insertion shows that a new solution to the system will be $k\bar{p}_i$, $k\bar{P}$, all relative prices and real demands and supplies being unaffected, with the demand for and the supply of money in money terms increasing in the proportion k. Although money is now fully integrated into the system, in equilibrium it is still neutral, as the neoclassicists insisted. (See Chapter 5, Section 1.) In this sense Patinkin's system is entirely compatible with neoclassical thinking.

In setting up the demand and supply equations we based the form of the equations upon the deliberations in Chapter 7; we have carried the form of the demand and supply functions of the individual household or enterprise over to the demand and supply functions of the aggregated market. This gives rise to problems only with respect to the variable M. When we add all the individual demand functions for a specific commodity we obtain an expression that depends upon all relative prices and all individual cash holdings. The relative prices are the same for all individuals; therefore, we can also write the aggregated function as dependent upon relative prices. In Equations 8.2 and 8.3, however, we have replaced the individual cash holdings by M, the sum of the individual cash holdings. This procedure is permissible only if distribution of the cash holdings among the individuals does not affect total demand for the individual goods. This assumption is obviously disputable; if it cannot be upheld various difficulties arise.[2]

---

[1] Hahn (1965) has discussed the problem of a solution to monetary systems of Patinkin's type and has shown that with the assumptions Patinkin actually makes concerning the demand for money, his system will indeed have a solution. Hahn questions, however, whether it is legitimate to make such assumptions *a priori*. He argues that in assuming, as Patinkin does, that there will be a positive demand for money at any positive value of money, we have in fact begged the question of a solution to an equilibrium system with money.

[2] For example, since the establishment of equilibrium generally leads to a redistribution of cash holdings, as compared with the initial distribution, the equilibrium of the next period will, *ceteris paribus*, be different in all respects if the distribution of cash matters. A process will continue until a stationary state is reached where at the beginning of the period each individual holds the cash that he desires to hold, considering the equilibrium prices. The system will only move toward such a final stationary state if it is stable (see

2 / Patinkin's system and the exchange equation

Patinkin's system determines the price level directly and there is no need for the exchange equation. On the other hand, since the system leads to the same result as the exchange equation, the two cannot be contradictory. Indeed, it is easily seen that the contradiction that arose in Chapter 5, Section 4, when we interpreted the exchange equation in terms of demand for and supply of money and related it to the simplified Walrasian system, does not arise in dealing with the exchange equation in relation to the Patinkin system. It will be recalled that the Fisher equation (see Equation 5.6) implied an excess demand function for money (in money terms) $(1/V)\Sigma p_i q_i - M$, which is homogeneous of degree 1 in all prices and the quantity of money, whether we consider it in relation to the Walrasian system or Patinkin's system. The excess demand function for money (in money terms) contained in the Patinkin system has exactly the same homogeneity property, however. From the explicit real demand and supply functions for money in Equations 8.2 and 8.3 we have directly

$$[8.5] \qquad P(m^d - m^s) = Pm^d\left(\frac{p_1}{P}, \ \cdots \ , \frac{p_n}{P}, \frac{M}{P}\right) - M$$

which is homogeneous of degree 1 in all prices and the quantity of money. We obtain the same result if we consider the excess demand for money (in money terms) implied by the other demand and supply functions through Walras' law

$$[8.6] \qquad P(m^d - m^s) \equiv \sum_{i=1}^{n} p_i q_i^s - \sum_{i=1}^{n} p_i q_i^d$$

where the right side also is homogeneous of degree 1 in prices and quantity of money.

The exchange equation, interpreted in terms of demand for and supply of money, is thus fully compatible with the Patinkin system. Indeed, there is nothing to prevent $(1/V)\Sigma p_i q_i - M$ from being the excess demand function for money (in money terms) of the Patinkin system. The same reasoning applies, of course, to the Cambridge equation. It is interesting to note also that V (or the Cambridge k) does not need to be constant. It suffices that V (or k) is a function of degree zero in the prices and the quantity of money, that is,

$$[8.7] \qquad V = V\left(\frac{p_1}{P}, \ \cdots \ , \frac{p_n}{P}, \frac{M}{P}\right)$$

Archibald and Lipsey, 1958). Instead of assuming that the distribution of cash does not matter, we could also assume that the equilibrium situations considered are of this long-term stationary character. Alternatively, if a short-term state is considered, we could assume that in case of changes in the quantity of money, all individual cash holdings are changed in the same proportion.

Patinkin's system is thus compatible with the Fisher equation and the Cambridge equation and permits, but does not necessarily require, a constant velocity of money.

3 / The real balance effect and the dynamics of the price level

A final problem with the Walrasian system was its inability to explain how changes in the quantity of money cause the price level to change, and its lack of stability around the price level determined by the equation of exchange. The Patinkin system solves this problem, however. The difference is in the so-called "real balance" effect.

Consider the demand for a certain commodity. Traditional demand theory teaches us that the effect of a change in the price of a certain commodity on the quantity in demand of that commodity may be divided into a substitution and an income effect. With demand and supply functions like those in Patinkin's system we still have these effects. But now we also have the real balance effect. The demand functions have the form

[8.8]
$$q_i{}^d = q_i{}^d \left(\frac{p_1}{P}, \ \cdots \ , \frac{p_n}{P}, \frac{M}{P} \right)$$

Assume, then, that p_i increases, everything else being equal. Due to the increase in the relative price of commodity i (the increase of p_i/P), and the fall in the other relative prices (p_j/P; $j \neq i$) we should normally expect a fall in $q_i{}^d$. This is the effect that traditional analysis divides into income and substitution effects. The fall in M/P, given M, will also influence demand, however. This is the real balance effect. Generally, this effect may be expected to be positive, although cases of "inferior" goods cannot be excluded. The real balance effect is, of course, the same for a decrease in the quantity of money as for a proportionate increase in the price level. Moreover, the real balance effect applies not only to goods and services, but also to the demand for money itself. The same holds true for the supply functions except that here we should perhaps find negative real balance effects more often than not (the more cash you have, the less do you need to work). *A priori* it is difficult to say whether positive or negative effects should tend to dominate. Some proponents of neoclassical theory were fully aware of the real balance effects (Pigou, 1947, 1948). Quantity theorists must have had something similar in mind, but they never did succeed in formalizing it.

We are now prepared to explain how a change in the quantity of money causes a change in the price level, and to argue that the Patinkin system is stable around the equilibrium price level. We shall present no rigorous proof of these propositions, but intuitive reasoning should suffice to show the fundamental difference between the Walrasian system and the Patinkin system.

Assume that in the system shown in Equations 8.1 to 8.4, M doubles while prices for the moment remain unchanged. The system will obviously be thrown out of equilibrium; that is, the equilibrium conditions will have to be relaxed. The relative prices remain unchanged but the real balances have increased; we should therefore, in general, expect the demand for goods to increase and the supply to fall. We shall assume that excess demands do arise in all markets for goods. If we then add to the picture Walras' excess demand hypothesis for price changes, prices will tend to increase everywhere. The price increase will cause the real balances to begin falling, but as long as prices have not risen in proportion to the rise in the quantity of money, real balances will continue to be larger than in the initial situation, that is, in equilibrium, and excess demands will continue to exist everywhere. Prices must therefore continue to rise, albeit more and more slowly, and will come to rest when they have risen in proportion to the rise in the quantity of money and have brought real balances down to their initial value.[1] It will be recalled that at unchanged relative prices in the Walrasian system an increase in the quantity of money would not in itself create excess demands in the markets for goods.

The stability problem can be discussed in a similar vein. Assume that the system set forth in Equations 8.1 to 8.4 is in equilibrium and that, at given M all prices are suddenly quoted 10 per cent above the equilibrium level. All relative prices are thus unchanged, but the real balances fall. Demands therefore tend to fall, too, and supplies tend to rise; that is, excess supplies tend to arise in all markets for goods, and given Walras' excess demand hypothesis, prices will begin to fall. The price fall must continue until the excess supplies have been eliminated; this will not happen until prices have fallen to the equilibrium level. Real balances will also have been brought back to their original equilibrium level. There is nothing left, then, that can create excess supplies. In the Walrasian system there was no such mechanism to make prices begin falling again once they rose above the equilibrium level.

Needless to say, Patinkin's system may not be stable as we have assumed. In that case, the real balance effects will continue to work, but they, together with possible changes in the relative prices, will not bring the economy back to the equilibrium position (if an equilibrium position exists at all). Rigorous conditions for the stability of the Patinkin system can be established in the same way as for the Walrasian system.

4 / The demand for money

Patinkin's system contains an explicit demand function for money, but, as we pointed out earlier, this demand function could also be derived from

[1] This analysis presumes that all prices change in the same proportion so that relative prices remain unchanged during the move toward the new equilibrium.

the other demand and supply functions of the system through application of Walras' law. We have, in real terms (Equation 8.2)

$$[8.9] \qquad m^d = m^d\left(\frac{p_1}{P}, \ \cdots, \frac{p_n}{P}, \frac{M}{P}\right) \equiv \sum_{i=1}^{n} \frac{p_i}{P}\, q_i{}^s - \sum_{i=1}^{n} \frac{p_i}{P}\, q_i{}^d + \frac{M}{P}$$

or, in money terms,

$$[8.9'] \qquad Pm^d = Pm^d\left(\frac{p_1}{P}, \ \cdots, \frac{p_n}{P}, \frac{M}{P}\right) \equiv - \sum_{i=1}^{n} p_i q_i{}^x + M$$

where in both cases the expression to the right of the identity sign is the demand function as derived through Walras' law. Equation 8.9 is homogeneous of degree zero in all prices and the quantity of money, whereas Equation 8.9' is homogeneous of degree 1 in the same variables.

Quantity theory of money has often maintained that the elasticity of the demand for money is unity (Pigou, 1917–18). From the equation of exchange, $MV = PT$, we obtain

$$[8.10] \qquad M = \frac{T}{V}\frac{1}{1/P}$$

Defining the "value of money" as the inverted value of the price level, that is, $1/P$, and interpreting the right side of Equation 8.10 as the demand function for money, it follows immediately that the elasticity (with negative sign) of this demand curve is 1. The curve I-I in Figure 8.1 depicts this demand-for-money curve. Quite apart from the fact that we are here speaking about the demand for money in terms of money and not in real terms, this proposition is questionable and needs qualification. The curve I-I is not a demand curve as this concept usually is defined.

We have already seen that Patinkin's system, Equations 8.1 to 8.4, is in principle compatible with the exchange equation. We have seen that if in this system we let M change, P will change in the same proportion, and the product of M and $1/P$ will thus remain constant. This applies, however, only if we consider a change in M and the following change in P after a complete adaptation of the system to the new equilibrium position. But this is not the sort of question that the elasticity of demand is supposed to answer. When we ask for the price elasticity of the demand for a certain commodity, the question is always: what will be the percentage change in demand at a 1 per cent change in the price of the commodity, *ceteris paribus?* It would seem that we should do something similar in the case of money and accordingly ask what happens to the demand for money (in terms of money) if there is a change in the price level, *ceteris paribus?* The problem is how *ceteris paribus* should be interpreted in this context. We cannot change P the price average without changing at least one individual price p_i. A given change in P can be brought about by an infinite number of combinations of changes in the p_is, however. To simplify, let us assume that the price level changes through proportional changes in all money prices. *Ceteris paribus* can then only mean that the actually existing quantity of money M is kept constant.

Assume that in the system, Equations 8.1 to 8.4, the price level doubles through a doubling of all money prices, but that the quantity of money M is unchanged. The system is out of equilibrium, with all relative prices unchanged and the real balances diminished in proportion to the price increase. Thus there will tend to be an excess supply in all the markets for commodities and services, and the value of all these excess supplies is, according to Walras' law, equal to the excess demand for money. At a given supply (quantity) of money, however, an excess demand for money can only arise through an increase in the demand for money. We must determine, therefore, how much the demand for money increases. To answer this question we must consider the demand function for money (in terms of money) as shown in Equation 8.9'.

We start out from a total-equilibrium position, with the quantity of money M_0 and the value of money $1/P_0$. (See Figure 8.1.) At a doubling of all prices, the value of money falls to $1/(2P_0)$. If we assume that all prices and the quantity of money actually held in the system double, then the demand for money (in terms of money) will also double according to Equa-

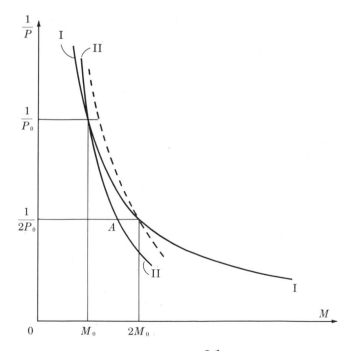

FIGURE 8.1

tion 8.9'. This brings us down curve I-I to the point $2M_0$, $1/(2P_0)$. This was the quantity theorists' way of viewing the situation. Point $2M_0$, $1/(2P_0)$ is a new equilibrium point for the system as a whole. Our problem is the change in the demand for money at a doubling of all p_i and P, given $M = M_0$. The right-hand side of Equation 8.9' consists of a value sum of excess demands with a negative sign, plus the quantity of money. The latter is unchanged. Everything depends, therefore, on the behavior of the value sum of excess demands. In equilibrium this value sum is zero. Relative prices are now unchanged but real cash balances have fallen. If the real balance effect is predominantly positive in the sense that with a fall in real cash balances excess supplies will dominate over excess demands in the markets for commodities and services, we can also be certain that a positive-value sum of excess supplies will arise, and that, accordingly, the demand for money will increase and become greater than M_0. In this way we arrive at the point A. The locus of all such points is curve II-II. We cannot exclude the possibility that curve II-II may have a positive slope. As a consequence of the fall in the real balances, excess demands may dominate over excess supplies; but such a situation does not appear very likely. Neither can we exclude the possibility that point A lies to the right of curve I-I, so that at an unchanged quantity of money and a doubling of all prices the demand for money more than doubles. This can only occur if money is an inferior good in relation to itself; that is, if the real balance effect on the demand for money (in real terms) is negative. Consider the explicit demand function for money in money terms $M^d = Pm^d$. P is doubled and if m^d increases, the demand for money (in money terms) will more than double; but m^d can only increase if the real balance effect on m^d is negative. This situation does not appear very likely either. *A priori* we therefore have good reasons for drawing the curve II-II as we have done.

Summarizing, we can thus say that in Figure 8.1, both curves I-I and II-II describe a relationship between the value of money and the demand for money. Both may be called demand curves, but they answer two entirely different questions. Curve I-I shows us the relationship between the value of money and the demand for money when the whole system moves from one general equilibrium to another as the consequence of changes in the quantity of money. Curve II-II shows us the relationship between the value of money and the demand for money when we imagine proportional changes in all individual prices and, thus, the value of money, keeping the quantity of money constant and letting the system move out of equilibrium. It is the latter curve that corresponds to traditional demand curves; it is a true "partial" demand curve. Curve I-I is the outcome of general equilibrium analysis; curve II-II is the outcome of partial analysis.

It may now readily be seen what happens to the demand for money when the supply of money, that is, the actual cash balance, doubles—but before money prices have begun to rise. The partial demand curve for money then shifts to a new position to the right of the old one, and as prices rise toward their new equilibrium level we follow the new curve (the dotted curve in Figure 8.1) from a value of money $1/P_0$ down to the point $2M_0$, $1/(2P_0)$, where the new curve cuts the general equilibrium curve I-I.

We note, finally, that the entire analysis in this section could be repeated in terms of real demand for money, and it may be a good exercise to do just that.

5 / Patinkin's system with credit market

Credit may be introduced into the system in various ways, but to simplify matters we shall assume that only one credit market exists. In this credit market (stock market) government bonds are bought and sold. The market rate of interest is r and the bonds are assumed to be perpetuaries. The market price of a bond with an annual interest payment of \$1 will then be $1/r$. The number of bonds, each bond having an annual interest payment of \$1, is given and equal to B. The total market value of all bonds held by the private sector is thus B/r.[1] Their real value is defined as $(B/r)/P$, that is, the money value deflated by the average price as defined below. The demand for bonds, expressed in the number of bonds, is B^d. The money value of the demand for bonds is B^d/r, and the demand for bonds in real terms is $b^d = (B^d/r)/P$. The supply of bonds is B^s, its money value is B^s/r, and the real supply of bonds is $b^s = (B^s/r)/P$. Otherwise the notation is the same as in the Patinkin system without credit.

The definition of the price level is now even more ambiguous, but we shall retain the previous definition

[8.11]
$$P = \sum_{i=1}^{n} w_i p_i \qquad \sum_{i=1}^{n} w_i = 1$$

The price level, or, rather, the average price, does not include the rate of interest or the price of bonds. Considering the homogeneity assumptions of the following demand and supply functions, it is easily understood that the rate of interest and the price of bonds must be excluded from the definition of the price level. Otherwise the homogeneity properties would not conform to the findings in Chapter 7.

We have now $n + 2$ "real" demand functions

$$q_i^d = q_i^d\left(\frac{p_1}{P}, \ldots, \frac{p_n}{P}, 1+r, \frac{B/r}{P}, \frac{M}{P}\right) \qquad i = 1, \ldots, n$$

[8.12] $\quad b^d = b^d\left(\frac{p_1}{P}, \ldots, \frac{p_n}{P}, 1+r, \frac{B/r}{P}, \frac{M}{P}\right)$

$$m^d = m^d\left(\frac{p_1}{P}, \ldots, \frac{p_n}{P}, 1+r, \frac{B/r}{P}, \frac{M}{P}\right)$$

---

[1] We disregard problems related to the distribution of bonds; they are in principle the same as money. See the final paragraph of Section 1.

All real demands are homogeneous of degree zero in all money prices, the number of bonds, and the quantity of money (cash holdings); and they are functions of the rate of interest. This is entirely in line with the models discussed in Chapter 7.

The $n + 1$ real supply functions are

$$q_i{}^s = q_i{}^s\left(\frac{p_1}{P}, \cdots, \frac{p_n}{P}, 1 + r, \frac{B/r}{P}, \frac{M}{P}\right) \qquad i = 1, \ldots, n$$

[8.13] $$b^s = \frac{B/r}{P}$$

$$m^s = \frac{M}{P}$$

The equilibrium conditions are

[8.14]
$$q_i{}^d = q_i{}^s \qquad i = 1, \ldots, n$$
$$b^d = b^s$$
$$m^d = m^s$$

The system shown in Equations 8.11 through 8.14 furnishes us with $3n + 7$ equations to determine $3n + 6$ unknowns, namely $n\ q_i{}^d$, $n\ q_i{}^s$, $n\ p_i$, b^d, b^s, r, m^d, m^s, and P. Walras' law assures us that one of the equations is dependent upon the rest so that we have the same number of independent equations and unknowns. We assume that it has a unique, meaningful solution.

We notice now that the homogeneity of degree zero in all prices, the number of bonds, and the quantity of money, that is, in p_i, P, B, and M, implies that a proportionate change in B *and* M will change all equilibrium prices in the same proportion and leave the equilibrium rate of interest unchanged. The proof runs as before: Assume $\bar{p}_i$, $\bar{P}$, and $\bar{r}$ to be a solution to the system at $B = \bar{B}$ and $M = \bar{M}$. Double B and M. The new solution to the system is, then, $2\bar{p}_i$, $2\bar{P}$, $\bar{r}$, all the real demands and supplies remaining unchanged. It follows, however, that an isolated change in the quantity of money M, given the number of bonds B, does *not* imply that prices in the new equilibrium have changed in proportion to the quantity of money or that the equilibrium rate of interest is unchanged. Assume that M doubles at unchanged B. Inserting prices equal to $2p_i$ and leaving the rate of interest unchanged, all relative prices, the rate of interest, and the real quantity of money will be unchanged; but the real value of bonds will have changed and the equilibrium is therefore disturbed. This means that money is no longer neutral, and it would seem that the basic neoclassic and quantity theoretical proposition has broken down.[1]

[1] This result has caused some concern, and various arguments have been brought forward to save the neoclassical view. It may thus be argued that the sole reason for the breakdown of the neoclassical proposition is a money illusion on the part of the government. When the government increases the quantity of money and prices increase, the real value

Let us also discuss the problem of the relationship between the system set forth above and the exchange equation. The system contains an explicit demand function for money in real terms m^d, which is homogeneous of degree zero in all prices, the number of bonds, and the quantity of money. The corresponding demand function in money terms Pm^d is homogeneous of degree 1 in the same variables. In deriving the demand function via Walras' law, we should of course find a demand function for money with the same properties; otherwise the system would not be consistent. Walras' law is now

[8.15]
$$M + \frac{B}{r} + \sum_{i=1}^{n} p_i q_i^s \equiv \sum_{i=1}^{n} p_i q_i^d + M^d + \frac{B^d}{r}$$

from which we find the demand function for money in money terms

[8.16]
$$M^d = Pm^d = -\sum_{i=1}^{n} p_i q_i^x - \frac{B_r^d}{r} + \frac{B}{r} + M$$

which is homogeneous of degree 1 in all prices, the number of bonds, and the quantity of money. Dividing through by P we find the demand function for money in real terms; it is of course homogeneous of degree zero in the same variables.

At this point we must call attention to a short cut we have taken throughout this section. Since government bonds exist at a number equal to B with interest payments equal to $1 per bond, the private sector must receive

---

of outstanding government bonds and real interest payments will fall. The absence of a money illusion might be said to imply that the government should be concerned only with the real value of the bonds and interest payments, and should thus increase the number of bonds in proportion to prices. This argument is very much a matter of semantics, however. It might be asked why the same reasoning does not apply to the quantity of money. The quantity of money is part of the public debt, and absence of a money illusion might imply that this part of the public debt should also be kept constant in real terms. This pattern of behavior implies that any change in preferences, productivity, and so forth, in the private sector, which at a given quantity of money would lead to a change in the price level, would be followed by a proportional change in the quantity of money, which would imply a policy of a constant price level.

Another argument (Christ, 1957) concentrates on the taxes necessary to cover the interests in a static setting. (See below.) If the taxpayers see the future correctly and capitalize future tax payments, the value of bonds held by the private sector will be offset by the corresponding negative capital value of future tax payments. If this negative capital value (debt) influences the taxpayers' demands and supplies in the same way as the positive capital value of government bonds, a price increase will diminish the taxpayers' "real debt" to the government by the same amount as the bondholders' real wealth diminishes, and the effects of each will be cancelled out (disregarding problems of distribution). The argument $(B/r)/P$ should accordingly be deleted from all the demand and supply functions. There is no doubt that future tax payments are to some extent capitalized, but it is doubtful whether foresight will be so perfect that this argument really holds water.

interest income from the government equal to $\$B$ per period. This interest income was not included in the left side of Equation 8.15. Nor does it appear as a determinant in the demand and supply functions in Equations 8.12 and 8.13. The reason for the omissions is that the government cannot pay interest without collecting the same amount in taxes per period. Otherwise our assumptions of a given quantity of money and a given number of bonds would break down. We have thus omitted these two payments, equal in size. In the aggregate budget restriction, Walras' law, the two payments do indeed cancel each other out, but not necessarily in the individual budget restrictions, which means that they do appear in the individual demand and supply functions. We have thus tacitly assumed that the effects of interest and tax payments on real demand and supply cancel out. Quite apart from the distribution of taxes, the nature of the taxes levied is important too. We could have tried taking this into account by introducing the real interest payments B/P and the corresponding tax payments, let us say T/P, as separate arguments in the demand and supply functions. Assuming that the government's budget is always balanced, that is $B = T$, nothing would be changed with respect to the homogeneity properties of the system, although it would, of course, affect the equilibrium solution. The distributional problem would remain, however, which leads to the much wider problem of government transactions in relation to the general equilibrium system. (See Section 7.)

After this digression, we can now write the exchange equation either as

$$[8.17] \qquad MV = \sum_{i=1}^{n} p_i q_i \qquad \text{or} \qquad MV = \sum_{i=1}^{n} p_i q_i + \frac{B}{r}$$

and interpret

$$[8.18] \qquad \frac{1}{V} \sum_{i=1}^{n} p_i q_i \qquad \text{or} \qquad \frac{1}{V} \left(\sum_{i=1}^{n} p_i q_i + \frac{B}{r} \right)$$

(see Chapter 5, Section 4) as the demand for money. The Fisher equation in the above interpretation is clearly compatible with this system, Equation 8.18 being homogeneous of degree 1 in the prices, the number of bonds, and the quantity of money. We may assume that the velocity of money V is constant. Equation 8.18 is compatible with the system set forth in Equations 8.11 to 8.14, however, even if we assume that the velocity is a function homogeneous of degree zero in p_i, B, and M, and dependent upon the rate of interest, that is

$$[8.19] \qquad V = V \left(\frac{p_1}{P}, \; \cdots \; , \frac{p_n}{P}, 1 + r, \frac{B/r}{P}, \frac{M}{P} \right)$$

Both the demand for money and the velocity of money may thus be functions of the rate of interest. This is the essence of Keynes' liquidity-preference theory of money, which accordingly is fully compatible with Patinkin's system with credit markets. We shall return to this point in Chapter 11.

6 / Real assets and the Patinkin system

Without a number of important amendments the Patinkin system cannot possibly pretend to describe the real world in which we live. We shall devote the remaining part of this chapter to discussing briefly a number of possible amendments.

One amendment would be the incorporation of real capital stocks into the system of demand and supply functions. We thereby include total private wealth as arguments in the functions (Metzler, 1951). In one sense this amendment would not change the structure of the system in any significant way. If we assume that initial stocks of physical capital exist, it will, of course, affect demand and supply and the equilibrium position. Merely to include these physical assets as determinants in the demand and supply functions analogous to real cash holdings and real bond holdings, however, would not bring about an essential change in the behavior of the system. It would remain homogeneous of degree zero in prices, money, and number of bonds, and what has been said about the neutrality of money would still hold true.

We cannot include initial stocks of physical capital without considering the desired stocks and the investments explicitly, however. We would either have to add conditions for the economy to remain stationary, or we would have to study the accumulation and growth process over time. The first is a problem of neoclassical capital theory, the second belongs to modern growth theory. We shall return to both later, in Chapters 17 and 18.

7 / The role of government

Government begins to appear when we introduce money. Money was assumed to be issued by a government authority, or at least somebody outside the private sector. Government did not have any other economic function than to determine the quantity of money, however. The introduction of government bonds led us to consider government in a more significant way. Government interest payments had to be covered by tax revenues in the same amount. Government had thus a balanced current budget with interest payments as the only expenditure item and some kind of lump-sum taxes as its only revenue item, and the private sector held government bonds issued at an earlier date in a way not explained by the system. There is no reason why we should not proceed to introduce full-scale government activity. Relatively little has been done in the way of discussing government in relation to the general equilibrium system, however. Such discussion has occurred mainly in connection with aggregated systems of the Keynesian type.

We shall here follow the standard national accounting terminology and exclude from government all public-sector activities that lead to sales of commodities and services in the market. We thus disregard public enterprises and trading agencies (which can be dealt with as other enterprises), and are left with public administration (in a wide sense, including education and defense). Government expenditures consist, then, of purchases of goods and services and transfer payments (including interest payments on the public debt), and government revenues are various kinds of taxes, income from property, and perhaps transfer revenues that cannot be classified as either taxes or property income. Further, the government may be active in the credit market, taking and giving loans. We may include the central bank in the government, which means that money is issued by the government. All these activities should be considered in the general equilibrium system.

Two problems should be separated clearly. One problem is how the government should behave under ideal circumstances to create maximum welfare, for example, a Pareto optimum, and what the structure of the general equilibrium system would be if the government behaved accordingly. Another problem is how governments actually behave, and how actual government behavior influences the structure of the general equilibrium system.

The solution to the first problem depends entirely upon how optimum welfare is defined. It is well known that under certain assumptions with respect to income distribution, the government should decide which quantities of goods and services it should purchase, given the preferences of the private sector, and finance the expenditures fully by lump-sum taxes. In a neoclassical equilibrium setting, the budget should be balanced. This would not essentially change the structure of the system. To the demand functions we would now have to add a constant quantity purchased by the government; the real value of the lump-sum taxes would appear as determinants in the private sector's demand and supply functions along with the real value of the services from the public sector. Demand and supply would thus be homogeneous of degree zero in prices, lump-sum taxes, government bonds, and the quantity of money. A change in the quantity of money, accompanied by a proportional change in the lump-sum taxes and the number of government bonds would thus lead to a proportional change in the equilibrium prices. Some difficult problems do arise, however, in connection with so-called "collective services" (Samuelson, 1954).

The second problem has a different solution. Governments may actually tend to fix purchases of goods and services in real terms and let money expenditures vary with money prices, but lump-sum taxes are, practically speaking, unknown in modern societies. Government revenues in advanced Western countries are dominated by progressive personal income taxes, proportional corporate income taxes, proportional social security contributions, proportional value added, turnover, or sales taxes, and specific indirect taxes on various goods and services. The proportional corporate income taxes, social security contributions, and value added taxes do not disturb the homogeneity properties of the Patinkin or Walras systems. They all enter the system as a constant coefficient by which prices on taxed commodities are multiplied, $(1 + t_i)p_i$, t_i being the tax rate. The equilibrium solution will be affected by their appearance, of course, but the homogeneity properties remain unchanged. Progressive income taxes and specific indirect taxes will not only affect the equilibrium solution, but will also change the homogeneity properties. For these taxes the rate is not a constant, but is itself a function of price. If all prices change proportionately, the tax rates will change. With progressive income taxation, a general (proportional) price increase in the system will lead to a more than proportional increase in tax revenues. It might be argued that to keep the budget in balance, which is necessary to prevent an induced change (fall) in the quantity of money, the government must change the scale of taxation to such a degree that after the proportional price increase and the cut in the tax scale, there is merely a porportionate increase in tax revenues. (We assume that the government's physical purchases are unchanged.) This change can be accomplished in many ways, however, and the method chosen will be decisive for the new equilibrium.

As we have already noted, a state of general equilibrium requires that the government's budget balances in the sense that revenues and expenditures balance, and that net borrowing remains at zero. Otherwise the stocks of government money and/or claims will change continuously. The requirement of a balanced budget places an important restraint on the system, and in some respects limits its applicability. Thus we cannot analyze the effects of a permanent change in a certain tax without assuming a compensating change in the current budget of the government. This leads to an ambiguity in the notion of the effects of a tax, well known from the theory of shifting and incidence of taxation (Hansen, 1958, Chapter II). It has similar consequences for the analysis of government asset and debt operations, for example, open-market operations. Even at a balanced budget the government may buy or sell bonds in the market. The quantity of government money outstanding will then change by the same amount in the opposite direction. The current expenditures for interest payments will also change, however, and a compensating change in the budget will have to be undertaken. This compensating change may be a tax change, but in principle there is nothing to prevent us from considering a compensating change in government purchases. The precise assumptions about this compensatory change in the current budget may be decisive for the effects of open-market operations (Mundell, 1960).

A final implication of the assumption of a balanced budget is that isolated changes in the quantity of money or government claims can be accomplished only through gifts or confiscation once and for all, that is, in national accounting terminology, through capital transfers. If we were prepared to relax temporarily the assumption of a balanced budget, we could assume that money were injected or withdrawn through a temporary expenditure or revenue, taking place in one single period, after which the temporary expenditure or revenue would be abolished and the budget again balanced. We cannot be sure, however, that the following equilibrium would not be influenced by what took place in the budget during the period we allowed it to become off balance. The effects of a change in the quantity of money accomplished in this way may therefore depend on the way in which it was done.

8 / Inside money and claims. Private net wealth

The discussion of money and credit has so far concentrated exclusively on government bonds and money and their place in the general equilibrium system. Credits given and taken within the private sector, and money created by the private sector itself, have been left aside. In a modern society the bulk of credit market transactions take place through financial intermediaries— in particular, private banks—and modern monetary theory has paid increasing attention to the role played by intermediaries in the economic system. This has given rise to a distinction between so-called "outside" claims and money, that is, claims and money issued by somebody (government or foreign country) outside the private sector, and "inside" claims and money, issued by private individuals, enterprises, or institutions (Gurley and Shaw, 1960).

The existence of inside claims and financial intermediaries means that we have to consider a number of interrelated credit submarkets where various types of inside claims are bought and sold. These claims may differ with respect to maturity, security, yield, and liquidity, and their market rates of interest may therefore differ. In principle, there is nothing to prevent the general equilibrium system from being expanded to include all these individual credit submarkets. For each additional credit market, we get three new variables: the number of claims in demand, the number supplied, and their rate of interest. Provided that buyers and sellers, including the intermediaries, are utility or profit maximizers, we shall still find that all real demand and supply functions are homogeneous of zero degree in all prices, and physical and financial assets and debts (in value terms), and functions of the many rates of interest or return (see, for instance, Lindbeck, 1963; Tobin, 1969). A special portfolio theory has been developed for handling problems related to demand and supply of such assets and debts; problems related to uncertainty about the future become particularly important in this context. We shall not enter upon this theory here (see Markowitz, 1959).

The functioning of the general equilibrium system, and its solution (assuming that it has a solution), will greatly depend upon the nature of the intermediaries and the control to which they may be subjected from the side of the government with respect to entrance, current business, interest rates, and so forth. Even under perfectly competitive conditions, we have no reason to believe that the existence of financial intermediaries and inside claims should be neutral to the system in the sense that they leave relative prices and quantities of commodities bought and sold, and interest rates, unchanged. The situation is parallel to the introduction of commodity or fiat (government) money (see Chapter 5, Section 1).

The existence of intermediaries and inside claims does, however, give rise to special problems as soon as some kind of aggregation is attempted. Thus, the appropriate definition of money in a quantity theoretical setting may no longer be obvious (Friedman and Schwartz, 1963). Some inside claims may be so liquid and secure that they are perfect substitutes for government money; deposits on checking accounts in private banks are a case in point. There may be little doubt that such deposits should be included in the definition of money. Much less obvious is how to deal with the whole range of other more or less liquid and secure, interest-bearing private claims that exist in modern credit markets.

Another important aggregation problem arises in relation to the definition of total private net wealth (to be entered as an argument in the demand and supply functions). In a barter economy private wealth is identical with the stock of physical assets (disregarding so-called "human wealth"). When commodity money (gold, for instance) or fiat money (government notes) is added to the picture, private wealth equals the value of physical assets plus money. If interest-bearing net claims on the government exist, they should be added to private net wealth, although it may be argued (see above, p. 88, note 1) that if the private sector correctly foresees and capitalizes the tax payments necessary (in a static setting) to cover the government's interest payments, the interest-bearing net claims on the government will be canceled out by a corresponding "debt." The latter argument does not apply to net claims on foreign countries; they clearly add to the private net wealth. It has been argued that inside claims cannot add to private net wealth. A debt corresponds to each claim, and in the process of consolidation for the private sector as a whole, they cancel each other out (Gurley and Shaw, 1960). This argument overlooks, however, that the capitalized value of the profits of the financial intermediaries represents a net addition to private wealth (Pesek and Savings, 1967). If, for instance, a bank receives check deposits at zero interest rates, lends at a certain positive interest rate, and has given costs, the value of deposits and loans certainly cancel each other out on aggregation for the private sector; but there is nothing to offset the capitalized value of the banks' profits. This situation can only arise in the case of imperfect credit markets, however. In competitive markets the financial transactions will be expanded (through lower loan rates and, perhaps, higher deposit rates) until the marginal and average costs in the long run are equal to the interest margin; profits will then become zero. In a perfectly competitive long-term equilibrium, inside claims and intermediaries should thus not in themselves represent an addition to total private net wealth. This is not to deny, however, that indirectly they may affect private net wealth through their effects on the equilibrium stock of physical assets. Even if in an accounting sense inside claims and debts cancel each other out, the same does not need to be true with regard to their effects; the distribution of assets and debts and, thus, of private wealth may have important consequences for the general equilibrium system and its solution.

References

ARCHIBALD, G. C., and R. G. LIPSEY: "Monetary and Value Theory: A Critique of Lange and Patinkin," *Review of Economic Studies*, vol. 26, no. 69, 1958.

CHRIST, C.: "Patinkin on Money, Interest, and Prices," *Journal of Political Economy*, vol. 65, no. 4, August, 1957.

FRIEDMAN, M., and ANNA J. SCHWARTZ: *A Monetary History of the United States, 1867–1960*, N.B.E.R., Princeton University Press, Princeton, 1963, Appendix B.

GURLEY, J. G., and E. S. SHAW: *Money in a Theory of Finance*, The Brookings Institution, Washington, D.C., 1960.

HAHN, F. H.: "On Some Problems of Proving the Existence of an Equilibrium in a Monetary Economy," in F. H. Hahn and F. P. R. Brechling (eds.), *The Theory of Interest Rates*, St. Martin's Press, New York, 1965.

HANSEN, BENT: *The Economic Theory of Fiscal Policy*, George Allen and Unwin, London, 1958.

LINDBECK, A.: *A Study in Monetary Analysis*, Almqvist and Wiksell, Stockholm, 1963.

MARKOWITZ, H.: *Portfolio Selection*, John Wiley & Sons, New York, 1959.

METZLER, L. A.: "Wealth, Saving, and the Rate of Interest," *Journal of Political Economy*, vol. 59, no. 2, April, 1951.

MODIGLIANI, F.: "The Monetary Mechanism and Its Interaction with Real Phenomena," *The Review of Economics and Statistics*, vol. 45, no. 1, part 2, supplement, February, 1963.

MUNDELL, R. A.: "The Public Debt, Corporate Income Taxes, and the Rate of Interest," *The Journal of Political Economy*, vol. 48, no. 6, December, 1960.

PATINKIN, D.: *Money, Interest, and Prices: An Integration of Monetary and Value Theory*, Row, Peterson, Evanston, Ill., 1956. Second edition, Harper and Row, New York, 1966.

PESEK, B. P., and T. R. SAVINGS: *Money, Wealth, and Economic Theory*, Macmillan, New York, 1967.

PIGOU, A. C.: "The Classical Stationary State," *The Economic Journal*, vol. 53, no. 212, December, 1943.

—: "The Value of Money," *The Quarterly Journal of Economics*, vol. 32, no. 1, 1917–18. Reprinted in F. A. Lutz and L. W. Mints (eds.), *Readings in Monetary Theory*, George Allen and Unwin, London, 1951.

—: "Economic Progress in a Stable Environment," *Economica*, N.S., vol. 14, no. 55, August, 1947. Reprinted in F. A. Lutz and L. W. Mints (eds.), *Readings in Monetary Theory*, George Allen and Unwin, London, 1951.

SAMUELSON, P. A.: "The Pure Theory of Public Expenditures," *The Review of Economics and Statistics*, vol. 36, no. 4, November, 1954.

SCITOVSKY, T.: "Capital Accumulation, Employment, and Price Rigidity," *Review of Economic Studies*, vol. 8, no. 2, February, 1940.

TOBIN, J.: "A General Equilibrium Approach to Monetary Theory," *Journal of Money, Credit, and Banking*, vol. 1, no. 1, February, 1969.

Investments and savings, price level and activity level

9

This chapter discusses the relationship between the general system of demand and supply and certain aggregates that are well known from macroeconomic analyses and national accounting. We will demonstrate the definitional relationship between total investments and savings, and demand for and supply of commodities and services, loans and money. We shall discuss thereafter the dynamic implications that the existence of equality or discrepancies between investments and savings have for the general system.

1 / An excess demand identity

Before introducing aggregates we shall rewrite Walras' law in a way that is useful in discussions of money and credit market problems. For the Patinkin system, extended to include a credit market (namely, the market for government bonds), Walras' law can be written (compare Equation 8.15):

$$[9.1] \qquad \sum_{i=1}^{n} q_i^d p_i - \sum_{i=1}^{n} q_i^s p_i \equiv \frac{B}{r} - \frac{B^d}{r} + M - M^d$$

Recalling that $q_i^d - q_i^s = q_i^x$, and writing $B^d - B = B^x$ and $M^d - M = M^x$,

Walras' law becomes

[9.2]
$$\sum_{i=1}^{n} q_i^x p_i \;\equiv\; \left(\frac{-B^x}{r}\right) + (-M^x)$$

| Sum of value of all excess demand or supply in markets for commodities and services | Value of excess supply of bonds = excess demand for loans (credit) | Excess supply of money |

2 / Aggregation of the general system

The general system of demand and supply may be aggregated in many different ways. Aggregates must always be formed so that they can fulfill a specific analytical purpose. For the purpose at hand it is convenient to classify all goods into six groups: consumer goods, capital goods, produced intermediary inputs, factor services, bonds, and money. The economy is thus conceived of as six corresponding, aggregate markets with their aggregate demands and supplies. For each particular aggregate market we can form the value sum of all individual demands or supplies belonging to that market. Each value sum defines an aggregate, as shown in the list of definitions on the next page. The definitions, with Equation 9.1, lead directly to

[9.3] $$C^d + I^d + R^d + F^d - C^s - I^s - R^s - F^s \equiv \frac{B}{r} - \frac{B^d}{r} + M - M^d$$

Assuming that all factors are owned by the households that sell their services, and that production takes place in separate units called business, income and savings may be defined:

Business' expected income (gross profit) $Y_b = (C^s + I^s + R^s) - (R^d + F^d)$
                                                           Expected sales   Planned costs

Households' expected income[1] $Y_f = F^s$

Business' planned savings $S_b = Y_b$

Households' planned savings $S_f = Y_f - C^d$

Note that all the aggregate concepts that have been defined in this section are measured in terms of value, in dollars for example, and are homogeneous functions of degree 1 in prices, number of bonds, and quantity of money; all are functions of the interest rate. Applying these definitions to Equation 9.3, we obtain (compare Equation 9.2):

[9.4] $$I^d - (S_b + S_f) \equiv (-B^x/r) + (-M^x)$$

| Planned investments | Planned savings | Excess supply of bonds | Excess supply of money |

Value of all excess demand or supply for commodities and services

---

[1] The remarks in Chapter 8, Section 5 concerning interest payments on the government bonds apply here, as well. We assume that all bonds are owned by the households, which pay an income tax equal to the interest payments. Dividends from businesses to households are considered payments for factor services.

LIST OF DEFINITIONS

Consumer goods $i = 1, \ldots, h$: $\sum\limits_{i=1}^{h} q_i^d p_i = C^d = $ planned consumption

$\sum\limits_{i=1}^{h} q_i^s p_i = C^s = $ expected sales of consumer goods

Capital goods $i = h + 1, \ldots, j$: $\sum\limits_{i=h+1}^{j} q_i^d p_i = I^d = $ planned (fixed[1]) investment (gross)

$\sum\limits_{i=h+1}^{j} q_i^s p_i = I^s = $ expected sales of capital goods

Intermediary inputs $i = j + 1, \ldots, m$: $\sum\limits_{i=j+1}^{m} q_i^d p_i = R^d = $ planned purchases of intermediary inputs

$\sum\limits_{i=j+1}^{m} q_i^s p_i = R^s = $ expected sales of intermediary inputs

Factor services $i = m + 1, \ldots, n$: $\sum\limits_{i=m+1}^{n} q_i^d p_i = F^d = $ planned purchases of factor services

$\sum\limits_{i=m+1}^{n} q_i^s p_i = F^s = $ expected sales of factor services

Bonds (perpetuaries): $B^d/r = $ planned purchases of bonds (gross) = planned lending (gross)

$B/r = $ expected sales of bonds (gross) = planned borrowing (gross)

Money: $M^d = $ planned cash balances

$M = $ existing cash balances

---

[1] Inventory changes are not considered in this chapter. They could easily be included in the analysis but would not change the conclusions in any essential way.

The difference between planned investments and planned savings is thus equal to the total value of excess demand for commodities and services, and equal to the sum of the value of the excess supply of bonds and the excess supply of money.

3 / Investments and savings, *ex ante* and *ex post*

Investments and savings, as defined in Section 2, may differ in size. When the system is in complete equilibrium so that demand and supply tally everywhere, the amount of savings and investments must of course be equal. They can only differ if the system is in disequilibrium. Even in that case they may be equal; namely, when the value of excess demands and the value of excess supplies in the markets for commodities and services happen to cancel each other out. Investments and savings in this particular sense are called *ex ante* investments and *ex ante* savings, respectively.

Investments and savings may be defined alternatively *ex post*. The *ex post* definitions are also based on demand and supply of commodities and services. Whereas the *ex ante* definitions are related to intended demand and supply, which may differ, the *ex post* definitions are based on demand and supply in the sense of actual turnover, and in this sense demand and supply cannot differ.

Let Figure 9.1 represent an arbitrary market for a commodity or service, all other prices being given. At $\bar{p}$ the market is in equilibrium and the intended (*ex ante*) demand $\bar{q}^d$ and the intended (*ex ante*) supply $\bar{q}^s$ are equal,

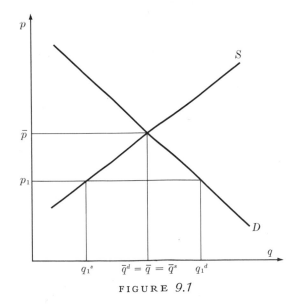

FIGURE *9.1*

and are also equal to actual (*ex post*) turnover $\bar{q}$. At equilibrium demand and supply coincide on all definitions. At p_1 the market is in disequilibrium. *Ex ante* demand q_1^d exceeds *ex ante* supply q_1^s and there is an excess demand, *ex ante*, whose value $(q_1^d - q_1^s)p_1$ contributes to build the difference between *ex ante* investments and *ex ante* savings. (Compare the left sides of Equations 9.2 and 9.4.) But what is the actual turnover when the price is equal to p_1? We are unable to answer this simple question without additional assumptions. If there are no inventories, actual sales cannot exceed q_1^s, and actual turnover will thus be equal to q_1^s. With sufficient inventories from which unexpected sales can take place, total sales may become equal to q_1^d. In other cases actual turnover may fall between q_1^s and q_1^d. No matter what size the actual turnover may be, actual purchases must be equal to actual sales. This means that *ex post* demand and supply are equal, whether or not the system is in equilibrium.

It follows that if we apply the definitions of investments and savings given in Section 2, but interpret all demands and supplies as *ex post* demand and supplies, then investments and savings must be equal in all circumstances. *Ex post* investments must be equal to *ex post* savings simply because *ex post* demand is equal to *ex post* supply in all individual markets. The following table is now easy to understand, I denoting investments and S savings:

	Ex ante	Ex post
General equilibrium	$I = S$	$I = S$
General disequilibrium	$I \gtreqless S$	$I = S$

Equality of investments and savings is a necessary but not sufficient condition for general equilibrium. It would seem, therefore, that a comparison between investments and savings cannot tell us very much about the general state of the economy. Although the difference between planned investments and planned savings tells us something about the economy (namely, the sign and size of the sum of the value of all excess demand or supply in the markets for commodities and services), it is clear that equality of *ex ante* investments and savings does not exclude there being an excess demand for commodities and an excess supply of labor, for instance. Equality of investments and savings may coexist with all kinds of partial disequilibria within the group commodities and services. It follows also from Equation 9.4 that equality of *ex ante* investments and savings tells us nothing directly about the state of the market for loans (credit), or about the "money market."[1]

---

[1] The term "money market" is used here as a shorthand expression meaning demand for and supply of money. It should not be confused with everyday use of the term wherein money market means the organized short-term credit market. Demand for and supply of money exist in all markets for goods, services, and credit; there is no special market for money, with the exception of foreign-exchange markets. Hicks expressed this special position of money by saying that the money market in the present sense serves as a mirror of all other markets.

With investments and savings equal *ex ante* there may be excess demand for loans, and thus an increasing rate of interest, if only at the same time there is an excess demand for money.

We notice in passing that the state of the credit market (or the money market) permits us to draw only one conclusion: if there is disequilibrium in the credit market (or the money market) there must be disequilibrium in at least one other market in the system. The existence of equilibrium in the credit market, or, the money market, implies nothing about the rest of the economy. We may have equilibrium in the money market with a positive excess demand for all commodities and services; that is, with investments exceeding savings, and a positive excess demand for loans. We may have an excess supply of money, through an increase in the supply of money, for instance, with an excess supply of all commodities and services, provided that there is a sufficient excess demand for bonds.

Nevertheless, monetary theory has always attached great importance to the difference between investments and savings as an indicator of present tendencies of change in the economy. Neoclassical monetary theory, from Wicksell (1898) onward, insisted that the difference between investments and savings indicates the direction and size of the price level's tendency to change. A recent example is Stein (1969). After Keynes, this statement was modified to say that investments and savings tell us something of the economy's tendency to expand or contract. More concretely, if investments exceed savings the economy should tend to expand; with idle resources, production and employment expand, otherwise prices increase. We shall now show under what conditions such statements may be true (Hansen, 1951; Enthoven, 1956; Schultze, 1959).

4 / Dynamic macroconditions for a constant price level

Consider a Laspeyres' price index $P(t)$ with $P(0) = 1$. The index includes all commodities and services. It will be understood, therefore, that all summations in the following expressions extend from 1 to n. We have then

[9.5]
$$P(1) = \frac{\Sigma p_i(1)q_i(0)}{\Sigma p_i(0)q_i(0)}$$

where the numbers 0 and 1 refer to the base period 0 and to period 1, respectively. Equation 9.5 may also be written

[9.6]
$$P(1) = \frac{\Sigma[p_i(0) + \Delta p_i]q_i(0)}{\Sigma p_i(0)q_i(0)} = 1 + \frac{\Sigma \Delta p_i q_i(0)}{\Sigma p_i(0)q_i(0)}$$

where Δp_i is defined as $p_i(1) - p_i(0)$.

We shall then assume that relative price change is determined by relative excess demand. This assumption is nothing more than a special version of Walras' excess demand hypothesis for price changes. We have, then,

[9.7]
$$\frac{\Delta p_i}{p_i(0)} = k_i \frac{q_i^x(0)}{q_i(0)} \qquad k_i > 0$$

Solving Equation 9.7 for Δp_i and inserting (dropping the time variable), Equation 9.6 may then be written as

[9.8]
$$\Delta P = \frac{\Sigma k_i q_i^x p_i}{\Sigma p_i q_i}$$

If all k_i, the so-called "price flexibility coefficients," are equal, we have (compare with Equations 9.2 and 9.4)

[9.9]
$$\Delta P = k \frac{\Sigma q_i^x p_i}{\Sigma p_i q_i} = k \frac{I - S}{\Sigma p_i q_i}$$

with the implication that

[9.10]
$$\Delta P \gtreqless 0 \qquad \text{as} \qquad I - S = \Sigma q_i^x p_i \gtreqless 0$$

In other words, the price index will rise, remain unchanged, or fall accordingly as the sum of the value of the excess demands for commodities and services is positive, zero, or negative; that is, as the difference between investments and savings is positive, zero, or negative. The price level's rate of change will be in proportion to the difference between investments and savings.[1]

Earlier we discussed the first basic assertion of neoclassical monetary theory; namely, that assuming equilibrium, an increase in the quantity of money will imply a proportional increase in the level of all prices. We have now proved the second basic assertion of neoclassical monetary theory. Note, however, how many assumptions were necessary to bring about this result.

First, we must work with a rather unusual price index. It is true that Laspeyres' price indexes are widely used, but it is not usual to include the prices of all commodities and factor services in the same index. The proof requires that all commodities, whether consumer goods, capital goods, or intermediary inputs, and all factor services be included in the index.

Secondly, relatively little is known about the realism of price change equations such as Equation 9.7. From what is known about the determinants of money-wage changes, it seems clear that Walras' excess demand hypothesis does not hold true without important modifications (Chapter 10, Section 8). It may be objected here that modern labor markets are not competitive, and that neoclassical monetary theory worked on the assumption of perfectly competitive markets.

---

[1] It should be emphasized that there is no immediate connection between the amount of the excess supply of money and the price level's rate of change. To establish such a relationship it must be assumed that the credit market is always in equilibrium.

Finally, we have the assumption of equal price flexibility coefficients. Little is known about the actual size of such coefficients. On commodity bourses, however, they must be large, whereas in administered markets they are low if we consider a time period of the same length in both cases. Again it may be objected that administered markets are not competitive, and that in truly competitive commodity or labor markets, such as the Middle Eastern bazaar, prices are known to react very fast and vigorously. Such objections, of course, imply that neoclassical monetary theory may not have much relevance for a modern society.

5 / Dynamic macroconditions for a constant activity level

It is usually taken for granted that neoclassical theory is insufficient for purposes of discussing activity levels and their changes at given productive resources. It is believed to be one of the basic differences between neoclassical and Keynesian theory. This assertion is not quite correct, however. At given resources, tastes, and so forth, the general equilibrium system can, of course, determine only one activity level, granted that it has a unique solution. When we drop the equilibrium conditions, however, it is certainly possible to discuss activity-level changes instead of price-level changes; the demand and supply relations need not be changed for that purpose. Instead we must reconsider our assumptions about the system's dynamics. Indeed, we must switch from Walras' excess demand hypothesis for price changes to Marshall's excess price hypothesis for quantity changes.

We are now interested in activity levels, so let us consider a Laspeyres' quantity index including all commodities and services.

[9.11] $$Q(1) = \frac{\Sigma q_i(1)p_i(0)}{\Sigma q_i(0)p_i(0)} = 1 + \frac{\Sigma \Delta q_i p_i(0)}{\Sigma q_i(0)p_i(0)}$$

Recalling that $p_i{}^d$ and $p_i{}^s$ denote demand and supply prices, respectively, we then postulate the following special version of Marshall's excess price hypothesis:

[9.12] $$\frac{\Delta q_i(0)}{q_i(0)} = k_i \frac{p_i{}^d(0) - p_i{}^s(0)}{p_i(0)} \qquad k_i > 0$$

Writing $p_i{}^x = p_i{}^d - p_i{}^s$ and dropping the time indication, which is now superfluous, we find

[9.13] $$\Delta Q = \frac{\Sigma k_i q_i p_i{}^x}{\Sigma q_i p_i}$$

or, assuming that all $k_i = k$,

[9.14] $$\Delta Q \gtreqless 0 \qquad \text{as} \qquad \Sigma q_i p_i{}^x \gtreqless 0$$

The sum $\Sigma q_i p_i{}^x$ could be called the *total excess profit* in the system. The word "profit" must then be used in a very broad and unusual sense, however.

Market i, for instance, may be the labor market. Following Marshall's terminology, it would be more appropriate to speak about the total *quasi*-rent in the system. We shall show that total excess profit, or *quasi*-rent, is equal to the difference between planned investment and saving.

In working with Walras' excess demand hypothesis it is assumed that both buyers and sellers know the market price at which transactions will actually take place; at that price the quantity in demand and the quantity in supply may then differ. This assumption cannot be upheld when we work with Marshall's hypothesis. The crucial point here is the difference between the buyers' price and the sellers' price at a given supply and turnover. We shall assume, therefore, that sellers always expect to be paid the supply price, and that buyers always expect to pay the demand price (both being defined on the market demand and supply curves); both parties are assumed to know the quantity supplied and actually bought and sold in the market. With these assumptions Walras' law must be written

[9.15]
$$M + \frac{B}{r^s} + \sum p_i^s q_i \equiv M^d + \frac{B}{r^d} + \sum p_i^d q_i$$

or

[9.16]
$$\sum p_i^x q_i \equiv \left(\frac{-B}{r^d} + \frac{B}{r^s} \right) + (-M^x)$$

r^d and r^s being the demand and supply rates of interest, respectively. We must then redefine all the aggregates introduced in Section 2.

$$C^d = \sum_{1}^{h} p_i^d q_i \qquad \text{and} \qquad C^s = \sum_{1}^{h} p_i^s q_i$$

$$I^d = \sum_{h+1}^{j} p_i^d q_i \qquad \text{and} \qquad I^s = \sum_{h+1}^{j} p_i^s q_i$$

$$R^d = \sum_{j+1}^{m} p_i^d q_i \qquad \text{and} \qquad R^s = \sum_{j+1}^{m} p_i^s q_i$$

$$F^d = \sum_{m+1}^{n} p_i^d q_i \qquad \text{and} \qquad F^s = \sum_{m+1}^{n} p_i^s q_i$$

Income and savings Y_b, Y_f, S_b, and S_f may hereafter be defined as they were previously. Through insertion in Equation 9.16 we find:

[9.17]
$$\Sigma p_i^x q_i \equiv I - S \equiv (-B/r^d + B/r^s) + (-M^x)$$

| Total excess profit or *quasi*-rent on commodities and services | Planned investment minus saving | Excess supply of bonds | Excess supply of money |

It follows, then, that

[9.18]
$$\Delta Q \gtreqless 0 \qquad \text{as} \qquad I - S \gtreqless 0$$

The quantity of commodities and services as measured by a Laspeyres' index will thus tend to expand, remain unchanged, or contract according to whether *ex ante* investments are larger than, equal to, or smaller than *ex ante* savings.

Depending upon the assumptions about market dynamics and expectations, the difference between investments and savings may thus say something about the tendency for the price level, or, alternatively, the activity level (the quantities of commodities and services) to change. In both cases it is a question of *ex ante* investments and *ex ante* savings; it is the underlying assumptions that differ. In both cases rather strong assumptions are needed in order to arrive at the conclusions.

6 / The inflationary gap

The concept of the inflationary gap was originally set forth by Keynes (1940), who defined it as being equal to the sum of the value of the total excess demand (at full employment) for commodities and services satisfying final demands. Under conditions similar to those discussed in Section 4, the inflationary gap indicates the direction and size of the rate of change in a Laspeyres' index for prices of commodities and services entering final demand. On the other hand, it may tell us nothing about the tendencies of factor and other input prices to change. The inflationary gap as conceived by Keynes must therefore be supplemented by a corresponding gap, the factor gap, for factor services and other inputs. The sum of these two gaps will be equal to the difference between investments and savings (Hansen, 1951).

References

ENTHOVEN, A. C.: "Monetary Disequilibrium, and the Dynamics of Inflation," *The Economic Journal*, vol. 66, no. 262, June, 1956.

HANSEN, BENT: *A Study in the Theory of Inflation*, Chapter IX, George Allen and Unwin, London, 1951.

KEYNES, J. M.: *How to Pay for the War*, Macmillan, London, 1940.

SCHULTZE, C. L.: "Recent Inflation in the United States," Joint Economic Committee, U.S. Congress, *Study of Employment, Growth, and Price Levels*, Study Paper no. 1, 1959.

STEIN, J.: " 'Neoclassical' and 'Keynes-Wicksell' Monetary Growth Models," *Journal of Money, Credit, and Banking*, vol. 1, no. 2, May, 1969.

WICKSELL, K.: *Interest and Prices*, Macmillan, London, 1936. Originally published in German as *Geldzins und Güterpreise*, Göttingen, 1898.

Inflation,
general equilibrium,
and *quasi*-equilibrium

10

In the previous chapter we discussed the conditions for the general system to be in a *state* of equilibrium, inflation, or deflation in an aggregate, or average, sense. We shall now explore the process of inflation as it relates to the general equilibrium system.

1 / General equilibrium and inflation

The static general equilibrium system cannot by itself give an adequate description of the inflationary or deflationary processes. This applies also to Patinkin's systems. These systems can only solve problems in comparative statics. Thus, we can allow the quantity of money to increase and compare the new equilibrium with the old one. If the system is homogeneous in prices and quantity of money, the price level will increase but nothing will happen in real terms. If a public debt exists and the system is homogeneous in prices, quantity of money, and the number of government bonds held by the private sector, a comparative static analysis of the increase in the quantity of money may suffice to describe at least some important aspects of inflation: the fall in the public debt in real terms, the losses inflicted upon owners of fixed money claims, the gains of the taxpayers who enjoy correspondingly falling real tax payments, and the consequences for relative prices and the rate of interest. In Hicks' model of a perfect futures economy (Chapter 7, Section 5) we can, moreover, analyze the effects of expectations about future developments on the spot and forward prices of the system. This will give us important insight regarding the present state of the economy. It will only tell us something about the actual developments over time if the expectations are correct, however; and inflation with perfect foresight is, after all, a rather special case. (But see Chapter 18, Sections 2 and 6.)

It would thus be unfair to say that comparative static general equilibrium analysis has nothing to offer with respect to inflation analysis. In general, however, we are interested in what happens during the process when money prices move upward or downward and the system is thrown out of equilibrium. To analyze such processes we not only need to specify some dynamic mechanism; we must also specify the basic cause of the inflation. A process in which the government increases its purchases of military equipment and borrows from the central bank will differ from one in which the loan rate of interest is kept below the equilibrium rate, allowing credits to the private sector expand accordingly. Three different cases will be discussed. We will consider first an elementary example where money is given to people like manna from heaven. Then we will discuss the case wherein the central bank finances government purchases. Finally we will discuss the instance of easy-money inflation.

The last example presents an opportunity to relax an assumption concerning the behavior of the central bank that has been carried over to both the neoclassics, Patinkin, and even to Keynesian economics. The assumption stems from the days when the currency consisted of gold or silver coins, which were struck and issued by the sovereign, but it is of little relevance under modern institutional conditions. Today, the quantity of available money is not determined exogenously by the government or the central bank in the simple way these systems assume.

Modern central banks conduct business with the government, with the banking system, and with foreign countries. The government usually has accounts with the central bank where its surplus liquidity is kept temporarily; in most countries the government has more or less liberal drawing rights on the central bank. This circumstance makes the government's net position with the central bank tend to move automatically with the cash surplus or deficit of the budget, over which neither the central bank nor the government has any direct control. Similarly, the banking system deposits surplus liquidity with the central bank and may borrow at the official discount rate. Indeed, it is inherent in the concept of the central bank as the "bank of banks" that it should never allow private banks to run out of cash. Finally, most modern central banks buy and sell foreign exchange at pegged rates and must supply or take up the difference between demand and supply in the foreign-exchange market in order to peg the rates. To a large extent development of the supply of money is therefore determined by transactions in which the central bank is more or less passive. The central bank may nonetheless follow the development of the supply of money closely, even from day to day, and influence its course through open-market operations, changes in the rate of discount, reserve requirements, and so forth, or, occasionally, through the foreign-exchange rates. This does not change the basic fact that the supply of money is an endogenous variable in modern economic systems, however. Monetary theory has tended to ignore this aspect of money supply (Brunner, 1961).

2 / The *quasi*-equilibrium system

Let us take Patinkin's system without credit markets (Equations 8.1 to 8.4) as a starting point. Money is here integrated with the demand and supply equations and Say's law does not hold. We have already discussed the dynamics of this model for the simple case wherein a single injection of money occurs (Chapter 8, Section 3). An increase in the quantity of money leads to an increase in the real balances, at unchanged prices, creating a general excess demand, and prices begin to rise. The process of price increase continues until the real balances have returned to their initial size. A limited inflation has thus taken place.

We shall now make this limited inflationary process permanent by assuming that after the initial increase in the quantity of money, the government allows the quantity of money to continue to increase in proportion to the price level. This means that the government maintains the real balances constantly above the equilibrium level. Excess demands will therefore continue to exist and prices will continue to rise. Here, as well as in the following cases, expectations are assumed to be static. Current prices are expected to continue unchanged in the future so the price increase is therefore unexpected. This is extreme case but it serves to emphasize the characteristics of all inflations not fully foreseen, which must, after all, be the usual case.

Formally, in the system set forth in Equations 8.1 to 8.4, M/P is replaced by a constant $M/P = \bar{m}$ larger than the equilibrium M/P. The demand and supply functions of the system therefore become:

[8.2']
$$q_i^d = q_i^d \left(\frac{p_1}{P}, \ldots, \frac{p_n}{P}, \bar{m} \right) \qquad i = 1, \ldots, n$$

$$m^d = m^d \left(\frac{p_1}{P}, \ldots, \frac{p_n}{P}, \bar{m} \right)$$

[8.3']
$$q_i^s = q_i^s \left(\frac{p_1}{P}, \ldots, \frac{p_n}{P}, \bar{m} \right) \qquad i = 1, \ldots, n$$

$$m^s = \bar{m}$$

while the definition of P (Equation 8.1), and the equilibrium conditions (Equation 8.4), are unchanged. There remain $3n + 4$ equations, of which one is dependent upon the rest by virtue of Walras' law. We have lost one unknown, however. The number of unknowns has decreased to $3n + 2$; namely, $2n + 2$ real demands and supplies, and the n "real" prices p_i/P. Since $\bar{m}$ differs from the equilibrium value of M/P, the system does not have a static equilibrium solution. The natural thing to do, then, is drop the equilibrium conditions and turn to the dynamics of the system.

The set of n equations

[10.1] $$\frac{dp_i}{dt} = f_i\left[q_i^x\left(\frac{p_1}{P}, \ldots, \frac{p_n}{P}, \bar{m}\right)\right] \qquad f_i' > 0 \qquad f_i(0) = 0$$

(with Equation 8.1) is a dynamic system corresponding to Equations 8.1, 8.2′, 8.3′, and 8.4. We ask for its stationary solution by setting $dp_i/dt = 0$, implying that $q_i^x = 0$, which (considering Walras' law) is nothing more than the static system shown in Equations 8.1, 8.2′, 8.3′, and 8.4. This system does not have a solution, however, and Equation 10.1 therefore has no stationary solution. Here we are discussing a stationary solution in the absolute money prices. Considering that Equations 8.1, 8.2′, 8.3′, and 8.4 actually is a system in the relative prices, it might be more appropriate to ask for a stationary solution in the relative prices; that is, equilibrium in the relative prices. Since equilibrium in the relative prices simply means constant relative prices, the conditions for such an equilibrium are

[10.2] $$\frac{dp_i/dt}{p_i} = \frac{dp_n/dt}{p_n} \qquad i = 1, \ldots, n - 1$$

all absolute prices being positive. Inserting Equation 10.1 we obtain

[10.3] $$\frac{f_i(q_i^x)}{p_i} = \frac{f_n(q_n^x)}{p_n} \qquad i = 1, \ldots, n - 1$$

This is a system of $n - 1$ independent equations in the n relative prices. With the definition of P, Equation 8.1, we thus have n equations for determining our n price ratios. Note that Equation 10.3, with Equation 8.1, is a purely static equilibrium system. We shall assume that it has an economically meaningful solution. Equation 10.3 is the *quasi*-equilibrium system (Hansen, 1951), so called because it determines the relative prices without being in equilibrium in the traditional sense. The excess demands will not be zero, and the absolute prices are continuously increasing or falling. Whereas the forces at work on the absolute prices do not cancel each other out (see the definition of equilibrium, Chapter 1, Section 2), those at work on the relative prices do. From Equation 10.1 it follows that there must either be excess demands or excess supplies everywhere, although as a borderline case, excess demands may be zero everywhere, with the system thus in traditional equilibrium. With excess demands in all markets for commodities and services there is a permanent constant inflation; with excess supplies there is a permanent deflation. Since in our case M/P is kept above the equilibrium level, we should expect excess demands, price increases, and permanent inflation. If the functions f_i are homogeneous of degree 1 in the prices so we can write $\dot{p}_i/p_i = f_i$, the prices will increase or fall at a constant rate; even deflation can then continue indefinitely.

The system in Equation 10.3 and its underlying "corresponding" dynamic system in Equation 10.1 can be studied with respect to stability conditions and *quasi*-equilibrium properties. It can be shown that it functions much like the static general equilibrium system, which may indeed be conceived of as a special case of the system in Equation 10.3. For instance, if the system is stable, an increase in the demand for a commodity will lead to an increase in the relative price of that particular commodity (Hansen, 1951, Chapters VII and VIII). This result is well known from the general equilibrium system. (See Chapter 4, Section 4.)

The inflationary system discussed in this section, however, is primitive in the sense that the quantity of money is exogenously determined by the authorities who inject money into the system through gifts (transfers) to the private sector. Such a situation could certainly occur even under modern conditions, but inflationary policies are usually more complex, and are often related to government purchases or credit market policies. We shall now see to what extent and under what conditions the concept of *quasi*-equilibrium and permanent, constant inflation carries over to these cases.

3 / Inflation through government purchases

Let us first consider the case of inflation propelled by government purchases based on central bank credit. To simplify, we assume that there is no government debt, so that the private sector keeps no government bonds; this assumption will be relaxed later. Moreover, in the initial situation there are no government purchases or taxes. The initial equilibrium situation may thus be described by the system shown in Equations 8.1 to 8.4.

Assume, then, that the government decides to purchase a certain commodity j at a constant quantity $q_j{}^g$ per period, and to finance the purchase by borrowing from the central bank or, more directly, by issuing notes. The amount borrowed per period is $p_j q_j{}^g$, where p_j is the price actually ruling during the period. The amount borrowed is thus proportional to the price of commodity j. The deficit of the budget is $p_j q_j{}^g$ and the quantity of money will increase by this amount per period.

The immediate effect on the system is an excess demand for commodity j equal to $q_j{}^g$, and a corresponding excess supply of money $p_j q_j{}^g$. The price of commodity j will thus begin to increase immediately. Provided that the government succeeds in buying (note that the market is now a sellers' market), private real cash balances will increase and a general excess demand for commodities and services will arise. If the government should now withdraw from the market, the injection of new money would stop and the familiar process would develop wherein prices increase and real balances fall until a new equilibrium is reached at a higher price level. The government continues to purchase the same quantity of commodity j at increasingly higher prices, however. The excess supply of money increases by the corresponding amount, and in this way the process continues. At an instantaneous adaptation of the price system to the equilibrium prices, the system would shift from equilibrium to equilibrium; after an adjustment of the relative prices in the first period they would remain unchanged, and only the absolute prices would increase. By assumption we rule out instantaneous adaptation, however. Therefore, an equilibrium with demand equal to supply everywhere in the system cannot be reached, simply because the quantity of money is continuously increasing. We may imagine, however, that the process moves toward a state in which there is just enough excess demand in each market so that all prices increase in proportion to the increase in the quantity of money. Real cash balances, relative prices, and real excess demands will then be constant, as the absolute prices race upward. A *quasi*-equilibrium may thus be established. It may be described by Equation 10.3, recalling that now $q_j^x = q_j^d - q_j^s + q_j^g$. The relative prices determined by this *quasi*-equilibrium will deviate from those of the initial equilibrium; the relative price of commodity j will have increased. The relative prices will also deviate from those that would be reached if the government suddenly abandoned central bank financing and collected taxes to cover the budget deficit and permit static equilibrium to be established.

What would happen to the process just described if a public debt had existed in the initial situation? The real value of the bonds held by the public would diminish continuously as a result of the price increase, which would lead to a fall in private demand and put a brake on the rate of price increase.[1] It could never stop the process, however, because the quantity of money increases continuously. To cancel out the effect of an increasing quantity of money, the real value of the bond and money holdings must fall continuously, requiring increasing prices, which in turn require excess demand. A *quasi*-equilibrium may be reached, but only when the real value of the bond holdings has vanished will the rate of the price increase approach the rate of the increase in the quantity of money.

4 / Easy-money inflation

When money is injected into the private economy through the government's budget and inflation is created, it is impossible to determine whether the

---

[1] We disregard the problem of the capitalized value of the future tax payments needed to finance the interest payments (see Chapter 8, Section 5). This "debt" will, of course, diminish in real terms along with the fall in the real value of bonds and we might assume that this cancels out the effects of the fall in the real value of bonds.

inflation was created by fiscal or monetary policy. The two work hand in hand. It may even be argued that inflation cannot be created by pure fiscal policy. If all public-debt operations are classified as monetary policy so that pure fiscal policy requires a balanced budget (otherwise some kind of debt operations must be undertaken), inflation is impossible unless monetary policy is involved somehow, although distribution effects of fiscal operations within a balanced budget could conceivably lead to a shift in the price level. There is no doubt, however, that there are instances where monetary policy alone is responsible for inflation. This is a classic problem. It received its first modern analytical treatment by Wicksell in his famous model of the "cumulative process" in *Geldzins und Güterpreise* (1898, 1936). Wicksell assumed that the monetary authorities keep the loan rate of interest below the so-called "natural rate of interest," and demonstrated how this policy may generate an infinite inflationary process that does not end unless the loan rate is again made equal to the natural rate.

To discuss this case it is convenient to start out from the Patinkin system with a credit market (see Equations 8.11 through 8.14). Here money consists of central bank money, and the credit market is a market for government bonds. Initially the economy is assumed to be in equilibrium at a given quantity of money and a given number of government bonds. The only items on the government budget are the interest payments and a corresponding lump-sum tax that just balances the budget. We shall identify the natural rate of interest with the equilibrium rate determined by this system. It follows that, *ceteris paribus*, the natural rate of interest is dependent upon the number of government bonds existing in the system. Granted that interest payments and lump-sum taxes cancel out each other's effects on demand and supply (Mundell, 1960), we can safely assume that the natural rate of interest is positively related to the number of bonds in existence. The greater the number of bonds, the lower their equilibrium price, and the higher the natural rate of interest.

The central bank decides now to peg the market rate of interest at a level below the prevailing natural rate. To that end the bank offers to buy (or sell) an unlimited number of government bonds at a price $1/\bar{r}$ above the prevailing equilibrium price. The higher bond price implies an increase in the value of private bond holdings, and at unchanged commodity prices their real value increases correspondingly. It also leads to an excess supply of bonds from the private sector, which is automatically taken up by the central bank. There will presumably be an excess demand for commodities and services; both the lower rate of interest and the increase in real private wealth should tend to work in this direction. For the same reason we should expect an excess demand for money. The excess demand for money, however, must be smaller than the value of the excess supply of bonds from the private sector. This is a consequence of Walras' law (Equation 9.2). Considering the central bank's demand for bonds and its supply of new money, we find that whereas demand (including central bank purchases) and supply of bonds are equal at the new lower rate of interest, there is a general excess demand for commodities and services, and an excess supply of money, including the new central bank supply. As a reaction to the excess demand, the prices of commodities and services will begin to rise.

The following development depends upon what happens to the total private wealth; that is, to the total value of private money and bond holdings (disregarding real capital, which we assume given), and its composition. The money value of privately held government bonds rose initially because the rate of interest fell, and total private wealth rose accordingly. The central bank purchases leave the value of private wealth at this higher level. When bonds are sold to the central bank, private money holdings increase by the same amount, and the rate of interest remains contant at its low level. At unchanged real wealth the private sector would have no reason to convert additional bonds into money. But the falling real value of private wealth leads not only to a fall in the excess demand for goods and services and a fall in the excess supply of money; it also tends to create a new excess supply of bonds. Since any excess supply of bonds is taken up by the central bank at the pegged bond price, the composition of private wealth will continue to shift away from bonds and toward money. This shift tends to lower the potential equilibrium rate of interest, however. Apparently a state may be reached where the real value of private wealth has fallen so far that the excess demand for commodities and services disappears, and so few bonds are left with the private sector that the equilibrium interest rate has fallen to the rate fixed by the central bank. The inflationary process would then stop at a new natural rate of interest equal to the loan rate of interest.

It may be useful at this point to consider what the conditions must be for such a new equilibrium to be established. As an example, consider a system with only one commodity, one type of government bond, and central bank money. The commodity supply is q, and in the initial situation the number of bonds is B_0 and the quantity of money M_0. The demand and supply functions for the commodity market are

[10.4] $$q^d = \alpha + \beta(1 + r) + \delta\frac{B_0/r + M_0}{p} \qquad q^s = q$$

The functions for the credit market are

[10.5] $$\frac{B^d/r}{p} = a + b(1 + r) + d\frac{B_0/r + M_0}{p} \qquad \frac{B^s/r}{p} = \frac{B_0/r}{p}$$

The equilibrium conditions are

[10.6] $$q^d = q^s \qquad \frac{B^d/r}{p} = \frac{B^s/r}{p}$$

We need not write the equations for money; they are easily derived from the other equations. "Normal" responses require $\alpha > 0$, $\beta < 0$, $\delta > 0$,

$a > 0$, $b > 0$, and $d > 0$, and for the demand for money to be inversely related to the rate of interest and directly related to wealth, we must also require $\beta + b > 0$ and $1 - \delta - d > 0$. We assume there is a solution at a positive price and rate of interest. Let the rate of interest be fixed at a positive value $\bar{r}$ below the initial equilibrium value r. This increases the money value of total private wealth from $W_0 = B_0/r + M_0$ to $\bar{W} = B_0/\bar{r} + M_0$, at which higher value it remains unchanged. We then ask whether a new equilibrium may exist with a positive commodity price $\bar{p}$ and a positive number of bonds $\bar{B}$ such that, utilizing the equilibrium conditions,

[10.7]
$$q = \alpha + \beta(1 + \bar{r}) + \delta \frac{\bar{W}}{\bar{p}}$$
$$\frac{\bar{B}/\bar{r}}{\bar{p}} = a + b(1 + \bar{r}) + d \frac{\bar{W}}{\bar{p}}$$

This system has the solution

[10.8]
$$\bar{p} = \frac{\delta \bar{W}}{q - \alpha - \beta(1 + \bar{r})}$$
$$\bar{B} = \bar{r} \left\{ \left[a + b(1 + \bar{r}) \right] \frac{\delta \bar{W}}{q - \alpha - \beta(1 + \bar{r})} + d\bar{W} \right\}$$

$\bar{p}$ will be positive (and higher than the old equilibrium price) if $r - \bar{r} < \delta W_0/(-\beta p)$. The right side of this expression is positive, so that if the rate of interest is pegged above the old equilibrium rate, there will always be a new equilibrium. If it is pegged below the old rate there may be a new equilibrium, although not necessarily. The existence of a public debt does not guarantee that the process will stop. If the demand for commodities reacts too strongly to a fall in the rate of interest (that is, if the numerical value of β is too large, or private wealth W_0 is too small, and/or its effect on the commodity demand δ is too weak) there will not be a new equilibrium at a positive price level with a natural interest equal to $\bar{r}$.

The example serves also to show that the inflationary process must continue infinitely if from the beginning private financial wealth has been zero (Modigliani, 1963, p. 183). This may be the case if instead of a public debt, the government has claims on the private sector corresponding to the quantity of money. Such a situation would have arisen if in the past money had been issued only against claims on the private sector. In the above example, the natural rate of interest would then be exclusively determined in the commodity market by the relation $q = \alpha + \beta(1 + r)$; if the rate of interest is fixed at any other level there is nothing that can bring the commodity market into equilibrium again. We must assume, however, that the loans extended to the private sector resemble bank loans so that the claims held by the government are nonnegotiable debt certificates. The value of the existing debts to the government is then independent of the current rate of interest. On the other hand, if there were an open market for these claims, the net wealth of the private sector would change from zero to something positive if the rate of interest were pegged below the initial equilibrium rate. It is appropriate, therefore, to replace B^d/r with D^d, the demand for claims, and B^s/r with D^s, the supply of claims, in the demand and supply equations. At an interest rate below the equilibrium rate there will now be constant excess demand for the commodity, and the price will increase at a constant rate. The real private supply of claims to the government (central bank) may be described by an equation similar to Equation 10.5

$$\frac{D^s}{p} = a + b(1 + r)$$

but the policy of the central bank is to let demand be equal to supply automatically, whatever the supply may be.[1] The real supply is constant, given the rate of interest as fixed by the central bank, but the money value will increase in proportion to the price of the commodity. This means that if the loan rate of interest is fixed at the natural level, the supply of claims in both real and money terms will be constant. There will be a constant excess supply of money equal in value to the excess demand for commodities. Accordingly, we would have the system

[10.9]
$$\frac{\dot{p}}{p} = f[\alpha + \beta(1 + \bar{r}) - q] \qquad f' > 0$$
$$\frac{D^d}{p} \equiv \frac{D^s}{p} = a + b(1 + \bar{r})$$
$$M^x = p[q - \alpha - \beta(1 + \bar{r})]$$

which is a very simple version of Wicksell's cumulative process.

Wicksell assumed that a so-called "ideal bank" made loans and held deposits for the private sector at a given rate of interest fixed by the bank. The private sector's money (deposits) and debts therefore canceled each other out and the financial net worth was zero. In the terminology of Gurley and Shaw (1960), the deposits in Wicksell's ideal bank would presumably be called "inside" money, but the distinction is blurred in this case because the government (central bank) may behave in exactly the same way. Be this as it may, we have here the case where the "cumulative process" will go on infinitely with a constant excess demand for commodities. The example we have given is so simple that there are no relative commodity prices, there being only one commodity, but it may be considered a degenerated *quasi*-equilibrium model. Indeed, it is easy to extend the model to comprise any number of commodities in a *quasi*-equilibrium process. If in the system set forth in Equations 8.11 to 8.14 we assume that B/r and M enter the demand

---

[1] The qualifications set forth in note 1 on p. 88 apply here, as well, *mutatis mutandis*.

and supply functions as $B/r + M$, and that $M = -B/r$, the real balances vanish. Since the rate of interest is pegged, we are back to a system like that shown in Equations 8.1, 8.2', 8.3', and 8.4 in the relative prices, and we can form a *quasi*-equilibrium system such as the one shown in Equation 10.3. We have only to add to this a bond market identity such as that shown in Equation 10.9 and the system will be complete.

5 / An aggregate *quasi*-equilibrium inflation model

The simple, aggregated model presented here serves as an illustration to the systems discussed in Sections 3 and 4.

We assume that the quantity of labor is given and that productive capacity is unlimited. Thus there is an upper limit $\bar{q}$ for production determined by the supply of labor. Only one commodity is produced, and it may be used for both investment and consumption. With given technique and equipment, the volume of planned production q^s is a function of the ratio between price and wage rate p/w; that is,

[10.10]
$$q^s = f\left(\frac{p}{w}\right) \qquad f' > 0$$

As to the demand for commodities, assume that the demand for investment purposes is given, determined by the fixed interest rate. Demand for consumer goods will be determined by the price-wage ratio, which determines the distribution of income. If the profit earners' propensity to consume is lower than that of the wage earners', demand for consumer goods will be inversely related to the price-wage ratio. Total planned demand for commodities is thus

[10.11]
$$q^d = g\left(\frac{p}{w}\right) \qquad g' < 0$$

In Figure 10.1 we have drawn the two curves corresponding to Equations 10.10 and 10.11, and the vertical line $\bar{q}$. Reading horizontally we have, in line with the traditional definitions:

$q^d - q^s$ = excess demand for commodities
$q^s - \bar{q}$ = planned but unrealizable production
= index of excess demand for labor

At all values of p/w above B there is an excess demand for labor; below B there is an excess supply of labor. At B the labor market is in equilibrium. At A planned demand and supply of commodities is equal, the excess demand is zero, and there should be equilibrium in the market for commodities. This does not take into account the breakdown in production plans. Nevertheless, we shall assume that it is the excess demand that is decisive for changes in the

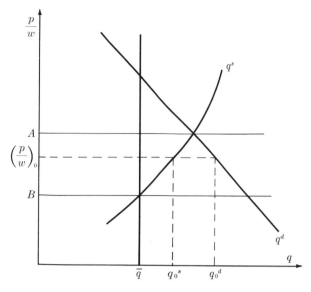

FIGURE *10.1*

commodity price.[1] Above A we have an excess supply, and below A an excess demand for commodities. Only between A and B do we have excess demands in both markets.

   To determine the static equilibrium position of this model we should search for a p/w at which both $q^d = q^s$ and $q^s = \bar{q}$. Such a value of p/w does not exist. At A, $q^d = q^s$, but $q^s > \bar{q}$ and wages are rising. At B, $q^s = \bar{q}$, but $q^d > q^s$ and prices are rising. We note, however, that whereas $dp/dt = 0$ at A and becomes positive and larger the smaller p/w becomes, $dw/dt = 0$ at B and becomes positive and larger the larger p/w becomes. Since neither becomes infinite, it is obvious that there must be a value of p/w between A and B, for example, at $(p/w)_0$, at which prices and wages increase in the same proportion. This is the *quasi*-equilibrium value of p/w. It is also easily seen that this *quasi*-equilibrium position is stable. At a higher level of p/w wages increase proportionately faster than prices, and p/w must fall. The opposite applies at a lower level of p/w.

---

[1] In the original formulation of this model, the excess demand for commodities was defined as $q^d - \bar{q}$; that is, the difference between demand and actual production (Hansen, 1951, Chapter VII). This definition was based on the simple theory that if production plans break down, a planned supply cannot help prevent a price increase. Although it may be more appealing, this definition of excess demand is not compatible with the neoclassical definition. Since it does not change anything essential in the model, we prefer to remain with the same definition and the same price-change dynamics adopted in the first part of this chapter. We touch here upon a difficult problem that has never received satisfactory treatment in economic theory; that is, what is it, exactly, that determines the rate at which a price will change? (See Arrow, 1959, and Section 8.)

Let us seek the effects of an increase in the demand for commodities, as through an increased government demand. Both $\bar{q}$ and q^s are unaffected by this, but q^d shifts to the right. It is easily seen that the result must be a new *quasi*-equilibrium position at a higher price-wage ratio and at greater excess demands for both labor and commodities. We thus find a result well known from studies of comparative statics: the relative price of the commodity has risen. We find, in addition, that the general rate of inflation has increased.

6 / The adjustment of plans and expectations

The inflation analysis presented here is incomplete in at least two important respects. *Quasi*-equilibrium systems remain forever in a state with permanent excess demand (in case of inflation) in all markets for commodities and services, and excess supply of money; purchasing plans are thus continuously breaking down. In addition, price expectations are continuously disappointed; we have assumed static expectations (current prices are thus always expected to remain unchanged) but actual prices are continuously rising. It stands to reason that people should realize this and subsequently learn from their bad experience.

Neoclassical inflation theory of Fisher's and Lindahl's vintage was fully aware of the importance of price expectations for the inflationary process but did not succeed in formulating precise hypotheses about the formation of price expectations and their revisions. Beginning with Cagan's study of hyperinflation (1956) modern monetary theory has suggested various concrete hypotheses of price expectations and the way people learn from experience in this field. The revision of price expectations can easily be incorporated into the *quasi*-equilibrium processes (Nagatani, 1969). Let us call the expected price p^e. The expected rate of change of price is $dp^e/dt = \dot{p}^e$. So far we have assumed $\dot{p}^e = 0$. We may now assume that the expected rate of price change is modified on the basis of actual experience in such a way that if the actual price change exceeds the expected rate of price change, the latter will be revised upward in proportion to the experienced unexpected price increase. This hypothesis may be written as $\ddot{p}^e = c(\dot{p} - \dot{p}^e)$ where c is a positive constant and the double dots indicate the second derivative with respect to time. It is natural to let $\dot{p}^e$ appear as an argument in the excess demand functions for commodities and services, and money. This gives us one more unknown $\dot{p}^e$ (which may be conceived of as a price vector) and one more *quasi*-equilibrium condition $\dot{p} = \dot{p}^e$. In *quasi*-equilibrium the expected rate of price change is equal to the actual rate of price change. Granted that the excess demands are increasing functions of the expected rate of price change, and the revision of expectations is gradual ($c < 1$), this should not essentially change the functioning of the systems.

Concerning the breakdown of purchasing plans, and hence production, investment, and consumption plans, matters are more complex. Little seems to have been done on this problem. It would be reasonable to assume that during the course of an inflationary *quasi*-equilibrium process, purchasers slowly realize that they are confronted with sellers' markets where purchasing plans cannot be fulfilled completely. They may then begin to scale down their purchasing plans below optimum, although the opposite reaction cannot be excluded (purchasers may line up in several queues at the same time). We may perhaps even visualize a final state wherein purchasing plans have been reduced so much below optimum that demand and supply become equal and the price increase is brought to an end. Society would then be locked in an apparent equilibrium position with constant prices and wages and all demands below what is optimal at present prices, interest rates, and supply of money. This would be a perfect antithesis to the Keynesian under-employment situation in which supply is assumed to adjust itself to effective demand (Chapter 11, Section 7); in our case, demand adjusts itself to effective supply. A better answer to the problem may, however, be to apply the concept of "search costs," well known from the theory of employment and wages (Stigler, 1962; Phelps et al., 1970). Purchasers would be assumed to extend their purchasing plans and attempts to the point where marginal search costs (which may be entirely subjective) equal expected gains. This is a field, however, where research has only recently begun to develop.

7 / Demand-pull and cost-push

Traditional inflation theory was a monetary theory based either upon the hypothesis that the difference between investments and savings governs the rate of change of the price level, or upon the quantity theory of money. As we have seen in both cases, the inflation theory was ultimately based upon the hypothesis that price changes are governed by excess demand. The inflation theory so far discussed in this chapter is therefore a rationalization of traditional theory.

Before World War II, J. M. Keynes (1930) observed that there are cases or aspects of inflation that are not readily explained by traditional theory. Keynes spoke about "income inflation" as a phenomenon that occurs when factor owners raise their remuneration despite the existence of equilibrium between investments and savings, or, more precisely, in spite of equilibrium between demand for and supply of factors. Keynes had in mind labor and money wages in particular. This idea has been developed since World War II under the catchwords of "demand-pull" and "cost-push," or "demand inflation" and "cost inflation." This terminology has not helped clarify the issue. Because of interdependencies in the economic system, the distinction between inflation from the demand side and from the cost side is not clearly defined. Nonetheless, there exists here a phenomenon that traditional inflation theory cannot handle. Actual developments since World War II have made it overwhelmingly clear that the price level may rise although the conditions for traditional equilibrium seem to be fulfilled. Since Walras' excess demand hypothesis for price changes is fundamental to the traditional approach, this phenomenon leads us to reconsider Walras' hypothesis. In so doing it should be made clear that a main factor behind nontraditional inflation is monopoly and other limitations of competition. A reconsideration of Walras' hypothesis does not necessarily imply a critique of it as a description of price behavior in competitive markets.

8 / Walras' excess demand hypothesis reconsidered

In its simplest form, Walras' excess demand hypothesis, which we have met so many times, states that

$$[10.12] \qquad \frac{dp_i}{dt} = f_i(q_i^x) \qquad f_i(0) = 0 \qquad f_i' > 0 \qquad i = 1, \ldots, n$$

where the notation is as usual.

The discussion in the previous section suggests that the condition $f_i(0) = 0$ should be replaced by $f_i(0) > 0$ at least for some markets, notably the labor market. Equation 10.12 should therefore be changed to

$$[10.12'] \qquad \frac{dp_i}{dt} = f_i(q_i^x) \qquad f_i(0) \geqq 0 \qquad f_i' > 0 \qquad i = 1, \ldots, n$$

This change of hypothesis is shown graphically in Figure 10.2. The traditional hypothesis is represented by the curve (line) I, which passes through the origin and has a positive slope. Curve II is the modified hypothesis with $f_i(0) > 0$. It may or may not cut the abscissa to the left of the origin.

It should be pointed out that in spite of a great interest in wage dynamics in recent years and a host of empirical studies in the field, little is known about the empirical relevance of Walras' hypothesis. The possible existence of a so-called "Phillips' curve" does not really prove or disprove Walras' hypothesis. The Phillips' curve is a relationship between aggregate unemployment (that is, total excess supplies in the labor market) and the rate of money-wage change. Even if in the aggregate the Phillips' curve shows that a certain per cent of unemployment is necessary for money wages to remain constant, it does not prove that in Walras' hypothesis $f_i(0) > 0$. The labor market is heterogeneous, with many noncompeting or only weakly competing groups of labor, and normally we should expect to find excess demand in some submarkets simultaneously with excess supplies in other submarkets. To the aggregate unemployment observed when average wages are constant,

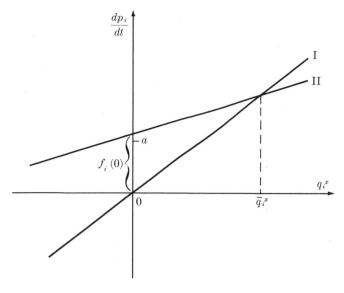

FIGURE *10.2*

there may have thus existed a corresponding, nonobserved excess demand in other submarkets (Lipsey, 1960, and Hansen, 1970).

This is only part of the story, however. What about the *slope* of curve II in Figure 10.2 as compared with that of curve I? If as we draw the curves in Figure 10.2 the slope of curve II is smaller than the slope of curve I, there will exist an excess demand $\bar{q}_i^x$ beyond which the rate of wage increase will be slower with curve II than with curve I. In this case we cannot use $f_i(0)$ as a unique measure of the degree of cost-push. Assuming (by definition) that in a perfectly competitive market as depicted by curve I there is no cost-push, we must admit that there is also no cost-push at $\bar{q}_i^x$; for larger excess demands the slope of curve II even shows a negative cost-push. The question of the slopes of curves I and II can only be answered empirically, but if curve I depicts an ideal competitive market that does not exist, how shall we be able to measure its slope? Nevertheless, Scandinavian labor economists maintain that although the trade unions cause wage rates to increase faster than they would at equilibrium between demand and supply for labor, or at unemployment, at a higher level of demand for labor the unions prevent money wages from increasing as fast as they would otherwise do. This possibility complicates the picture and deprives the cost-push concept of its apparent simplicity.

To fully define the cost-push concept we must also consider the rate of productivity increase. If the rate of productivity increase is equal to a (see Figure 10.2), then at zero excess demand the cost-push is equal to $f_i(0) - a$; the difference between the rate of wage-rate increase and the increase in productivity will indicate the rate of the price increase in markets for produced goods. If $f_i(0) - a$ is positive, there may exist a certain level of excess supply (unemployment) at which the money wages increase at the same rate as productivity. Here the cost-push is zero and prices can remain constant. This, then, is the basis for the theory of a necessary trade-off between price increase and unemployment. Introduction of the rate of productivity increase does nothing to further clarify the notion of cost-push. With curve I it would seem that at equilibrium there is a negative cost-push, and that a certain amount of excess demand would be necessary to keep the price level stable. We also still have the problem of the different slopes of curves I and II. In addition, it appears likely that the rate of productivity itself may be dependent upon the level of excess demand in the labor market.

Other modifications of Equation 10.12 are possible. A particularly important one is to allow the rate of price increase to be dependent not only upon the excess demand of the market, but also upon the rate of price increase in other markets. This modification would lead us to

[10.12″] $$\frac{dp_i}{dt} = f_i\left(q_i^x, \frac{dp_j}{dt}\right) \quad \text{or} \quad = f_i\left(q_i^x, \frac{dP}{dt}\right)$$

dp_j/dt being a vector of all rates of price increase. Appropriately specified with respect to $f_i(0,0)$, and the partial derivatives, Equation 10.12″ may be looked upon as a description of trade union behavior, and perhaps of enterprise behavior as well. A number of econometric studies of wage behavior point in this direction (see Bodkin et al., 1967). Trade unions may seek compensation for the rise in cost of living, and enterprises may pass cost increases directly on to the consumer, even under competitive conditions. If expectations about future price development are governed by the current rate of increase in prices, the inclusion of dP/dt allows price expectations to enter the picture. (See Section 6, above.) The argument that expectations of future price and wage increases tend to shift the Phillips' curve upward is a case in point (Phelps, 1967; Friedman, 1968). It has also been suggested (Patinkin, 1952) that excess demand in other markets may enter the price change function for a particular market as a kind of spillover effect, but this hypothesis is open to criticism.

9 / Generalized inflation theory

A modified Walras' excess demand hypothesis such as that in Equation 10.12′ is inconsistent with the traditional general equilibrium system. The condition $dp_i/dt = 0$ does not imply $q_i^x = 0$, and vice versa. Equation 10.12″, on the other hand, is consistent with the traditional equilibrium system if it is specified so that $f_i(0,0) = 0$. Turning to the *quasi*-equilibrium system, it will be easily understood that the existence of *quasi*-equilibrium (that is, constant relative prices) does not require that $f_i(0) = 0$, and is consistent with Equation 10.12′. If $f_i(0) > 0$ for the labor markets but not for the other markets, we may obtain *quasi*-equilibrium solutions with excess supply in the labor markets, with prices and wages increasing proportionately (disregarding productivity changes). Empirically, this is probably a highly relevant case.

We note, finally, that *quasi*-equilibrium is also consistent with Equation 10.12″. If we begin to include the rate of price change as a determinant in the price change equations, however, we should presumably include it in the demand and supply functions themselves. We could then incorporate all the effects of price expectations in the system, still assuming that price expectations are linked to the current rate of price change. A typical demand function might then become

$$[10.13] \qquad q_i^d = q_i^d \left(\frac{p_1}{P}, \, \cdots \, , \frac{p_n}{P}; \, r - \frac{\dot{P}}{P}; \, \dot{p}_1, \, \ldots \, , \dot{p}_n; \, \frac{B/r}{P}, \, \frac{M}{P} \right)$$

Even after this change in the demand and supply functions *quasi*-equilibrium would still be possible. It thus permits a large variety of price change functions.

References

ARROW, K. J.: "Towards a Theory of Price Adjustment," in M. Abramovitz, *The Allocation of Resources*, Stanford University Press, 1959.

BODKIN, R. G., et al.: *Price Stability and High Employment: The Options for Canadian Economic Policy*, An Econometric Study, Queen's Printer, Ottawa, Canada, 1967.

BRUNNER, K.: "A Schema for the Supply Theory of Money," *International Economic Review*, vol. 2, no. 2, January, 1961.

CAGAN, P.: "The Monetary Dynamics of Hyperinflation," in M. Friedman (ed.), *Studies in the Quantity Theory of Money*, University of Chicago Press, 1956.

DICKS-MIREAUX, L. A., and J. C. R. DOW: "The Determinants of Wage Inflation: United Kingdom, 1946–56," *Journal of the Royal Statistical Society*, series A (general), part 2, 1959.

FRIEDMAN, M.: "The Role of Monetary Policy," *The American Economic Review*, vol. 58, no. 1, March, 1968.

GURLEY, J. G., and E. S. SHAW: *Money in a Theory of Finance*, The Brookings Institution, Washington, D.C., 1960.

HANSEN, BENT: *A Study in the Theory of Inflation*, George Allen and Unwin, London, 1951.

—: "Excess Demand, Unemployment, Vacancies, and Wages," *The Quarterly Journal of Economics*, vol. 84, no. 1, February, 1970.

—, and G. REHN: "On Wage Drift, a Problem in Money Wage Dynamics," *25 Essays in Honour of Erik Lindahl*, Ekonomisk Tidskrift, Stockholm, 1957.

KEYNES, J. M.: *A Treatise on Money*, Macmillan, London, 1930.

LIPSEY, R. G.: "The Relation Between Unemployment and the Rate of Change of Money Wage Rates in the United Kingdom, 1862–1957," *Economica*, vol. 27, no. 1, February, 1960.

MODIGLIANI, F.: "The Monetary Mechanism and Its Interaction with Real Phenomena," *The Review of Economics and Statistics*, vol. 45, no. 1, part 2, supplement, February, 1963.

MUNDELL, R. A.: "The Public Debt, Corporate Income Taxes, and the Rate of Interest," *The Journal of Political Economy*, vol. 48, no. 6, December, 1960.

NAGATANI, K.: "A Monetary Growth Model with Variable Employment," *Journal of Money, Credit, and Banking*, vol. 1, no. 2, May, 1969.

PATINKIN, D.: "The Limitations of Samuelson's 'Correspondence Principle,' " *Metroeconomica*, vol. 4, no. 2, 1952.

PHELPS, E. S.: "Phillips Curves, Expectations of Inflation and Optimal Unemployment over Time," *Economica*, vol. 34, no. 135, August, 1967.

—, et al.: *Microeconomic Foundations of Employment and Inflation Theory*, New York, 1970.

STIGLER, G.: "Information in the Labor Market," *Journal of Political Economy*, vol. 50, no. 5, part 2, October, 1962.

WICKSELL, K.: *Interest and Prices*, Macmillan, London, 1936. Originally published in German as *Geldzins und Güterpreise*, Göttingen, 1898.

—: *Lectures on Political Economy*, Routledge and Kegan Paul, London, 1935, vol. 2.

The Keynesian system

11

This chapter will discuss the structure of the Keynesian model and its relationship to the neoclassical general equilibrium theory. It will not give a detailed exposition of the Keynesian system and its application (the multiplier theory and so forth), since such expositions can be found in any current intermediate textbook on macroeconomic theory. Keynes presented his theory in opposition and as an alternative to what he called "classical theory," that is, neoclassical theory. There is some disagreement, however, about what significant differences, if any, exist between Keynes and the neoclassicists. Opinions differ about what is *the* Keynesian model and *the* neoclassical model, and these are in turn related to basic ambiguities in both Keynes' *General Theory* (1936) and the neoclassical literature.

Keynes' theory is cast in terms of aggregates, national income, private investments, consumption, and so forth, and the relationships between these aggregates, such as the investment function, the consumption function, and the liquidity-preference function. The concept of aggregation does not by itself distinguish Keynesian theory from neoclassical theory, however. Aggregation was by no means alien to neoclassical thinking, which, indeed, did contain some aggregate theory. We have already discussed the investments-savings theory for changes in the price level (Chapter 9). Another example is the Cambridge version of the quantity theory of money $M = kY$, which is a very simple theory of aggregate money income determination. But the neoclassicists never presented a complete aggregated general equilibrium model corresponding to their disaggregated system. Even today, when the simple neoclassical theory of money income determination is undergoing a sort of renaissance under Milton Friedman and his followers, the theory is not presented in the framework of a complete aggregated model. To have presented such a model is an achievement ranking Keynes among the greatest of economists, even if his model is found to be fully consistent with neoclassical thinking, or the differences should prove to be only minor.

In comparing Keynesian and neoclassical theory we must select a Keynesian model that is not too simple. Keynesian models of the 2-equation type $S(r,Y) = I(r,Y)$ and $M = L(r,Y)$, with well-known notation, do not include prices, which play such an important role in neoclassical thinking. And the simplest neoclassical aggregate theory of the 1-equation type $M = kY$ tells us nothing about the real part of the economy, which was Keynes' basic concern. The present controversy between Keynesians and Friedmanians does tend to be in terms of these noncommensurable simplistic models, but nothing compels us to follow this bad example.

Here we shall select from among the many existing Keynesian models one presented by L. R. Klein in his book, *The Keynesian Revolution* (1947, 1966). Klein's book on the Keynesian revolution is the unsurpassed masterpiece of this genre, and his model is sufficiently differentiated to permit a meaningful comparison, yet simple enough to be analyzed without elaborate technical apparatus. Another choice would be the well-known model of Modigliani (1944). This model is marred, however, by some peculiar assumptions about the homogeneity properties, in which respect Klein's model is particularly satisfactory; it was for this reason that Modigliani later denounced his own model (1963). We shall let Patinkin represent the neoclassicists; for our purpose it suffices to consider his disaggregated system (Chapter 8). Our choice is not an obvious one. Patinkin's contribution came after Keynes', and it was not Patinkin's system that Keynes attacked. Our purpose is not to clarify issues of doctrinal history, however, but rather to compare the structures of theories relevant to modern economics.

1 / Klein's Keynesian model

With a few unimportant changes, Klein's Keynesian model is:[1]

[11.1]
$$\frac{S}{p} = f\left(r, \frac{Y}{p}\right)$$

[11.2]
$$\frac{I}{p} = g\left(r, \frac{Y}{p}\right)$$

[11.3]
$$I = S$$

[11.4]
$$\frac{M}{p} = L\left(r, \frac{Y}{p}\right)$$

[11.5]
$$Y = pq$$

[11.6]
$$q = \phi(N)$$

[1] This is the model presented in Klein (1947, p. 202). Following Keynes, Klein expressed his models in terms of wage units; that is, he deflated throughout by w rather than p. This method does not change the homogeneity properties of the model, however, and it was one of Keynes' less constructive ideas.

[11.7] $$\frac{w}{p} = \phi'(N)$$

[11.8] $$N^s = \psi\left(\frac{w}{p}\right)$$

In this system f, g, L, ϕ, and ψ are function symbols; the variables are:

$$S = \text{savings (in money terms)}$$
$$I = \text{investments (in money terms)}$$
$$Y = \text{national income (in money terms)}$$
$$r = \text{rate of interest}$$
$$p = \text{price of output (national product)}$$
$$w = \text{money-wage rate}$$
$$M = \text{quantity of money}$$
$$q = \text{national product}$$
$$N = \text{employment}$$
$$N^s = \text{supply of labor}$$

The first two equations of this system are the savings and investments functions, both expressed in real terms; the third equation is an equilibrium condition. Equation 11.4 contains the liquidity-preference theory. Equation 11.5 is a definitional relationship that could be dropped if q were substituted for Y/p in Equations 11.1, 11.2, and 11.4. Equation 11.6 is the aggregate production function, and Equation 11.7 is the condition for profit maximum, it being noted that there is only one variable input, labor. A stock of capital exists, of course, but the period considered is presumed to be so short that current investments do not affect the productive capital stock. (We shall drop this assumption in Chapter 18, Sections 1 and 2.) Equation 11.8, finally, is the households' supply function for labor.

With the quantity of money M and the money-wage rate w exogenously given, we thus have eight equations in eight unknowns; namely, S, I, Y, r, p, q, N, and N^s.

2 / Klein's neoclassical model

In addition to his Keynesian model, Klein presented a neoclassical model, which consisted of the same eight equations as the Keynesian model, with the addition of an equilibrium condition for the labor market.

[11.9] $$N = N^s$$

If we add one more equation to the system, and the new equation does not contain any additional unknown, we must obviously let one of the previously exogenous variables appear as an unknown to be determined by the system. There are two such variables: the quantity of money and the money-wage rate. It is entirely in the spirit of neoclassical thinking to let the money-wage rate be the additional unknown. In Klein's neoclassical model the quantity of money is thus the only exogenously determined variable, and we have nine equations to determine the nine unknowns, S, I, Y, r, p, w, q, N, and N^s.

3 / Demand and supply in Klein's models

The first observation we shall make is that the models presented by Klein are systems of demand and supply functions and conditions of equilibrium between demand and supply, and that all the demand and supply functions are fully consistent with neoclassical thinking. This is not always recognized and it may be a little difficult to see it directly from the system set forth in Equations 11.1 to 11.8. We shall therefore rewrite the system so that all demands and supplies in real terms appear as functions of relative prices (that is, of the price-wage ratio) and of the rate of interest. In so doing we shall add no new assumptions.

Since neoclassical models usually run in terms of demand for and supply of commodities and services, we shall first eliminate S savings. For that purpose we introduce the total expenditures for consumption C and have by definition $Y = C + S$ from which we obtain $C = Y - S$. Utilizing Equation 11.1 it follows that $C/p = Y/p - f(r,Y/p) = f^*(r,Y/p)$. In Equation 11.3, $I = S$ may be rewritten as $Y/p = C/p + I/p$. Instead of Equations 11.1, 11.2, and 11.3, we thus have:

[11.1′]
$$\frac{C}{p} = f^*\left(r, \frac{Y}{p}\right)$$

[11.2′]
$$\frac{I}{p} = g\left(r, \frac{Y}{p}\right)$$

[11.3′]
$$\frac{Y}{p} = \frac{C}{p} + \frac{I}{p}$$

The consumption function, Equation 11.1′, is an aggregate demand function for consumer goods. Real income and the rate of interest are the determinants of the demand for consumer goods in real terms. There is nothing in this relationship that contradicts neoclassical theory. Modern consumption-function theory is actually based on the same idea of utility maximization by the households as that used in neoclassical theory in deriving individual demand functions for consumer goods. There is perhaps now a greater stress on the intertemporal aspects of utility maximization, however. (See, for instance, Modigliani and Brumberg, 1954.) The argument Y/p could be replaced by a term in the price-wage ratio. Y is equal to wage income plus profits. Expected wage income equals $wN^s = w\psi(w/p)$. Expected profits may be written as $pq - wN$. From Equations 11.6 and 11.7 we have for the aggregate supply of produced goods $q = \phi(\phi'^{-1}(w/p))$, and for planned employment $N = \phi'^{-1}(w/p)$. We have thus

$$Y = w\psi\left(\frac{w}{p}\right) + p\phi\left[\phi'^{-1}\left(\frac{w}{p}\right)\right] - w\phi'^{-1}\left(\frac{w}{p}\right) = pF\left(\frac{w}{p}\right)$$

Y/p can thus be replaced by an expression in the wage-price ratio.

Similarly, the investment function can be written as a function of r and w/p, so that here also we have a demand function typically neoclassical in appearance. The neoclassicists never worked with investment functions, however. Their main interest was in the stationary society where the stock of capital had reached an equilibrium, and their interest was directed more toward the determinants of the equilibrium stock of capital than the demand for additional capital goods. The question has been subject to some discussion, and it has been maintained that neoclassical capital theory did not imply a theory of demand for investment goods (Haavelmo, 1960). It has been shown, however, that within the framework of a full-scale intertemporal production theory (Chapter 7, Section 4), neoclassical investment functions of the type used by Keynes can, indeed, be derived (Jorgenson, 1967).

The equilibrium condition in Equation 11.3' states that the total supply (itself a function of w/p) must be equal to the total demand for produced goods.

Furthermore, if we let M^d stand for demand for money and M^s for supply of money (both in terms of money), we can expand Equation 11.4 to

[11.4'a]
$$\frac{M^d}{p} = L\left(r, \frac{Y}{p}\right)$$

[11.4'b]
$$\frac{M^s}{p} = \frac{M}{p}$$

[11.4'c]
$$M^d = M^s$$

where Equation 11.4'a is the demand for money (in real terms). Since Y/p also can be replaced here by $F(w/p)$, we find that the Keynesian demand function for money, based on his concept of the transactions, precautionary and speculative motives, is entirely consistent with neoclassical demand theory, insofar as the determinants of money demand are concerned. We have several times called attention to this circumstance. The rest of the money market equations are, of course, entirely neoclassical.

Equation 11.5 can be written as

[11.5']
$$\frac{Y}{p} = q^s$$

which states that real national income is equal to the total supply of produced goods q^s. Equation 11.5' may still be considered a definitional relationship, but this definitional procedure is not entirely innocent. We shall return to it below when we discuss the Keynesian underemployment equilibrium (Section 7).

Let us now also make a clear distinction between the demand for labor N^d, which can be called planned employment, and the supply of labor N^s. Equation 11.6 may then be written

[11.6'] $$q^s = \phi(N^d)$$

Considering the following Equation 11.7', we could also, as we have already noted, write the total supply of produced goods q^s as a function of the wage-price ratio $q^s = \phi(\phi'^{-1}(w/p))$. The profit maximization condition in Equation 11.7 is the inverse demand function for labor, and we have

[11.7'] $$N^d = \phi'^{-1}\left(\frac{w}{p}\right)$$

Equation 11.8 is the supply function for labor and we shall simply repeat it

[11.8'] $$N^s = \psi\left(\frac{w}{p}\right)$$

all the labor market functions thus being pure neoclassical theory.

If we stop here we have a system of ten equations, of which the first three, with Equations 11.5' and 11.6', are the demand and supply relationships for produced goods and their equilibrium condition. Equations 11.4'a to c are the demand and supply functions for money and the related equilibrium condition. Equations 11.7' and 11.8', finally, are the demand and supply functions for labor. The ten equations determine the ten unknown variables C, Y, I, r, p, M^d, M^s, q^s, N^d, and N^s. There may be unemployment because nothing ensures $N^d = N^s$. This is the Keynesian model on an explicit demand and supply form.

We may once again add the equilibrium condition for the labor market

[11.9'] $$N^d = N^s$$

and consider the wage rate w as an additional unknown. We then have a complete system of demand and supply equations and equilibrium conditions for three interdependent markets determining absolute prices, the rate of interest, and quantities in demand and supply. In other words, we have an explicit neoclassical model.

4 / Common features of the Keynesian and the neoclassical models

To summarize, we have found that both the Keynesian and the neoclassical models are systems of demand and supply equations, and equilibrium conditions.

Further, the systems consist of real demand and supply functions, which are homogeneous of degree zero in prices, wages (income), *and* the quantity of money. The homogeneity properties are actually the same as in the Patinkin model, disregarding the problem of government bond holdings. The homogeneity properties are very unevenly distributed over the systems, however. Only the (real) supply function for money is homogeneous in prices and quantity of money. All other demand and supply functions are homogeneous in prices and wages (income) only; apparently we find no real balance effects in the system. We shall return to this problem in the next section. The homogeneity in prices, wages (income), and the quantity of money is perhaps most easily recognized if we write the excess demand for money in real terms

[11.10]
$$\frac{M^x}{p} = L\left(r, \frac{Y}{p}\right) - \frac{M}{p}$$

Equation 11.10 suffices to make Klein's neoclassical model conform to the quantity theory of money; a doubling of the quantity of money implies a doubling of all prices, money income, and money values, leaving all real quantities and the rate of interest unchanged. Klein's Keynesian model, on the other hand, does not conform to the quantity theory. On certain natural assumptions concerning the sign of the derivatives of the functions in the system, an increase in the quantity of money leads to a fall in the equilibrium rate of interest, an increase in the price of produced goods, and an increase in real demand for produced goods, production, and employment. An increase in money wages, given the quantity of money, will have the opposite effect. Note that in the neoclassical system it does not make sense to ask for the effects of an increase in money wages since money wages are endogenously determined. It follows that a proportional increase in the quantity of money *and* the money-wage rate in the Keynesian system will lead to a proportionate increase in money income and prices, and leave all real quantities and the rate of interest unchanged. In this special sense the Keynesian model also conforms to the quantity theory of money.

A further important conclusion is that if Klein's neoclassical model does have a meaningful solution at all with positive price, interest rate, and so forth, it will be a full-employment solution in the sense that at going money and real wages, demand and supply of labor are equal. Then there must also exist in Klein's Keynesian model a positive money-wage rate that makes demand for labor equal to supply, and thus creates full employment. There will be unemployment in the Keynesian model only if the money-wage rate differs from (that is, is higher than) this full-employment equilibrium rate. Conversely, only when the corresponding neoclassical system has no solution will there be no (positive) money-wage rate that can create full employment in the Keynesian system.

Finally, we note that the systems contain no equations for the credit market, although the presence of a money rate of interest makes it clear that a credit market must exist.[1] We know that by virtue of Walras' law one market does not need to be presented explicitly, and following Keynes' own exposition in the *General Theory*, Keynesian models have usually omitted this market. The credit market ought to be presented explicitly, however, not only for the sake of completeness, but also because it may be that the rest of the system implies demand and supply functions for the credit market that for *a priori* reasons may be difficult to accept. This circumstance may in turn suggest revisions of the assumptions upon which the rest of the system is based, which is exactly what happens when we begin looking at the Keynesian system's implicit demand and supply functions for the credit market.

5 / The hidden credit market equations

To formulate the credit market equations implied by the rest of the model, we must first write Walras' law. Klein's models obviously assume the existence of both households and enterprises. We must therefore formulate their aggregated budget restrictions. For that purpose we shall assume that the total national income accrues to the households, that is, to the factor owners. No profits are retained in the enterprises.

As to the nature of the credit market, we shall first assume that it is a market in government bonds and that the total number of bonds actually in the possession of the private sector B is distributed between households B^h and enterprises B^e, where $B^h + B^e = B$. We assume also that the quantity of government money M is distributed between households M^h and enterprises M^e, $M^h + M^e = M$. There is no borrowing and lending within the private sector, and no private banks. We shall relax this assumption in Section 6.

The budget restriction of the households is then[2]

[11.11] $$M^h + \frac{B^h}{r} + Y \equiv C + \frac{B^{hd}}{r} + M^{hd}$$

---

[1] Some critics of Keynesian models assume that in omitting the credit market equations the Keynesians have tacitly assumed that a credit market does not exist. (See, for example, Hahn, 1955, pp. 56 et seq.) This interpretation is a strange one, considering that Keynes' liquidity-preference theory is a theory of substitution between claims and money. Claims do exist. Why should there be no market for claims? Admittedly, Keynes and his followers were never explicit as to why the credit market was omitted from the formal models, thus leaving the field open to interpretation; the one suggested here is presumably the most natural. In the prolonged discussions that followed publication of the *General Theory*, the credit market did in fact play an important role.

[2] We do not consider the problem of interest payments and corresponding taxation. (Chapter 8, Section 5.)

where M^{hd} and B^{hd}/r are the households' demand for cash and bonds, respectively. For the enterprises we have

[11.12]
$$M^e + \frac{B^e}{r} + q^s p = Y + I + \frac{B^{ed}}{r} + M^{ed}$$

where M^{ed} and B^{ed}/r are the enterprises' demand for cash and bonds, respectively. We define $B^d = B^{hd} + B^{ed}$ and $M^d = M^{hd} + M^{ed}$. Adding Equations 11.11 and 11.12 and using Equations 11.1', 11.2', 11.4'a and 11.5', we obtain

[11.13]
$$\frac{B^d}{r} = M + \frac{B}{r} + Y - pf^*\left(r, \frac{Y}{p}\right) - pg\left(r, \frac{Y}{p}\right) - pL\left(r, \frac{Y}{p}\right)$$

so that real demand for bonds has the general form

[11.13']
$$\frac{B^d/r}{p} = \Phi\left(r, \frac{Y}{p}, \frac{M + B/r}{p}\right)$$

The real supply of bonds is, of course

[11.14]
$$\frac{B^s/r}{p} = \frac{B/r}{p}$$

and the equilibrium condition is

[11.15]
$$B^s = B\dagger$$

We saw earlier that Klein's two systems are homogeneous in prices and quantity of money; in this respect they resemble the Patinkin system. But nowhere in Klein's system do we find the real balance effects that characterize Patinkin's system. We see now that Klein's systems do, in fact, include real balance, or real wealth, effects, but only in the "hidden" demand function for bonds. This assumption is logically possible, and it may be empirically true; but *a priori* it looks peculiar, indeed. It is most natural that in the market for bonds we finally find real balance effects in relation to the Keynesian model. Keynes' liquidity-preference theory is a theory of substitution between money and bonds; the margin of substitution depends on both the amount of money and the amount of the bonds. It is more difficult to see why real balance, or real wealth, effects should only appear in the demand function of the bonds, a circumstance that has strange consequences for the *modus operandi* of the system.

Let us first determine the effects of an isolated change in the quantity of money, which can be gauged from the system set forth in Equations 11.1' to 11.8', or, 11.9', as the case may be. As we have already seen, in the Keynesian model it leads to a fall in the rate of interest, an increase in the

† Adding Equations 11.13', 11.14, and 11.15 to the Keynesian or the neoclassical system, we have three new equations and two new unknowns, B^d/r and B^s/r. One of the equations depends upon the rest *via* Walras' law, however, which was how we constructed Equation 11.13'.

price level, and an increase in all real demands and employment. In the neoclassical model it leads to an increase in the price, wage rate, and money income, but leaves all real magnitudes unchanged. An isolated change in the quantity of bonds, on the other hand, has no effect whatever! This result follows from the fact that B does not appear anywhere in that part of the system(s), Equations 11.1' to 11.8', or 11.9', which suffices to determine all the unknowns. A glance at the demand and supply functions for bonds explains why this is so. If the number of bonds changes from B to $B + \Delta B$, the supply of bonds in real terms increases by $\Delta B/(rp)$. The demand for bonds will increase automatically (that is, at given interest rates, prices, and so forth) by the same amount because $B/(rp)$ enters as a demand determinant with the coefficient 1. Klein's models thus assume a peculiar kind of Say's law for bonds: the supply of bonds creates its own demand. It follows that an isolated increase in the quantity of money will have the same effects as open-market operations (purchases of bonds).

We cannot possibly accept all of this, and must therefore make some revision in the rest of the system. The natural procedure, entirely in line with Keynes' liquidity-preference theory as a theory of substitution between money and bonds, is to let the real (financial) wealth $(M + B/r)/p$ enter as an argument in the demand function for money, too:

[11.4'a']
$$\frac{M^d}{p} = L\left(r, \frac{Y}{p}, \frac{M + B/r}{p}\right)$$

This revision reacts on the demand function for bonds where the quantity of bonds will now enter with a coefficient that is smaller than 1 (assuming a positive real wealth effect on the demand for money), which is what we should expect a priori. Incidentally, this result shows that a Patinkin system need not have real balance, or real wealth effects with respect to demand for and supply of commodities and services. These effects may be restricted to the financial part of the system, in which case the effects of a change in the quantity of money on demand for and supply of commodities and services must work via the rate of interest, as Keynes always maintained. Once the real balance, or real wealth, effects have been extended to the demand for money, it is difficult to understand, however, why they should not be extended in principle to all demands and supplies in the system. This would make Klein's neoclassical model very similar to Patinkin's system.

So far we have assumed that there are only government bonds and government money; that is, "outside" money, in the system. "Inside" money and debts play an important role in modern societies and must be considered, as well. Assume first that M is government money, but that bonds are issued by enterprises and kept by households, and vice versa. This would mean that B^h is equal to B^e with opposite sign $B^h = -B^e$ with the result that on the right side of Equations 11.13 and 11.13' $B/r = 0$; this term therefore disappears. We still have a real balance effect from government money, but there is no real bonds effect. The demands for bonds B^{hd} and B^{ed} do not necessarily cancel each other out, however. Entity $B^{hd} + B^{ed} = B^d$ may be positive or negative, and must be interpreted as the *net* demand for bonds, the net supply of bonds being zero because $B^s = B = 0$. The real bonds effect disappears in Equations 11.13 and 11.13′ only because we have assumed that bond holdings do not appear as determinants of demand and supply elsewhere in the system. This assumption is very difficult to defend under the present assumptions. If bonds are issued by enterprises and kept by households, we cannot assume that the positive holdings of households and the negative holdings of enterprises tend to cancel each other out automatically with respect to their effects on the demand for produced goods and services. Consumer goods are purchased exclusively by households and should be influenced by the positive holdings of households, whereas investment goods are purchased only by enterprises and should be influenced by the enterprises' negative holdings. It is difficult to understand how the positive holdings of the households should enter the picture in relation to investment demand, and vice versa for consumer demand and the negative holdings of enterprises. We may assume that the effects of the positive holdings of households on consumer demand and of the negative holdings of enterprises on investment demand cancel each other out in total effective demand for produced goods. But *a priori* there is no reason why they should.

We meet the same kinds of problems if we introduce inside money into the systems. We must then consider an intermediary, private banks, for example, which loan money to and keep deposits for the private sector. In addition, it might keep positive or negative balances with the central bank. Again, it may be argued that (with a competitive banking system) from a national accounting viewpoint claims and debts within the private sector cancel each other out so that total private wealth is unaffected by the existence of inside money and claims. We still have the problem of possible "distribution" effects, however; there is no reason why the effects of claims and debts should cancel each other out exactly everywhere in the system. (See Chapter 8, Section 8.)

6 / A Keynesian model with wealth effects and inside money

In the last section we showed that the Keynesian system, even in carefully constructed versions such as Klein's Keynesian model, is unsatisfactory in its treatment of credit and the embryonic role played by real balances, or wealth. Patinkin's criticism of the neoclassical system has had very useful spillover effects on Keynesian theory; considering the above discussion we should, at the least, try to expand Klein's Keynesian and neoclassical models to include wealth effects and inside money. In so doing we shall draw upon a model presented for a similar purpose by Modigliani (1963); our model integrates the private banks with the real system, however, which Modigliani's model does not really do.

We begin with the explicit demand and supply system set forth in Section 2. Defining total private wealth W as the sum of the value of real capital K, government bonds kept by the private sector, and central bank money (defined as notes and private sector net claims other than notes on the central bank), we have $W = pK + B/r + M$. W is partly predetermined, partly exogenously determined. We then modify Equations 11.1′ to 11.8′ as follows, keeping the functional signs unchanged for the sake of convenience:

[11.1″]
$$\frac{C}{p} = f^*\left(r, \frac{Y}{p}, \frac{W}{p}\right)$$

[11.2″]
$$\frac{I}{p} = g\left(r, \frac{Y}{p}, \frac{W}{p}\right)$$

[11.3″]
$$\frac{Y}{p} = \frac{C}{p} + \frac{I}{p}$$

which together with the definitional relation

[11.5″]
$$\frac{Y}{p} = q^s$$

and the production function

[11.6″]
$$q^s = \phi(N^d)$$

take care of the markets for produced goods. By including total private wealth in the demand functions, we obviously disregard problems related to the distribution of wealth between individuals, but we do not assume that the wealth effects on total demand cancel each other out.

For the sake of convenience we proceed to the market for labor, where the equations remain unchanged, although real wealth might have been included in the supply and demand functions for labor.

[11.7″]
$$N^d = \phi'^{-1}\left(\frac{w}{p}\right)$$

[11.8″]
$$N^s = \psi\left(\frac{w}{p}\right)$$

The changes with respect to money are more extensive. We assume now that there exist private banks that receive interest-free deposits from the private sector and as assets keep either central bank money (interest-free claims on the central bank) or bonds.[1] The private, nonbank sector there-

---

[1] We assume that the banking system is perfectly competitive so that no profits are paid from the banks to households and the capitalized value of the banks is zero. The banks are supposed to employ real resources and their operations are extended to the point where marginal (and average) costs are equal to the interest margin. We do not specify this explicitly in the system. Equation 11.7″ is supposed to include the demand for labor from the banks. This means that we actually ought to include the bond rate of interest as an argument in the demand function for labor. For the same reason the real wage rate w/p ought to appear in 11.4″f and 11.4″g.

fore keeps cash either as deposits in the private banks or as central bank money (notes). We let M^{pd} and M^{ps} denote total private, nonbank demand for and supply of cash, respectively. We assume that the private, nonbank sector is indifferent as to the composition of its cash holdings on notes and deposits, both being interest free, and thus have for the real demand for cash

[11.4″a]
$$\frac{M^{pd}}{p} = L\left(r, \frac{Y}{p}, \frac{W}{p}\right)$$

The real supply of cash to the private, nonbank sector is now

[11.4″b]
$$\frac{M^{ps}}{p} = \frac{D + M^p}{p}$$

where D represents deposits in private banks and M^p represents central bank money (notes) with the private, nonbank sector. As an equilibrium condition we have

[11.4″c]
$$M^{pd} = M^{ps}$$

Counting equations and unknowns in this modified Keynesian system we find that it contains ten equations and twelve unknowns. The hitherto given M on the right side of Equation 11.4′b has in Equation 11.4″b been replaced by two new unknowns D and M^p. Of course, we shall still assume, as an expression of the official monetary policy, that the total quantity of central bank money M is given, which furnishes us with the relationship

[11.4″d]
$$M = M^p + M^b$$

where M^b is the quantity of central bank money (claims) held by the private banks. This relationship gives us one more equation, but also one more unknown M^b. Thus, we are still short two equations, and must therefore turn to the behavior of the private banks. Their liabilities are the deposits D and their assets the holdings of central bank money M^b and bonds at a value of B^b/r, where B^b is a new unknown. The following definitional relationship holds[1]

[11.4″e]
$$D = M^b + \frac{B^b}{r}$$

In accordance with traditional theory (Chapter 6, Section 5) we shall assume that the banks allow their cash reserves to vary with the amount of deposits (although not necessarily in the same proportion), regard being paid to the opportunity cost of keeping cash, the foregone interests. We have thus

[11.4″f]
$$\frac{M^b}{p} = G\left(\frac{D}{p}, r\right)$$

---

[1] This is the balance sheet of the banks. We might have written a more complete budget restriction by including assets and debts at the beginning of the period, and interest payments and factor purchases. This procedure would force us to show these items explicitly in the rest of the model, however, which would unnecessarily complicate the picture.

Note that we let the real demand for central bank money depend on real deposits. As to the bond holdings of the private banks, we assume similarly that

[11.4″g] $$\frac{B^b/r}{p} = H\left(\frac{D}{p}, r\right)$$

the rationale of this equation is that D/p may be seen as a "wealth" effect, and r represents a speculative motive.

Given r and p, the last three equations determine the three items on the balance sheets of the private banks. We shall assume that at any positive r and p they have a unique positive solution in D, M^b, and B^b.

We have now the same number of equations as unknowns, and shall assume that the system has a meaningful solution. As before, we can add the equilibrium condition for the labor market

[11.9″] $$N^d = N^s$$

and letting the money-wage rate w be endogenously determined, we have then a neoclassical system with inside money and a banking system.[1]

A glance at the homogeneity properties of this neoclassical system shows that a proportional change in the quantity of central bank money M and the number of government bonds B will lead to a proportional change in price, wage rate, money income, and all other value entities, money supply to the private, nonbank sector, and so forth, and leave the rate of interest and all real quantities unchanged (with the usual reservation for distribution effects). In this respect the inclusion of a private banking system and inside money does not change the characteristics of the neoclassical system. This does not mean that the existence of private banks is neutral with respect to the real economy. The private banks' preference for central bank money and bonds influences the rate of interest and thus the equilibrium solution for the system in general. Although a change in the quantity of money and government debt is neutral, the existence of a banking system is not (Gurley and Shaw, 1960). For the Keynesian system, the same holds true, provided that the money-wage rate changes in proportion to the quantity of central bank money and government bonds.

It should be noticed that we can easily change the assumptions of the behavior of the central bank from fixing the quantity of government money to fixing the rate of interest. We need then only to let M be an endogenous variable, and r exogenously given. Moreover, it is clear that if the central

---

[1] To complete the system it would be necessary to add the demand function for bonds of the private, nonbank sector, and the supply function and equilibrium condition for bonds. We would then have three more equations and two more variables. One of the equations would follow from the rest of the system, as usual. We shall not write out these equations. The reader may convince himself that the private, nonbank sector's demand function for bonds now is well behaved. Let us only add that this demand function may be interpreted as a *net* demand function, implying that the private nonbank sector may issue bonds on itself (Modigliani, 1963, p. 81).

bank in its policy interferes with, for instance, the reserve ratio of the private banks—that is, interferes with Equation 11.4"f—the real variables of the system, interest rates, relative prices, etc., will be affected.

7 / Unemployment and general equilibrium

According to Klein's interpretation of the Keynesian and neoclassical systems, the main difference between them is not in the general form of the demand and supply equations for the invididual markets. Moreover, Klein's neo-classical model does not deviate in any essential way from the neoclassical system in Patinkin's version. It is true that Klein's version of the two systems is very special with respect to the appearance of real balance effects. Follow-ing Patinkin, we should in principle expect these effects to appear every-where. For the adjustment toward equilibrium, Klein's model therefore depends more heavily upon the rate of interest. But this is a matter of degree rather than of kind. Patinkin's system does not exclude the fact that there may be markets where, for all practical purposes, the real balance effects are negligible. There is, however, an important difference between the two systems: unemployment exists in the Keynesian system, and it does not in the neoclassical system.

Among other variables, Klein's neoclassical model determines the money-wage rate. Assuming that the neoclassical model has an economically meaningful solution, we know that if the money-wage rate is fixed above its equilibrium value (by the government, by trade unions, and so forth), the system cannot be in general equilibrium, *ceteris paribus*. Discarding the equi-librium equation for the labor market, Equation 11.9, we then have one unknown and one equation less; the remaining system determines a new set of equilibrium values for all variables with the equilibrium level of employment below the supply of labor. Formally, this was all that was needed to pass from Klein's neoclassical model to his Keynesian model. It might be argued that the explanation of permanent unemployment in the Keynesian system should then simply be that money wages are fixed at a level above that at which, taking into account repercussions through the rest of the system, de-mand and supply of labor would tally. Most Keynesians, Klein among them, object to this interpretation because it is exactly the explanation of permanent unemployment (over and above frictional and certain other forms of dynamic short-term unemployment) offered by the neoclassicists. The neoclassicists maintained that permanent unemployment can only exist if money wages are fixed at too high a level, typically as the result of monopolistic trade union policy or government minimum-wage legislation.

A neoclassical general equilibrium system with unemployment can easily be constructed by adding a Phillips' relation to Patinkin's system. The Phillips' relation may, for instance, be $\dot{w}/w = -au + b$, where $\dot{w}/w$ is the rate of change of the money-wage rate, u the unemployment percentage, and *a* and *b* positive constants. It follows that money wages are constant at an unemployment percentage equal to b/a. If, therefore, in the system described by Equations 8.1 to 8.4, market *n* is the labor market, we can simply change the equilibrium condition of this market $q_n{}^d = q_n{}^s$ to $q_n{}^d = q_n{}^s(1 - b/a)$. The rest of Patinkin's system remains unchanged.

Klein therefore argues that the neoclassical system may not have an economically meaningful solution at positive values of prices, wages, production, interest rates, and so forth. If this is true, there will be no positive money-wage rate that can bring about full employment equilibrium in the corresponding Keynesian model. It does not make sense, then, to single out the fixed money-wage rate as being *the* cause of the unemployment. Allowing money wages to fall will cause at most an increase in employment up to a certain maximum. The road to full employment should be that lower wage rates imply lower prices, that, at a given quantity of money, imply both a lower rate of interest and larger real balances, which would tend to increase the demand for consumer and investment goods, thereby permitting a higher rate of employment. A fall in wages in relation to prices would at the same time increase the optimum level of production and employment. This chain of events may be blocked, however, either because an infinitely elastic demand for money prevents the rate of interest from falling below a certain minimum, or because the rate of interest has fallen to zero without stimulating a demand sufficient to create full employment. If real balance effects are also too weak, even though prices fall toward zero and real balances grow infinitely, full employment equilibrium may never be reached. Another possibility, usually not considered by Keynesians, is that there may not exist any price-wage relationship that would induce producers to employ the entire labor force. Such a situation could occur in the event of a vertical marginal-cost curve, or, stated another way, in the case of zero marginal labor productivity before full employment is reached. This possibility is usually disregarded in discussions of developed economies. In any case, it is taken for granted that if no solution exists in the neoclassical system, the equilibrium condition for the labor market must be deleted; it is then assumed that the Keynesian model thus established will in fact have an economically meaningful solution, which may be questioned (Hahn, 1965).

This argument contains some dubious points that deserve comment.

First, the argument is based on the assumption that the neoclassical model may not have a meaningful solution. As we have seen, Klein's Keynesian model is really a special version of Patinkin's model. The question is therefore whether the latter has a solution. We have touched upon this question earlier (see Chapter 8, Section 1; also Hahn, 1965) and shall only repeat that with Patinkin's assumptions it does in fact have a solution.

Secondly, even in the Keynesian model there must be some money-wage rigidity. Otherwise wages and prices would fall continuously and we could not reasonably talk about an equilibrium system. Some critics therefore prefer to interpret the Keynesian system simply as a neoclassical model (perhaps modified à la Patinkin) proceeding slowly toward a full employment equilibrium, with only the labor market out of equilibrium.

Thirdly, it should be noted that, from a purely formal point of view, we could just as well drop any one of the other equilibrium conditions; the one belonging to the market for produced goods, for instance. We would then have a system wherein full employment existed, with the enterprises continuously producing more or less than they sell. From a short-term point of view (and the Keynesian system is a short-term model) dropping that condition may be just as plausible as dropping the labor market equilibrium condition. To some extent the hypothesis describes what has actually happened during the short-term fluctuations in postwar Europe. During recessions firms have been reluctant both to dismiss their workers and lower their prices. Instead they have preferred to let their inventories or their labor productivity, or both, fluctuate.

Fourthly, there is a crucial question to be asked: How is it possible for the Keynesian system to include unemployment and yet be in equilibrium in all other markets? Walras' law tells us that if one market, for example, the labor market, is out of equilibrium in that demand and supply are unequal, at least one other market must also be out of equilibrium. It may be argued that the credit market, not shown explicitly, must be the other market in disequilibrium. This argument is invalid, however. An excess supply in the labor market should mean that there is an excess demand in the market for bonds; even though money wages are prevented from falling despite the excess supply of labor, there should be a continuous rise in bond prices and a continuous fall in the rate of interest. This assumption leads us to a contradiction, however: according to the rest of the model the rate of interest is at its equilibrium level. There is no doubt that Keynesian theory assumes that *all* other markets are in equilibrium. The only solution to this dilemma, therefore, is to assume that the labor market must also be in equilibrium, despite the existence of unemployment. To see how this assumption can be made, let us consider the labor market and its demand and supply relationships.

With the quantity of labor on the abscissa and the money-wage rate on the ordinate, Figure 11.1 shows the demand curve for labor

$$N^d = \phi'^{-1}\left(\frac{w}{p}\right)$$

and the supply curve of labor $N^s = \psi(w/p)$, assuming p to be given at p_0. The actual money-wage rate is w_0, and the entire Keynesian system is presumed to be in equilibrium with the price of produced goods at p_0 with actual employment equal to N_0^d. In this situation the supply of labor equals N_0^s and unemployment is $N_0^s - N_0^d$. Note that the demand and supply curves tell us only how demand and supply for labor would change if the money-wage rate changed, but the price p is kept at its initial equilibrium

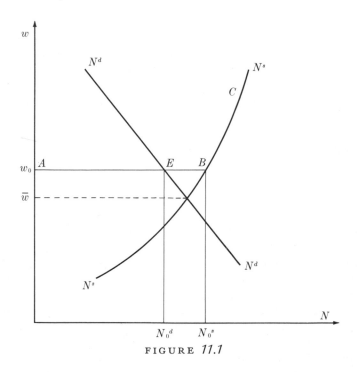

FIGURE *11.1*

level p_0. The money-wage rate $\bar{w}$ is therefore not an equilibrium rate in the sense that at this rate the whole system would be in equilibrium with no unemployment. Nevertheless, Figure 11.1 helps us understand the nature of the equilibrium position at the money-wage rate w_0. Our problem is: In what sense can we maintain that the labor market is in equilibrium without an excess supply of labor, despite the fact that unemployment is equal to $N_0^s - N_0^d$.

A very common interpretation, supported by Klein (1947, pp. 74–75), is that since the trade unions (or, as it may be, the government) have fixed the money-wage rate at w_0 and enforced it so that no labor is sold below that wage rate, the supply curve is really the kinked curve ABC, and not the curve $N^s = \psi(w/p_0)$. At the demand curve $N^d = \phi'^{-1}(w/p_0)$ and the actual employment N_0^d, labor is actually on its supply curve at E, which must mean that households only expect to sell N_0^d, although they would like to sell N_0^s. Their demand for consumer goods, money, and bonds must therefore also be determined by an expected income corresponding to actual employment N_0^d. This conclusion has consequences for the interpretation of Y/p in the demand functions of Klein's Keynesian model. In Section 3 we explained briefly how the argument Y/p in the consumption function could be replaced by an expression $F(w/p)$ to make the demand functions appear completely neoclassical. It will be understood now that expected wage income must be equal to wN^d and not to wN^s as we maintained in Section 3. This circumstance does not change the fact that demand is a function of w/p, and it solves the problem with Walras' law and the equilibrium of the remaining markets. There can be no doubt that the supplies that enter Walras' law are the expected sales; therefore if expected sales of labor equal planned purchases, all other markets may be in equilibrium, as the Keynesian system insists that they are (Clower, 1965). The consequence, of course, is that unemployment is some sort of appendix to the system, with no real economic importance. The unemployed do not expect to be employed and have no income expectations related to sales of labor; they do not exert any pressure on money wages.

Instead of saying that the supply curve for labor is *ABC*, so that labor is on its supply curve even when there is unemployment, it might be more natural to say that even in this situation the households' supply curve is $N^s = \psi(w/p_0)$, but that the households are off their supply curve by the amount $N_0^s - N_0^d$. Their loyalty to the unions prevents them from bidding down money wages, and they adjust their sales expectations to actual sales.

The enterprises, on the other hand, are on their demand curve and produce what they find optimal at the equilibrium wage-price ratio in accordance with Equations 11.6 and 11.7. Employment can then only increase if the wage-price ratio falls. In unemployment equilibrium, the real wage rate is thus higher than it would be in full employment. This is a very neoclassical viewpoint, but it was explicitly accepted by Keynes (1936, Chapter II).

The above interpretation is often criticized in its entirety because it is presumed to imply a money illusion in the supply of labor. Keynes himself was extremely confused on this issue, but insisted actually that unions are only interested in money wages (1936, Chapter II). In fixing a certain money-wage rate and maintaining it irrespective of the price level, supply of labor is made a function of money wages rather than real wages, at least up to the point of full employment. In the second edition of his *Keynesian Revolution* (1966, p. 211) Klein seems to agree with this criticism, which, however, is not really devastating. As just mentioned, we can maintain that the labor supply curve is indeed $N^s = \psi(w/p)$, but that the households' expected sales adjust themselves to actual sales. This assumption does not mean that a money illusion is introduced. On the other hand, the fact that trade unions are assumed to fix money wages (which they actually do as a rule) and not real wages (which they can be said to do only if escalator clauses are included in the wage contracts), certainly does not imply that unions ignore prices. We need only to assume that unions fix money wages on the basis of certain expectations with respect to prices, and that they will insist upon changing money wages after a period of time if their price expectations should prove to be significantly wrong. Wage contracts are actually made for periods up to several years, and the Keynesian system is a short-term system; the fixed money-wage rate does not really give rise to problems within the framework of the Keynesian model itself. In addition, it should be emphasized that even if we assume that unions fix real wages rather than money wages, it does not necessarily require any other changes in the Keynesian model itself. With w/p constant (rather than w), the optimal level of production and employment will be given, too (Equation 11.7 or 11.7'). If total effective demand for produced goods falls short of production at this level, prices will fall and so will money wages because the real wage is fixed. Through a lower interest rate or higher real balances, or both, demand for goods will then adjust itself upward until the market for produced goods is in equilibrium at optimum production.

Patinkin (1966, XIII:2) presented a different interpretation of the Keynesian unemployment equilibrium situation in assuming that both households and enterprises are off their supply curves. This situation requires rigidity in both money wages and prices. If a real wage has been fixed, Patinkin assumes that enterprises try to produce the optimum quantity of goods. If they find that demand is insufficient they do not bid down prices but rather adjust their sales expectations to actual sales and bring production down below the optimum. Households will adjust labor-sales expectations to actual employment in the way we assumed above. Both households and enterprises are then to the left of their supply curves, but with sales expectations equal to actual purchasing plans in the markets for produced goods and labor, respectively. In a sense, this is a logical extension of the first interpretation, where only the households were off their supply curve for labor. The supply of goods would then no longer be determined by the price-wage ratio *via* profit maximization. Irrespective of the price-wage ratio, enterprises would produce for expected sales, the price-wage ratio being assumed constant (Patinkin, 1966, pp. 330–331). This interpretation presumes market imperfections not only in the labor market but also in the market for produced goods and, considering the frequency of market imperfections in modern economies, it should not in itself disturb us. Indeed, it might be argued that Patinkin's interpretation is a badly needed step toward a higher degree of realism in the Keynesian model. Once we introduce market imperfections, however, it would seem that the entire Keynesian model is in need of revision. It is not very satisfactory to assume that market imperfections rule the roost outside full employment equilibrium, and that in full employment equilibrium everybody, at least on the producer side, behaves as if there were perfect competition.[1]

The two interpretations of the Keynesian equilibrium with unemployment that we have described could be tested empirically. In the first interpretation real wages would fall and profit margins would increase as employment increased. With Patinkin's interpretation this relationship would be

---

[1] A simple way to introduce market imperfections in these models is to assume a constant degree of monopoly in the markets for produced goods. This assumption changes the optimum condition from $w/p = \phi'(N^d)$ to $w/p = (1 - \epsilon)\phi'(N^d)$, where ϵ is the degree of monopoly. It does not change the *modus operandi* of Klein's models, however.

reversed. Statistical studies (see, for instance, Tsiang, 1947) have been inconclusive on this issue, which is probably quite natural since both interpretations may oversimplify or even misrepresent enterprise and household behavior under conditions of disequilibrium. Indeed, our discussion of the Keynesian equilibrium and its meaning as to unemployment serves mainly to show what was noted in connection with our discussion of inflation in Chapter 10. We noted there that economic theory has so far been unable to present satisfactory theories of enterprise behavior with respect to production, employment, and price-*change* decisions in situations of disequilibrium, of household behavior with respect to labor sales expectations, and, finally, of the determination of money-wage change. Modern microtheory is working on this type of problem (Phelps, 1969), but until an adequate microtheory has been established, macrotheory concerned with disequilibrium situations will probably be left in its present unsatisfactory state.

References

CLOWER, ROBERT: "The Keynesian Counterrevolution: A Theoretical Appraisal," in F. Hahn and F. P. R. Brechling (eds.), *The Theory of Interest Rates*, Macmillan, London, 1965.

HAAVELMO, TRYGGVE: *A Study in the Theory of Investment*, University of Chicago Press, 1960.

HAHN, F. H.: "The Rate of Interest and General Equilibrium Analysis," *The Economic Journal*, vol. 65, no. 257, March, 1955.

—: "On Some Problems of Proving the Existence of an Equilibrium in a Monetary Economy," in F. H. Hahn and F. P. R. Brechling (eds.), *The Theory of Interest Rates*, Macmillan, London, 1965.

JORGENSON, DALE W.: "The Theory of Investment Behavior," in R. Ferber (ed.), *Determinants of Investment Behavior*, N.B.E.R., New York, 1967.

KEYNES, J. M.: *The General Theory of Employment, Interest, and Money*, Harcourt, Brace, New York, 1936.

KLEIN, L. R.: *The Keynesian Revolution*, 2d ed., Macmillan, New York, 1966.

MODIGLIANI, FRANCO: "Liquidity Preference and the Theory of Interest and Money," *Econometrica*, vol. 12, no. 1, January, 1944.

—: "The Monetary Mechanism and Its Interaction with Real Phenomena," *The Review of Economics and Statistics*, vol. 45, no. 1, part 2, supplement, February, 1963.

—, and RICHARD BRUMBERG: "Utility Analysis and the Consumption Function: An Interpretation of Cross-Section Data," in K. K. Kurihara (ed.), *Post-Keynesian Economics*, Rutgers University Press, New Brunswick, N.J., 1954.

PATINKIN, D.: *Money, Interest, and Prices*, Harper and Row, New York, 1966.

PHELPS, E. S.: "The New Microeconomics in Inflation and Employment Theory," *The American Economic Review*, vol. 59, no. 2, May, 1969.

TSIANG, S. C.: *The Variations of Real Wages and Profits Margins in Relation to the Trade Cycle*, Isaac Pitman, London, 1947.

Alternative
interest theories

12

After publication of Keynes' *General Theory* there arose an animated discussion about the determination of the rate of interest. Keynes believed that his was an entirely new theory of the rate of interest, which contradicted what he believed was classical, or neoclassical, interest theory. He maintained that the rate of interest is determined by demand for and supply of money, and that the neoclassicists erroneously believed that the rate of interest is determined by savings and investments. Against him stood such representatives of neo-classical theory as D. H. Robertson (1940), Bertil Ohlin (1937), and others, who maintained that the interest rate is determined by demand for and supply of credit, or, as they stated it, by loanable funds, and that this was the true neoclassical theory. We shall not discuss what the neoclassicists really meant with respect to interest determination, but shall limit ourselves to consideration of the theory problem itself. The discussion may serve as an exercise in general equilibrium theory. To systematize the discussion we must distinguish between total- and partial-interest theory; we shall begin with the former. Part of the discussion concerned stock-flow problems, but since no real issues were involved here (see Patinkin, 1958) we shall not consider this aspect of the debate.

1 / The "sham dispute"

Hicks (1939, pp. 153–154; see also, 1950, Chapter XI, where the same argument is repeated in a somewhat different form) disposed of the debate by showing that it was really a "sham dispute":

Any treatment which pretends to deal with the economic system as a whole (and it is with such general analysis that the whole controversy has been concerned) cannot possibly regard the rate of interest in isolation. It is a price, like other prices, and must be determined with them as part of a mutually interdependent system.

Disregarding whether the rate of interest really is a price "like other prices" (Chapter 7, Section 2), there can be no doubt that the rate of interest, with all money prices, is determined by the system as a whole, provided, of course, that we are seeking the general equilibrium rate of interest. This argument applies to neoclassical, Keynesian, and any other general equilibrium system wherein the rate of interest is an endogenous variable.

Hicks noted that by virtue of Walras' law, one market can always be omitted. We can discard the "money market" and its equations and keep the credit market equations, along with the rest of the system; or we can discard the credit market and keep the money market; or we can drop the market for peanuts (to repeat Abba Lerner's witticism) or any other commodity, and keep both the money market and the credit market with the rest of the system. The solution of the system is the same, of course, no matter how we proceed in solving the equations; it does not make sense to say that the rate of interest is determined by demand for and supply of credit, or by demand for and supply of money. The interest rate is determined by the system as a whole, and not by any one part of it, unless it happens to be a recursive, decomposable system, which we have no reason to expect.

2 / General equilibrium and the three theories of interest

We presented Walras' law in Chapter 9, Section 1 in a way that makes it easy to explain Hicks' disposal of the debate.[1] With government money and bonds we have (see Equation 9.2)

[12.1]
$$\left(\sum_{i=1}^{n} p_i q_i{}^x \equiv \right) I - S \equiv \left(\frac{B}{r} - \frac{B^d}{r} \right) + (M - M^d)$$

This formulation of Walras' law covers both the neoclassical and the Keynesian cases. We must remember, however, that in the latter, excess demand for labor is interpreted as the difference between demand for labor in the sense of planned employment, and supply of labor in the sense of expected sales of labor. By assumption, both are equal to demand for labor in the Keynesian equilibrium. We must remember also that the sets of equilibrium prices and the interest rates are different in the two cases, granted that both have a solution.

---

[1] For a similar Walrasian approach to the problem, see Fellner and Somers (1941), and Hahn (1955).

Let us assume, then, that all money prices are fixed at their equilibrium levels, and the rate of interest is fixed at an arbitrary value different from its equilibrium value. The system will then be in disequilibrium and, in general, we should expect $I \neq S$, $B^d/r \neq B/r$, and $M^d \neq M$. On the other hand, it is clear that if we now ascribe the equilibrium value to the rate of interest, equilibrium will be reached everywhere, so that, simultaneously, $I = S$, $B^d/r = B/r$, and $M^d = M$.

In line with the above, then, let us formulate three alternative interest theories: the savings-investments theory, the loanable funds theory, and the liquidity-preference theory. In formulating these theories we assume that all money prices for goods and services are kept at a fixed level, which means that all our variables, I, S, B^d/r, B/r, M^d, and M, are functions of the rate of interest only (or constants). Note that since we assume all prices on produced goods and services to be constant, we need not bother about the distinction between demand (and supply) in real and money terms.

We have then

[12.2] $$I = I(r)$$
[12.3] $$S = S(r)$$
[12.4] $$S = I$$

giving us three equations to determine three unknowns, I, S, and r, which is the savings-investments theory of the rate of interest. It states that the rate of interest is determined by the equality of investments and savings.

Further, we have (with our earlier notation in Chapter 8, Section 5)

[12.5] $$\frac{B^d}{r} = Pb^d(r)$$

[12.6] $$\frac{B^s}{r} = \frac{B}{r}$$

[12.7] $$\frac{B^d}{r} = \frac{B^s}{r}$$

giving us three equations to determine B^d, B^s, and r (P is given). This is the loanable funds or credit market theory of interest: the rate of interest equilibrates demand for and supply of credit, loanable funds, or claims on future payments.

Finally, we have

[12.8] $$M^d = Pm^d(r)$$
[12.9] $$M^s = M$$
[12.10] $$M^d = M^s$$

yielding three equations to determine M^d, M^s, and r, which is, of course, the liquidity-preference theory of the interest rate, where the rate of interest equilibrates demand for and supply of money.

With all money prices of goods and services fixed at their general equilibrium values, the above theories of interest will determine the same value of the interest rate; this rate of interest is the general equilibrium rate. In this sense, the three theories are *equivalent;* therefore, arguments pro and con are pointless. Each is by itself sufficient to determine the general equilibrium rate of interest, but only on the condition that all prices of goods and services have been fixed at their equilibrium levels in advance, which brings us back to Hicks' point. We cannot find the equilibrium rate of interest via any of these theories unless we first solve the general equilibrium system. If we solve the system for the prices of all produced goods and services we obtain, during the same process, the rate of interest as well; to return thereafter to any of the three above described theories would be a roundabout way of accomplishing what could be done directly. Moreover, if all prices are fixed at their equilibrium value, the equilibrium rate of interest can, in principle, be determined from the equilibrium condition of any market, even the peanut market, and we could establish a peanut theory of interest that, in this particular sense, would be equivalent to the savings-investments, and loanable-funds, and the liquidity-preference theories.

3 / The threefold margin

In a discussion of Keynes' interest theory, D. H. Robertson (1940) explained that whereas Keynes considered the rate of interest to be determined at one single margin (the convenience of holding money), earlier Cambridge writers insisted that the rate of interest was determined simultaneously at three different margins: resources can be consumed, invested, or added to cash holdings; that is, present consumption is balanced against future consumption, real investments are balanced against financial investments, and cash is balanced against interest-bearing claims. This is, of course, the basic reason why savings, investments, and the demand for money can be written as functions of the rate of interest; as a reflection we see that the demand for bonds is also a function of the rate of interest. Here again, however, we do not know the position of the marginal schedules unless we know all the equilibrium prices of goods and services. If these prices are known, any two schedules will suffice to determine the rate of interest.

4 / Partial-interest theory

Hicks did not really dispose of the entire issue, however, because part of it concerned partial- rather than total-interest theory. We are accustomed to partial-equilibrium theory in dealing with single, isolated markets, industries, commodities, or enterprises. It may be more difficult to defend the use of a partial-equilibrium theory of interest because the rate of interest is a phenomenon that pervades the economy as a whole and may influence it anywhere, or everywhere. From a purely methodological point of view, however, there is nothing in partial-interest theory that can be objected to.

Let us return to Walras' law as formulated in Equation 12.1 and again assume that all money prices for goods and services are fixed in advance. If we fix them at their equilibrium values, the three interest theories discussed in the previous section prove to be equivalent. Assume, therefore, that all prices (or at least some of them) have been fixed at values different from those of the equilibrium prices. Generally we find then that $I \neq S$, $B^d/r \neq B/r$, or $M^d \neq M$ at whatever level (including the general equilibrium level) we fix the rate of interest. There is nothing to ensure that under these assumptions there will exist a value of the rate of interest which will simultaneously make $I = S$, $B^d/r = B/r$, and $M^d = M$.

Walras' law (Equation 12.1) cannot, of course determine the rate of interest, because this relationship applies identically to all prices and interest rates. All the entities appearing in Walras' law appear also under the present assumptions as functions of the rate of interest (or as constants), however. It is therefore entirely legitimate to ask for the rate of interest that equilibrates investments and savings, *or* the rate of interest that equilibrates the market for bonds (credit), *or*, finally, the rate of interest that equilibrates demand for and supply of money, each "market" considered in isolation. It is tantamount to considering the three interest theories as three different partial-equilibrium theories, each one determining a partial-equilibrium rate of interest. Each of these three partial-equilibrium rates is well defined and may exist in the sense that positive solutions exist; in general each will be different and will be dependent upon the precise values ascribed to the prices of goods and services. In this sense there is no conflict between the three theories. They answer three different questions and define three different partial-equilibrium rates. We may ask, however, whether any one of these three partial-equilibrium rates should be considered the partial-equilibrium rate of interest *par excellence*.

It may appear strange for us to be confronted with a number of partial-equilibrium rates. To shed light on the problem, and to help us answer our question, it may be useful to turn for a moment to a less controversial field, for example, the price of butter.

When we ask for the partial-equilibrium price of butter we usually have in mind the price that, given all other prices and the rate of interest, makes demand for and supply of butter equal. But we may also ask for the price of butter that, given all other prices, including the price of margarine, makes demand for and supply of margarine equal. Normally, this butter price will exist, and usually it will differ from the butter price that makes demand for and supply of butter equal. Such questions are actually asked in connection with programs for agricultural support. Here the problem may be: how high should the price of margarine be, through taxation of margarine, to make demand for butter equal to supply at a certain given butter price. Similarly, we may even ask for the butter price that, given all other prices and the rate of interest, makes demand for and supply of money equal. Such a question may not be a usual one to ask; but such a butter price may exist. If it does, it will generally differ from the butter price that equilibrates demand for and supply of butter, and also differ from the butter price that equilibrates demand for and supply of margarine (or potatoes, or automobiles). When we discuss the price of butter, we thus find a multitude of well-defined partial-equilibrium prices. Accordingly we should not be surprised to find also a multitude of well-defined partial-equilibrium rates of interest.

Yet there is no doubt that it is toward the butter market itself that our attention usually turns when we speak about the partial-equilibrium price of butter. It may be only a silly habit, but there is probably more to it than that. When we refer to the equilibrium price, we do not only mean a price that makes demand for and supply of something equal, but rather a price that remains constant once it has been established, everything else remaining unchanged. Indeed, this is our basic definition of equilibrium in the prices. We are led, therefore, to ask for the determinants of the rate of change in the butter price; that is, the forces that work on the butter price. The standard answer is Walras' excess demand hypothesis, which here amounts to

[12.11] $$\frac{dp_b}{dt} = f(q_b{}^d - q_b{}^s) \qquad f(0) = 0 \qquad f' > 0$$

where p_b, $q_b{}^d$, and $q_b{}^s$ are the price, quantity in demand, and quantity in supply of butter, respectively. Given Equation 12.11, there is no doubt that *the* partial-equilibrium price of butter is the butter price that makes demand and supply of butter equal. It is the only butter price that, given the other prices and the rate of interest, will cause the butter price to remain constant.

Returning now to the rate of interest, we note first that we have not only three, but a multitude of well-defined partial-equilibrium rates of interest. We could talk about the rate of interest that, given all money prices of goods and services, makes demand and supply of houses, or automobiles, equal. Monetary policy authorities sometimes ask such questions. We could also ask for the rate of interest that makes demand for and supply of butter equal, although this may not be a very interesting problem. Nevertheless, limiting ourselves to the three partial-equilibrium rates defined by Equations 12.2-4, 12.5-7, and 12.8-10, the problem would then be: which one of these three partial equilibria will ensure constancy in the rate of interest? Again, this must be a question of the "law of motion" of the rate of interest.[1] Equation 12.11, together with common sense, suggests, for example,

[12.12] $$\frac{dr}{dt} = f(B^d - B) \qquad f(0) = 0 \qquad f' < 0$$

[1] For a somewhat different approach, see Baumol (1962).

which means that the excess demand for bonds governs the rate of change in the interest rate. The rate of interest will remain constant only if demand for and supply of bonds, or supply of and demand for credit, are equal. On this criterion, and given Equation 12.12, we come out in support of the loanable funds theory of interest: *the* partial-equilibrium rate of interest is determined in the market for bonds, or, loanable funds.

This solution depends, however, entirely upon Equation 12.12. The validity of this hypothesis must be proved empirically. *A priori* we cannot exclude the possibility that other endogenous factors, such as excess demands in other markets, may influence the movement of the interest rate. We are back to the general problem of the realism of Walras' excess demand hypothesis that we touched upon earlier (Chapter 10, Section 7). Should Equation 12.12 not hold true, we would have to search for another "law of motion" and repeat the discussion on this basis.

In the debate between Keynes and his opponents, the participants generally agreed that the equilibrium rate of interest must make demand and supply of credit equal. In this sense there was no real disagreement about the loanable funds approach. Keynes tried to argue that savings and investments have nothing to do with demand for and supply of credit. The loanable funds theorists maintained that although savings and investments do not alone determine the rate of interest, savings and investments are two of the components of demand for and supply of credit. The third component, they said, is hoarding or dishoarding, by which was meant planned changes in cash holdings. Under the assumptions adopted here the loanable funds theorists were obviously correct. Rearranging Equation 12.12 and considering also Equations 12.2, 12.3, 12.5, 12.8, we have

[12.1']
$$Pb^d(r) - \frac{B}{r} \equiv S(r) - I(r) + M - M^d(r)$$

Value of excess demand for bonds = excessive loanable funds	Planned saving minus planned investment	Excess supply of money = planned dishoarding

Granted that the partial-equilibrium rate of interest is the rate that equilibrates demand for and supply of credit, or loanable funds, we are left with two alternative, equivalent partial-interest theories; namely, the loanable funds approach, which states that the partial-equilibrium rate equilibrates the left side of Equation 12.1', or an alternative approach that says the partial-equilibrium rate (after a change of sign) is determined by

[12.13]
$$I(r) - S(r) \quad + M^d(r) - M = 0$$

Planned investment minus planned saving	Excess demand for money

Since Equation 12.1' is an identity in the rate of interest, the rate that makes the left side zero will also make the right side zero, and vice versa. Savings and investments certainly do affect the partial-equilibrium rate of

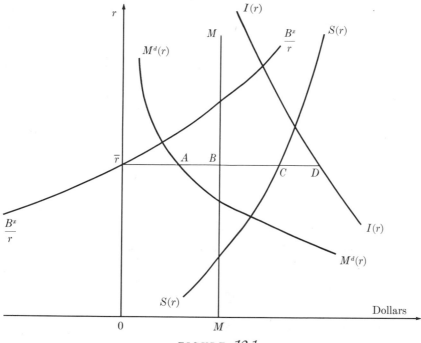

FIGURE *12.1*

interest. A rate of interest that equilibrates demand for and supply of money does not necessarily equilibrate demand for and supply of credit. Such would be the case only if savings and investments were assumed to be equal; there would be no reason to introduce this general equilibrium assumption in a partial-interest theory, however.

Abba Lerner (1938, Figure 1) has presented a useful diagrammatic picture of Equations 12.1′ and 12.13. With a certain modification[1] Lerner's diagram is shown in Figure 12.1.

---

[1] Lerner drew a demand curve for credit (and a supply curve for bonds) obtained through a horizontal summation of M^d and $I(r)$, and a supply curve equal to $M + S(r)$. The intersection between the two curves would, of course, lead to the very same partial-equilibrium rate of interest as in Figure 12.1, but the two curves thus obtained would not be the true demand and supply curves for bonds. Knowledge of the demand and supply functions of money and the investments and savings functions permits us to draw conclusions only about the excess demand for bonds. If we wish to draw a demand curve for bonds, special assumptions must be added, for instance, that the number of bonds is given. With given B, B/r would become a rectangular hyperbola in Figure 12.1, and B^d/r could be constructed. We have abstained from doing that, and have only shown the excess demand curve, $B^x/r = B^d/r - B/r$.

Lerner, in his following argumentation, abolished this figure by assuming that $I \equiv S$ identically in the rate of interest. In so doing he introduced a total-equilibrium condition, but this only confused the discussion.

We assume here that saving is an increasing and investment a decreasing function of the rate of interest. The quantity of money is constant, and the demand for money (Keynes' liquidity-preference function at given income) becomes very elastic at a certain low rate of interest. The excess demand for bonds, finally, which is constructed from the other four curves, is an increasing function of the rate of interest, as we should, of course, expect.

The partial-equilibrium rate of interest determined in Figure 12.1 is $\bar{r}$. Excess demand for bonds (credit) here is zero, but there is an excess supply of money equal to AB, and a corresponding excess of investment over saving $CD = AB$. Obviously, this is not only a partial equilibrium, it is a short-term equilibrium, as well.

We note, finally, that if all prices of goods and services had been fixed at their equilibrium prices, the investments and savings curves would have crossed each other at the same rate of interest as the demand and supply curves for money. At that rate the excess demand for bonds would be zero. This rate would be the general equilibrium rate of interest.

References

BAUMOL, W. J.: "Stocks, Flows, and Monetary Theory," *Quarterly Journal of Economics*, vol. 76, no. 1, February, 1962.

FELLNER, W., and H. SOMERS: "Alternative Monetary Approaches to Interest Theory," *The Review of Economics and Statistics*, vol. 23, no. 1, February, 1941.

HAHN, F. H.: "The Rate of Interest and General Equilibrium Analysis," *The Economic Journal*, vol. 65, no. 257, March, 1955.

HICKS, J. R.: *Value and Capital*, Clarendon Press, Oxford, 1939.

—: *The Trade Cycle*, Clarendon Press, Oxford, 1950.

LERNER, A. P.: "Alternative Formulations of the Theory of Interest," *The Economic Journal*, vol. 48, no. 190, June, 1938. Reprinted in A. P. Lerner, *Essays in Economic Analysis*, Macmillan, London, 1953.

OHLIN, B.: "Some Notes on the Stockholm Theory of Savings and Investment," *The Economic Journal*, vol. 47, no. 185, March, 1937.

PATINKIN, D.: "Liquidity Preference and Loanable Funds: Stock Flow Analysis," *Economica*, vol. 25, no. 100, November, 1958.

ROBERTSON, D. H.: "Mr. Keynes and the Rate of Interest," in *Essays in Monetary Theory*, Staples Press, London, 1940.

General equilibrium and foreign trade

13

Until now, our discussion has been limited to general equilibrium in closed economies without foreign trade. For a huge economy like the United States, where exports and imports only amount to about 5 percent of the GNP, foreign trade may not be an overriding concern, although at times the balance of payments is a decisive factor in economic policy. The impact of foreign trade is pervasive in small economies like the northwestern European countries, however, where it amounts to as much as half the GNP. Therefore, general equilibrium theory without foreign trade is of little relevance for such countries.

Walras did not really extend his system to include foreign trade, but the deficiency was remedied by V. Pareto (1896). A related system was presented by Yntema (1931), and later Ohlin (1935, Appendix I) extended Cassel's system to include foreign trade. J. Mosak (1944) finally formulated a purely neoclassical system on the basis of Hicks' simplified Walrasian system. It combines great elegance with a high degree of generality, and is the first system to be discussed here. Mosak's system is based explicitly on the assumption of Say's law and we must, of course, subsequently remove this assumption. We accomplish this by introducing real cash-balance effects in the manner of Patinkin. Until World War II foreign-trade equilibrium theory was mainly based on Marshall's "reciprocal demand" technique (1879), which is a kind of highly aggregated general equilibrium theory; we shall not discuss that theory here, however. It has proved to be very powerful in analyzing such problems as those of the terms of trade, but its degree of high aggregation makes it less interesting in this context. Keynesian analysis has also been extended to foreign trade, and here we shall present the Keynesian general equilibrium theory with foreign trade formulated by L. Metzler (1950).

In the discussion of international equilibrium problems a host of so-called "two-country," "two-commodity," "two-factor" models have been presented in which various features of the national economies and their international relations have been elaborated in a way not possible in the more general systems. By and large, these models follow the pattern set by Mosak or Metzler, or both.

1 / Mosak's neoclassical system

Mosak's general equilibrium system with foreign trade was developed directly from Hicks' excess demand system, which was described in Chapter 4, Section 2. It will be recalled that for a closed economy with n commodities and services, of which commodity n is used as a *numéraire*, the excess demand system is

$$[4.2] \qquad q_i^x(\pi_1, \ldots, \pi_{n-1}) = 0 \qquad i = 1, \ldots, n$$

where π_i are the *numéraire* prices. By virtue of Say's law, one of the equations follows from the rest. Considering Lange's criticism of neoclassical theory, Mosak was careful in postulating Say's law to abstain explicitly from presenting equations for demand for and supply of money.

We assume now that the world consists of m countries, each one with its own set of excess demand functions. Say's law is assumed to hold for each individual country. Disregarding transport costs, customs duties, local taxes, and other obstacles to full mobility, the *numéraire* prices must be the same in all countries. The set of excess demand functions for any country j are then

$$[13.1] \qquad {}_jq_i^x = {}_jq_i^x(\pi_1, \ldots, \pi_{n-1}) \qquad \begin{matrix} i = 1, \ldots, n \\ i = 1, \ldots, m \end{matrix}$$

and, thanks to Say's law,

$$[13.2] \qquad \sum_{i=1}^{n} {}_jq_i^x\pi_i \equiv 0 \qquad i = 1, \ldots, m$$

identically in the prices.

Since commodities and services move freely between countries, the equilibrium condition for a certain commodity must be that the excess demand is zero for the world as a whole. We need not have equality between demand and supply for the individual commodity within each country; the commodity may be exported or imported. For the world as a whole, however, exports and imports cancel each other out for each commodity, and global demand

and supply must be equal. We thus obtain the following world equilibrium system:

[13.3] $$\sum_{j=1}^{m} {}_{j}q_{i}{}^{x}(\pi_1, \ldots, \pi_{n-1}) = 0 \qquad i = 1, \ldots, n$$

which makes n equations to determine the $n - 1$ *numéraire* prices. One of the equations is dependent upon the rest, however. From Equation 13.2 we have

[13.4] $$\sum_{j=1}^{m} \sum_{i=1}^{n} {}_{j}q_{i}{}^{x}\pi_{i} \equiv 0$$

and we are left with $n - 1$ independent equations to determine $n - 1$ world prices.

The world equilibrium system (Equation 13.3) is obtained simply by summing the individual market excess demand equations of the national excess demand systems. The system seems almost too simple to be true. What, for example, ensures equilibrium in the balance of payments of the individual countries? What role do the foreign-exchange rates play, and how are they determined? Should we not expect to find equations for the foreign-exchange market? The answer is that all problems related to the balances of payments and their equilibria are ruled out by assumption in this neoclassical model. Say's law is assumed to hold for each single country, which means that for each country the sum of the value of all excess demand is zero (Equation 13.2) or, for each country total expenditure equals total revenue from sales of commodities and services. Therefore, if a country buys goods abroad it must have goods of the same value available for export. Having based the model explicitly on this assumption we need not look for any condition or mechanism to ensure its fulfillment. Neither do we need to know the exchange rates; what matters for demands and supplies are the *numéraire* prices, and they are by assumption the same everywhere.

It follows that the system is of rather limited application insofar as it is unable to deal with any problem related to the balance of payments equilibrium and the foreign-exchange markets. The system has proved useful, however, in studying changes in relative prices. Since we are concerned here with foreign trade, this means the terms of trade. The system has been studied with respect to its stability conditions, and so forth (Mosak, 1944), and is sufficiently flexible to permit a number of interesting questions to be answered, for instance, problems related to unilateral transfers or growth. (See Mosak, 1944, and Södersten, 1964.)

Although Mosak explicitly adopted Say's law, and thus by definition ruled out changes in cash holdings, he nevertheless introduced money to determine the absolute price level in the individual countries. If the money price of the *numéraire* in country j is ${}_{j}p_n$, the other money prices can be calculated from the relationships ${}_{j}p_i = \pi_i \cdot {}_{j}p_n$ (Chapter 3, Section 6). For each country we write an equation of exchange that must be comprehended as a simple definitional relationship without any interpretation in terms of demand for and supply of money (Chapter 5, Section 2). Using Fisher's equation we have thus

[13.5]
$$_jp_n \sum_{i=1}^{n} {}_jq_i\pi_i = {}_jM_jV \qquad j = 1, \ldots, m$$

where $_jM$ is the quantity of money in country j (measured in its own currency units), $_jV$ its transactions velocity (assumed given), and $_jq_i$ its equilibrium turnover (which must be determined from the demand or supply functions behind the excess demand functions). Equation 13.5 suffices to determine the money prices of the *numéraire* in all countries in terms of their own currency. From the money prices of the *numéraire*, all other money prices follow, given their *numéraire* prices.

The exchange rates $_jR_h$ defined as the price of a unit of the currency of country h in terms of the currency of country j must be

[13.6]
$$_jR_h = \frac{_jp_n}{_hp_n} \qquad \begin{array}{l} j = 1, \ldots, m \\ h = 1, \ldots, m \end{array}$$

Of these mm exchange rates, m definitionally $= 1$ (the exchange rates of the currencies against themselves), and of the remaining $m(m-1)$, $(m-1)^2$ follow from a set of $m-1$ rates, for instance $_jR_m$, $j = 1, \ldots, m-1$. Equation 13.6 must hold in equilibrium, otherwise arbitrage would be profitable. This equation may be considered a "purchasing power parity" theory of the foreign-exchange rates. The foreign-exchange rates are proportional to the price levels. Since the price level in each country is proportional to its own quantity of money, the foreign-exchange rates of a country are also proportional to its quantity of money. A change in the quantity of money of any country is neutral with respect to *numéraire* prices, real demand and supply, exports and imports. It affects only the price level and the exchange rates of the country itself. On the other hand, it is clear that both quantity theory and the theory of purchasing-power parity here are reduced to completely empty definitional relationships. We are faced with the same problems encountered in other neoclassical systems based on Say's law (Chapter 5).

2 / General equilibrium and the balance of payments

To study balance of payments problems in a general equilibrium setting we must discard Say's law, leading us to the same kinds of problems encountered in the closed Walrasian or Hicks' systems. They can also in this case be solved along the lines of the Patinkin system. The excess demand functions, shown in Equation 13.1, must be changed. Working with money prices rather than *numéraire* prices, and indicating the country with a prefix, we can define the price level for country j as

[13.7] $$_jP = \sum_{i=1}^{n} {_jw_{ij}p_i} \qquad \Sigma_j w_i = 1 \qquad j = 1, \ldots, m$$

The quantity of money of country j is $_jM$, and assuming for the moment that a country's currency is held exclusively by its own residents, we can write the excess demand functions as

[13.8] $$_jq_i^x = {_jq_i^x} \left(\frac{_jp_1}{_jP}, \ldots, \frac{_jp_n}{_jP}, \frac{_jM}{_jP} \right) \qquad \begin{array}{l} i = 1, \ldots, n \\ j = 1, \ldots, m \end{array}$$

homogeneous of degree zero in prices and quantity of money.

Since we measure each country's prices in terms of its own currency, but continue to assume that all commodities and services move freely between countries, we have

[13.9] $$_jp_i = {_jR_{mm}p_i} \qquad \begin{array}{l} i = 1, \ldots, n \\ j = 1, \ldots, m-1 \end{array}$$

We assume for the sake of convenience that all exchange rates are expressed on the basis of country m's currency, so that the prices of all countries can be expressed in terms of country m's prices. Even when the world economy is in disequilibrium we assume that (after conversion to a common currency) there is only one price in the world market for each good. Otherwise Equation 13.8 would have to be reformulated.

The world equilibrium system is now

[13.10] $$\sum_{j=1}^{m} {_jq_i^x} \left(\frac{_jp_1}{_jP}, \ldots, \frac{_jp_n}{_jP}, \frac{_jM}{_jP} \right) = 0 \qquad i = 1, \ldots, n$$

World excess demand for each single market (good) must be zero as before. In addition, however, we must add the equilibrium conditions for each country's balance of payments

[13.11] $$\sum_{i=1}^{n} {_jq_i^x} {_jp_i} = 0 \qquad j = 1, \ldots, m$$

These equations state that for each country the total value of demand for commodities and services must be equal to the total value of supply, or, total expenditures on commodities and services must be equal to total sales of commodities and services. Note the difference between Equations 13.2 and 13.11; the former is an identity in the prices, the latter a set of equilibrium conditions.

The world general equilibrium system consists of Equations 13.7, 13.9, 13.10, and 13.11, which gives us altogether $2m + nm$ equations to determine $2m + nm - 1$ unknowns, namely, the m price levels $_jP$, the mn individual money prices $_jp_i$, and the $m - 1$ foreign-exchange rates $_jR_m$. One of the equations, 13.11, is superfluous, however. If all countries but one have equilibrium in their balance of payments, the last one will be in equilibrium, too. This is not Walras' law, which we have used to delete the "money market" from the system. We could have added m real excess demand functions for money (of the same general form as Equation 13.8) which, put equal to zero, would have given us other m equations; they would, however, follow from the rest of the system by virtue of the m Walras' laws.

The system determines all money prices and price levels in the m countries, together with the exchange rates, and it ensures that the balances of payments are in equilibrium everywhere. The equilibrium conditions for the balance of payments may be interpreted as equilibrium conditions for the foreign-exchange markets. With no borrowing and lending between the countries, the value of exports equals the supply of foreign currency, and the value of imports equals the demand for foreign currency. A study of the system immediately reveals that it follows the quantity theory of money and its corollary, the purchasing-power parity theory. A change in the quantity of money in one of the countries will leave all relative prices of commodities and services unchanged, and increase the money prices and the price level of the country as well as the exchange rates, that is, the prices of foreign currency in proportion to the quantity of money.

The system is, however, based on assumptions that prevent us from discussing balance of payments disequilibria, and the dynamics and stability of the system. By assuming that each country's quantity of money is exclusively kept as cash in the country itself, we have in effect assumed that the countries have no claims upon one another. This is a highly restrictive assumption. In a situation of balance of payments disequilibrium, the surplus countries accumulate claims upon the deficit countries, and if no other claims exist, they must accumulate foreign currency.[1] The system we have outlined does not allow for that, however. Not only does it assume that holdings of foreign currency are zero everywhere in the initial situation, but it does not consider the possibility that a country might hold foreign currency. We must somehow allow for that.

3 / A system with foreign trade and foreign-exchange holdings

In this system (see Hahn, 1959; Kemp, 1964, Chapter XVI; and Meinich, 1968) there exists, as before, a given amount of each national currency, but it shall be assumed that the national currencies may be held also by foreigners. In this section we will assume that there are no official foreign-exchange reserves and no government intervention in the foreign-exchange

---

[1] We ignore the possibility of gold movements, which, in neoclassical balance of payments theory, played a key role as equilibrating factor (Viner, n.a.; Iversen, 1935).

markets. The exchange rates are "floating" and left to the market forces; this is entirely in the spirit of neoclassical theory. We do not introduce specialized foreign-currency dealers in the model; private firms must thus keep cash for transactions in both domestic and foreign currency. Presumably, domestic transactions must always be settled in domestic currency, but foreign transactions may have to be settled in some foreign currency. We may, then, include holdings of all currencies in the individual utility functions, and on this basis derive demand functions for all commodities and services, and for all currencies. An alternative method would be the payments technical approach applied to domestic money in Chapter 6. In any case we would, for each country, arrive at m demand functions for cash holding, one for each particular currency. By summing the m countries' demand functions for a particular currency, we would obtain the total world demand for this currency. For each currency we would have such a total demand function, a given supply, and an equilibrium condition. In this way we obtain the same number of equations for money as the previous system, but the form of the equations is different.

In addition, we must take into account that initial cash holdings consist of both domestic and foreign currency that, accordingly, must enter as arguments in the demand and supply functions, and thus the excess demand functions. It is obviously the real holdings that matter, but it is not quite obvious exactly how real holdings should be defined. With our general assumption of uniform world market prices, we can write country j's holdings of country h's currency $_hM_j$ in real terms as $_jR_h \cdot {}_hM_j/_jP$ or, with currency m as a basis for the exchange rates,

$$[13.12] \qquad {}_hm_j = \frac{_jR_m \, _hM_j}{_hR_m \, _jP} \qquad \begin{array}{l} j = 1, \ldots, m \\ h = 1, \ldots, m \end{array}$$

Note that $_hm_j = {}_hM_j/_hP$. Conversion to domestic currency and deflation by the domestic price level is equivalent to deflation by the foreign country's price level. This makes sense because it is in the foreign markets that the holdings of foreign currency are used for transactions.

We can then rewrite the excess demand functions shown in Equation 13.8 as

$$[13.8'] \qquad {}_jq_i^x = {}_jq_i^x\left(\frac{_jp_1}{_jP}, \ldots, \frac{_jp_n}{_jP}, {}_hm_j\right) \qquad \begin{array}{l} i = 1, \ldots, n \\ j = 1, \ldots, m \end{array}$$

where $_hm_j$ denotes a vector with m elements, $h = 1, \ldots, m$, defined by Equation 13.12. The real excess demand functions for cash holdings of the m currencies have the same form

$$[13.13] \qquad {}_hm_j^x = \frac{_jR_m \, _hM_j^d}{_hR_m \, _jP} - \frac{_jR_m \, _hM_j}{_hR_m \, _jP}$$

$$= {}_hm_j^x\left(\frac{_jp_1}{_jP}, \ldots, \frac{_jp_n}{_jP}, {}_hm_j\right) \qquad \begin{array}{l} h = 1, \ldots, m \\ j = 1, \ldots, m \end{array}$$

We are now in a position to write the complete world system. Equations 13.7 and 13.9 are unchanged. But the equilibrium equations for the commodities and services change to

$$[13.10']\qquad \sum_{j=1}^{m} {}_jq_i{}^x\left(\frac{{}_jp_1}{{}_jP}, \ \cdots \ , \frac{{}_jp_n}{{}_jP}, {}_hm_j\right) = 0 \qquad i = 1, \ \ldots \ , n$$

In addition, we have the equilibrium conditions for money

$$[13.10'']\qquad \sum_{j=1}^{m} {}_hm_j{}^x\left(\frac{{}_jp_1}{{}_jP}, \ \cdots \ , \frac{{}_jp_n}{{}_jP}, {}_hm_j\right) = 0 \qquad h = 1, \ \ldots \ , m$$

The equilibrium conditions for the balance of payments in Equation 13.11 remain the same.

The general world equilibrium system consists now of Equations 13.7, 13.9, 13.10', 13.10'', and 13.11; that is, $nm + 3m$ equations to determine $nm + 2m - 1$ unknowns, as before. Thanks to the m Walras' laws (one for each country), and the fact that the world is closed so that one of Equations 13.11 follows from the others, the number of independent equations reduces again to $nm + 2m - 1$.

Assume that the system has a unique, meaningful solution. A first problem, then, is whether this system also follows the quantity theory of money and the purchasing-power parity theory. Matters are complicated in this case by the fact that the currency of a certain country is kept both inside and outside that country. Let us assume, as usual, that the holdings of currency j are doubled everywhere. Consider then first cash holders in country j. Their holdings of the domestic currency have doubled. Therefore, if the domestic price level doubles, their real holdings of domestic currency will be unchanged. Their real holdings of foreign currency will be left unchanged provided that not only the domestic price level, but also the exchange rate of country j on country m, doubles (see Equation 13.12). Therefore, if in country j all money prices and the foreign-exchange rate on country m doubles, all real demands will be unchanged. This means that the demand for domestic money, in money terms, will double, and the demand for foreign currency in money terms will be unchanged. Consider then an arbitrary foreign country h. In this country holders of currency j have also suddenly experienced a doubling of their holdings of this currency. But its real value is unchanged if country j's exchange rate on country m doubles (see Equation 13.12). It follows that all real demands in country h will be unchanged, too. The basic postulates of the quantity theory and the purchasing-power parity theory must therefore carry over to this case, too: At an increase in the amount of a certain currency the world equilibrium will be preserved at a proportional increase in the price level and in the foreign-exchange rate of that country, leaving all price levels of other countries, all relative prices of commodities and services, and all real demands and supplies unchanged (Meinich, 1968). On the other hand, it is difficult to visualize a corresponding concrete economic policy. An isolated increase of the quantity of money can only take place as a gift, a capital transfer, from the government to the cash holders. There is nothing unusual in domestic capital transfers; capital transfers to foreign countries frequently take place (foreign aid, compensations, etc.). It is difficult, however, to imagine that a country should spray the world with such transfers in proportion to the individual country's holdings of its currency.

More important, however, is that this model permits a discussion of the process of adjustment to equilibrium and of the stability of the system. It is clear that the real balance of domestic and foreign currency must play an important role in such adjustment processes, and the equilibrating mechanism of this system is, indeed, very similar to the gold movements on which neo-classical balance of payments theory centered (Viner, n.a., and Iversen, 1935). Here we shall only indicate how the mechanism works. If for some reason a country has a surplus in its balance of payments, this will imply a continuous increase in the cash holdings of that country. At unchanged domestic prices and foreign-exchange rates this means increasing real cash balances and increased spending on both domestic and foreign goods; this will subsequently rectify the balance of payments. If the system is stable, changes in the relative prices should tend to move in the same direction. To work this out in detail necessitates a specification of the initial disturbance, however. The rest of the world will experience opposite effects. The process will continue until so much currency has been shifted to the surplus country that its total expenditure is again in line with total sales and the balance of payments is in equilibrium.

4 / Pegged exchange rates and other modifications

Since World War II, most countries have pegged the foreign-exchange rates, the governments (or their agencies) buying and selling foreign exchange at fixed prices. Should the rates by chance be pegged at their equilibrium levels nothing changes in the equilibrium position described by the last model. The interesting and realistic case, however, is the one in which the rates are pegged above or below their equilibrium values. The balance of payments will then be out of equilibrium with permanent surpluses or deficits. The governments are then obliged to accumulate foreign exchange or run down the official reserves, as the case may be.

Formally the introduction of pegged rates means that we must consider the $m - 1$ exchange rates as exogenously determined and drop the $m - 1$ (independent) balance of payments equilibrium conditions (see Equation 13.11). The functioning of the system changes radically, the most important feature being that accumulation or decumulation of reserves will go on continuously so that the system cannot be in stationary equilibrium. The accumulation may react back on the balance of payments, however, and create equilibrium in the long run. Everything depends upon the simultaneous monetary policy of the governments. If the governments peg the rates and buy or sell foreign exchange, the supply of money in the countries must increase or fall accordingly; this will have long-run effects on the balance of payments. At a different policy with respect to the supply of money, the long-run effects may become entirely different. (See Kemp, 1964, Chapter XVI.) On additional assumptions concerning the stability of the system, important conclusions can be drawn about the effects of changes in the exchange rates and the quantity of money (Kemp, forthcoming).

As soon as we raise the problem of alternative monetary policies it becomes obvious that the system is in need of a number of further modifications in order to permit a full-fledged discussion of modern balance of payments policies at pegged rates. First, the balance of payments is usually only one target amongst several others, and this means that measures taken to rectify balance of payments surplusses or deficits must be coordinated with measures taken for other purposes. It is well known from the modern theory of multitarget policy that we cannot isolate a single target and the measures taken for the sake of this target; a simultaneous determination of all measures is required (Tinbergen, 1952). This means that we must have both the public budget and the banking system built into the model. Considering the importance of capital movements for balance of payments disequilibria, any realistic general equilibrium model with foreign economic intercourse must include a number of short- and long-term credit markets. In principle one can well imagine a general world equilibrium model that takes all these factors into account simultaneously. Practically speaking, however, such models might not be manageable. Indeed, remarkably little has been done to formulate such all-inclusive international general equilibrium systems.

5 / International equalization of factor prices

In Mosak's system it was assumed that relative prices, that is, *numéraire* prices, are the same in all countries. In the system with foreign-exchange holdings the same assumptions were made with respect to prices in terms of money (after conversion to a common currency). The assumption requires that there be full mobility without transport costs and other obstacles to commodity and factor movements. It is impossible to keep this assumption if the existence of so-called "domestic," or national, commodities and services is admitted. It is difficult to assume that factors of production (or, rather, their services) move internationally without obstacles; land and other natural resources certainly cannot be moved from country to country. We may therefore be forced to abandon the assumption of uniform relative prices. Domestic commodities (housing and other services) have prohibitive transport costs and cannot be exported or imported. It is relatively simple to take this into account in the system. Mosak (1944) showed that the incorporation of domestic commodities necessitates only minor modifications of the formal structure of the neoclassical system (see also Kemp, forthcoming). An important problem remains, however; that is, to what extent is the price structure upset by the existence of immobility, or, to what extent does the assumption of uniform relative prices break down? Discussion of this problem has concentrated mainly upon the factor prices.

It is generally agreed that if factors can move freely, then factor prices (for identical factors) must become the same everywhere. In spite of emigration and capital movements, neoclassical theorists usually preferred to work with the standard assumption that factors are completely immobile, but argued (Heckscher, 1919; Ohlin, 1935) that even so, commodity trade will tend to equalize factor prices internationally. Loosely speaking their argument was that countries will tend to produce commodities with a relatively high content of those factors that are relatively abundant. The possibility of exports will therefore increase the demand for the abundant factors and increase their relative scarcity. P. A. Samuelson (1948, 1949, and 1965) and A. P. Lerner (1952) showed that the factor-price equalization will become perfect under certain conditions. Among them were that the number of commodities be at least equal to the number of factors, that all commodities move freely and be produced everywhere, that the technical knowledge (the production function) be the same everywhere, that constant returns to scale and decreasing returns to factors prevail, and finally, that the factor intensity differs in the sense that at given factor-price ratios, the factors be used in different proportions for the various commodities produced. Under such assumptions it is not difficult to understand intuitively that full factor-price equalization is possible. Since relative commodity prices are assumed to be the same everywhere, the same must be true for the relative marginal productivities. Therefore, the factor proportions in producing a particular commodity must also be the same in all countries, the production functions being identical; but with constant returns to scale this implies that the marginal productivities for any factor must be the same everywhere. Finally, if factor remunerations equal marginal productivities, factor remunerations must be the same everywhere, too. The assumptions are so restrictive, however, that we should probably never expect complete factor-price equalization. Be this as it may, for the purpose of discussing such problems the general equilibrium system must be specified with respect to the underlying conditions of production. Instead of the abstract demand and supply functions with which Mosak worked, we must return to the production possibilities upon which the system is based.

6 / Metzler's Keynesian multicountry system

The major contribution of Keynesian, or rather, post-Keynesian theory, to the field of foreign trade is the introduction of the import function, with the national income or product as a dominating determinant of imports. The import function is the basic relationship in Metzler's multicountry system, which shows the interrelationship between income formation in a number of countries.

Metzler (1950, 1951) assumes that total spending in a country can be divided into domestic spending and import, both of them functions of national income. If we let Y_j denote national income, D_j domestic spending, and M_j import of country j, we have then, by hypothesis

[13.14] $$D_j = a_{jj}Y_j + A_j \qquad j = 1, \ldots, m$$

where a_{jj} and A_j are constants, a_{jj} being the (marginal) propensity to spend domestically, and A_j autonomous domestic spending. The import function is

[13.15] $$M_j = \sum_{i=1}^{m} a_{ji}Y_j \qquad j = 1, \ldots, m \qquad i \neq j$$

where a_{ji}, $i \neq j$, is the propensity of country j to import from country i, the number of countries being m. Say's law does not hold; otherwise we would have

$$\sum_{i=1}^{m} a_{ji} = 1$$

Considering an individual country, we know that in equilibrium total income (product) must be equal to domestic spending plus exports; since the export of a country arises from the other countries' imports, we have in equilibrium for country j

[13.16] $$Y_j = a_{jj}Y_j + A_j + a_{1j}Y_1 + \cdots + a_{j-1j}Y_{j-1} + a_{j+1j}Y_{j+1}$$
$$+ \cdots + a_{mj}Y_m$$

or

[13.17] $$Y_j = A_j + \sum_{i=1}^{m} a_{ij}Y_i \qquad j = 1, \ldots, m$$

This is Metzler's system. It contains m equations to determine the m national incomes. Under certain conditions concerning the constants a_{ij}, the system will have a unique, meaningful solution. The system may then be used to study how shifts in demand will affect national income in all countries. Under additional assumptions with respect to the dynamics of the system (or, rather, of a "corresponding" dynamic model) it can be shown that a shift of demand onto a certain country will increase the equilibrium income of that country, even when all repercussions throughout the system have been taken into account, provided that the system is stable.

The system does not assume equilibrium in the individual country's balance of payments, and there are no mechanisms that can ensure balance of payments equilibrium. Neither prices nor exchange rates appear anywhere. The role of money and exchange holdings is not clear. Without modifications the system is therefore of limited value for discussing problems related to rectification of balance of payments disequilibria, foreign-exchange rates, and foreign-exchange market problems.

7 / Transport costs and spatial equilibrium

One of the important contributions of Ohlin (1935) was to show that foreign trade and interregional trade are basically identical phenomena, and to show that problems of trade are really caused by the existence of transport costs and other obstacles to commodity and factor movements. Nevertheless, modern "pure" theories of foreign trade pay relatively little attention to the problem of transport costs. Despite Ohlin's efforts, the theory of international equilibrium and the theory of spatial equilibrium (founded by von Thünen) have developed rather independently. Recently, however, attempts have been made to establish general equilibrium systems where transport costs and location in space are integral parts of the equilibrium problem (Samuelson, 1952 and 1954; Isard, 1956; and Lefeber, 1958).

References

HAHN, F. H.: "The Balance of Payments in a Monetary Economy," *Review of Economic Studies*, vol. 26, no. 70, February, 1959.

HECKSCHER, ELI: "The Effect of Foreign Trade on the Distribution of Income," in H. Ellis and L. Metzler (eds.), *Readings in the Theory of International Trade*, Blakiston, Philadelphia, 1949. Published originally in Swedish in *Ekonomisk Tidskrift*, vol. 21, 1919.

ISARD, W.: *Location and Space Economy*, M.I.T. Press, Cambridge, Mass., 1956.

IVERSEN, C.: *Aspects of the Theory of International Capital Movements*, Oxford University Press, London, 1935.

KEMP, M. C.: *The Pure Theory of International Trade*, Prentice-Hall, Englewood Cliffs, N.J., 1964.

—: "The Balance of Payments and the Terms of Trade in Relation to Financial Controls," *Review of Economic Studies*, forthcoming.

LEFEBER, L.: *Allocation in Space*, North-Holland Publishing Co., Amsterdam, 1958.

LERNER, A. P.: "Factor Prices and International Trade," *Economica*, vol. 19, no. 73, February, 1952. Reprinted in *Essays in Economic Analysis*, Macmillan, London, 1953.

MARSHALL, A.: *The Pure Theory of Foreign Trade*, London, 1879. Reprinted by London School of Economics, London, 1930.

MEINICH, P.: *A Monetary General Equilibrium Theory for an International Economy*, Universitetsforlaget, Oslo, 1968.

METZLER, L.: "A Multiple-Region Theory of Income and Trade," *Econometrica*, vol. 18, no. 4, October, 1950.

—: "A Multiple-Country Theory of Income Transfers," *The Journal of Political Economy*, vol. 14, no. 1, February, 1951.

MOSAK, J.: *General-Equilibrium Theory in International Trade*, Principia Press, Bloomington, Ind., 1944.

OHLIN, B.: *Interregional and International Trade*, Harvard University Press, Cambridge, Mass., 1935.

PARETO, V.: *Cours d'économie politique*, Rouge, Lausanne, 1896.

SAMUELSON, P. A.: "International Trade and the Equalization of Factor Prices," *The Economic Journal*, vol. 58, no. 230, June, 1948.

—: "International Factor-Price Equalization Once Again," *The Economic Journal*, vol. 59, no. 234, June, 1949.

—: "The Transfer Problem and Transport Cost," *The Economic Journal*, vol. 62, no. 246, June, 1952, and vol. 64, no. 254, June, 1954.

—: "Equalization by Trade of the Interest Rate along with the Real Wage," in *Trade, Growth, and the Balance of Payments*, Essays in Honor of Gottfried Harberler, Rand McNally, Chicago, 1965.

SÖDERSTEN, B.: *A Study of Economic Growth and International Trade*, Almqvist and Wiksell, Stockholm, 1964.

TINBERGEN, J.: *The Theory of Economic Policy*, North-Holland Publishing Co., Amsterdam, 1952.

VINER, J.: *Studies in the Theory of International Trade*, George Allen and Unwin, London, n.a.

Leontief's

input-output system

14

Two static general equilibrium systems have dominated modern macro-economics, Keynes' system and Leontief's input-output system. It is not difficult to understand why. Both systems deal in a simplified way with central problems of practical and political importance, and lend themselves to empirical application. Both systems have provided a convenient starting point for the study of the dynamic problems of economic growth and development, the great issue of the postwar era. Yet it is interesting to note that whereas Keynes' system was originally presented as a protest against and alternative to the neoclassical system (as we have seen, the difference did not prove to be very great), Leontief's system was a deliberate attempt to carry over the basic Walrasian concept of general interdependence to an empirically manageable model. In discussing Leontief's system it is convenient to distinguish between the "input-output table," a purely definitional set of relationships that play an important role in modern national accounting systems, and the "input-output model," which deals with the behavior of the economic system. The value of the input-output table is indisputable, whatever the merits of the input-output model may be.

Leontief presented the first version of his model in 1936, but set out the static system more fully in *The Structure of the American Economy, 1914–1939,* (1941, 1951). A dynamic version has later been presented (Leontief, 1953), and brief, summarizing presentation of input-output analysis has been given by him (1966, Chapter VII). The input-output literature is voluminous and special bibliographies are compiled (Taskin, 1961; U.N., 1964). For an elementary description of the system and its applications, see Miernyk (1965). A sophisticated analytical discussion is found in Dorfman, Samuelson, and Solow (1957, Chapters IX and X).

1 / The input-output table and national accounting

Table 14.1 is the input-output table. The square matrix in the NW corner is a table of interindustry transactions of so-called "intermediary products," that is, domestically produced goods used in current domestic production. The interindustry table has the same number of horizontal and vertical entrances, one for each industry (activity). The elements in a row consist of the outputs delivered by a certain industry to other industries for current use.

TABLE 14.1

		Inputs in industry						*Final demands*			*Total outputs and incomes*
		1	2	···	j	···	n	*Con-sump-tion*	*In-vest-ment*	*Ex-port*	
Outputs from industry	1	V_{11}	V_{12}	···	V_{1j}	···	V_{1n}	V_{1C}	V_{1I}	V_{1X}	V_1
	2	V_{21}	V_{22}	···	V_{2j}	···	V_{2n}	V_{2C}	V_{2I}	V_{2X}	V_2
	·	·	·		·		·	·	·	·	·
	·	·	·		·		·	·	·	·	·
	·	·	·		·		·	·	·	·	·
	i	V_{i1}	V_{i2}	···	V_{ij}	···	V_{in}	V_{iC}	V_{iI}	V_{iX}	V_i
	·	·	·		·		·	·	·	·	·
	·	·	·		·		·	·	·	·	·
	·	·	·		·		·	·	·	·	·
	n	V_{n1}	V_{n2}	···	V_{nj}	···	V_{nn}	V_{nC}	V_{nI}	V_{nX}	V_n
	Labor (wages)	V_{L1}	V_{L2}	···	V_{Lj}	···	V_{Ln}				ΣV_{Lj}
	Capital (profits)	V_{K1}	V_{K2}	···	V_{Kj}	···	V_{Kn}				ΣV_{Kj}
	Land (rents)	V_{R1}	V_{R2}	···	V_{Rj}	···	V_{Rn}				ΣV_{Rj}
	Imports	V_{M1}	V_{M2}	···	V_{Mj}	···	V_{Mn}				ΣV_{Mj}
	Indirect taxes	V_{T1}	V_{T2}	···	V_{Tj}	···	V_{Tn}				ΣV_{Tj}
	Total inputs and final demands	E_1	E_2	···	E_j	···	E_n	ΣV_{iC}	ΣV_{iJ}	ΣV_{iX}	V

Consequently, a column shows the current inputs delivered to a certain industry by all other industries. The symbol V_{ij} represents the outputs from industry i used as current inputs in industry j. In the diagonals we find those outputs of an industry that are used by the industry itself, such as seeds and animal feed in agriculture. These diagonal elements may be put equal to zero, as they are both inputs and outputs of the same industry and can be netted out, but this is an unsatisfactory method of procedure that may hide important technological facts.

Below the interindustry square is a rectangular matrix, its rows showing the deliveries of various factor services, labor, capital, land, that is, natural resources, to the individual industries, as well as imported inputs, which are called "primary" inputs. For purposes of national accounting we have added a special row for indirect taxes (minus subsidies) that, in a formal sense, may be considered an input.

To the right of the interindustry square is another rectangular matrix; its columns show deliveries from the various industries for the different kinds of final use consumption, investment, and export. Consumption and investment may be broken down in many ways to show public and private, military and civilian use, fixed investments and inventory changes, and so forth. Exports are often defined as net exports, that is, the exports *minus* the so-called "competing imports." Imports are classified as "complementary" imports, which consist of commodities not produced in the country, and "competing" imports, of which there is some production in the country. The input row of imports consists, then, exclusively of complementary imports. This method of classifying imports is advantageous in defining and measuring the so-called "technical coefficients" of the system (see below).

Finally, there is a marginal row and column for total outputs and inputs.

The SE rectangular matrix in Table 14.1 has been left empty. This is a matter of definition, however, and it is by no means obvious that it is the best method of procedure. Everything depends upon how industries and their activities are defined.

For national accounting purposes, Table 14.1 must, for various reasons, be measured in money terms. No matter how fine the classification of industries, primary inputs, and final demands, the individual elements of an empirical table will always be comprised of heterogeneous commodities and services that must be expressed in money terms to permit addition. Moreover, within the context of a national accounting, it is necessary to form totals by summing the individual elements, both horizontally and vertically. The latter can only be done if all commodities and services are expressed in value terms. Finally, we note that an item such as capital (services) is extremely difficult to measure in anything but money terms, and indirect taxes are by definition value sums. The table may be expressed either in terms of the prices of the current year or some other year, however. If the prices of another year are used we have constant price accounting, which in fact implies that the elements are broken down into a quantity and a price component. This breakdown causes a number of index problems, however (see Stone, 1956, 1961; U.N., 1968).

With the notation set forth in Table 14.1, we have for total output (horizontal summation)

$$[14.1] \qquad V_i = \sum_{j=1}^{n} V_{ij} + V_{iC} + V_{iI} + V_{iX} \qquad i = 1, \ldots, n$$

and for the inputs (vertically)

$$[14.2] \qquad E_i = \sum_{j=1}^{n} V_{ji} + V_{Li} + V_{Ki} + V_{Ri} + V_{Mi} + V_{Ti} \qquad i = 1, \ldots, n$$

We count all gross profit as input from capital. Total output value must then equal total input value for any industry, that is,

[14.3] $$V_i = E_i \qquad i = 1, \ldots, n$$

Horizontal and vertical summation of all elements in the table lead, of course, to the same total V. We have, therefore, identically,

[14.4] $$V = \Sigma V_i + \Sigma V_{Li} + \Sigma V_{Ki} + \Sigma V_{Ri} + \Sigma V_{Mi} + \Sigma V_{Ti}$$
$$= \Sigma E_i + \Sigma V_{iC} + \Sigma V_{iI} + \Sigma V_{iX}$$

where all summations are over the n industries. Recalling Equation 14.3 and defining as follows:

Consumption $= C = \Sigma V_{iC}$
Investment $= I = \Sigma V_{iI}$
Exports (net) $= X = \Sigma V_{iX}$
Wage income $= L = \Sigma V_{Li}$
Capital income (gross) $= K = \Sigma V_{Ki}$
Land rents $= R = \Sigma V_{Ri}$
Imports (complementary) $= M = \Sigma V_{Mi}$
Indirect taxes
    (minus subsidies) $= T = \Sigma V_{Ti}$

we can write Equation 14.4 as

[14.4'] $$L + K + R + M + T = C + I + X$$

By definition, we have GNP at factor cost $= L + K + R$ and at market prices $= L + K + R + T$. We thus have, at market prices,

[14.4''] $$GNP + M = C + I + X$$

which is the well-known "balance of resources."

Table 14.1 can be expanded to a complete national transactions matrix by adding columns and rows for all real and financial capital transactions. In the United Nation's new, complete national accounting scheme (U.N., 1968) the input-output table still occupies a prominent position.

2 / The open input-output model

Pure input-output theory starts out from an input-output table where all elements are measured in physical units. This obviously requires that each industry produces only one, well-defined commodity or service, and that the primary inputs be homogeneous, too. There is in principle nothing to prevent us from working with any number of primary inputs in order to obtain homogeneity. We could thus specify each machine, type of building, all equipment, each quality of labor and land, and so forth. In this way the problem of measuring labor, capital, and land physically would be solved. In a physical table there is no place for indirect taxes (minus subsidies), and the concept of total inputs does not apply; such a table permits horizontal, but not vertical, summation. For purposes of the model, however, this is not required, either.

If, as usual, we let q denote the quantity of a commodity or service, we can replace all the V's in Table 14.1 by q's, keeping the subscripts unchanged. Thus, q_{ij} denotes the quantity of output from industry i delivered to (used by) industry j, q_{Li} is the quantity of labor delivered to industry i, q_{iC} the quantity of output from industry i delivered for final consumption, and q_i (with one subscript only) the total output from industry i.

Instead of Equation 14.1 we have now, lumping together all final demands so that by definition $q_{iF} = q_{iC} + q_{iI} + q_{iX}$,

[14.1']
$$q_i = \sum_{j=1}^{n} q_{ij} + q_{iF} \qquad i = 1, \ldots, n$$

We define the technical coefficients, or input coefficients a_{ij} as the number of output units from industry i necessary to produce one unit of output from industry j. Similar input coefficients are defined for labor input a_{Lj}, capital services a_{Kj}, land services a_{Rj}, and (complementary) imports a_{Mj}. The input coefficients correspond to Walras' technical coefficients, the only difference being that in the original Walrasian system only primary inputs were considered. (See Chapter 3, Section 2.)

It follows directly from the definition of the input coefficients that

[14.5]
$$q_{ij} = a_{ij}q_j \qquad \begin{aligned} i &= 1, \ldots, n, L, K, R, M \\ j &= 1, \ldots, n \end{aligned}$$

Inserting Equation 14.5 in Equation 14.1' we obtain

[14.6]
$$q_i = \sum_{j=1}^{n} a_{ij}q_j + q_{iF} \qquad i = 1, \ldots, n$$

Moving the expression under the summation sign to the left side, we arrive at an equation system that, written out *in extenso*, becomes

[14.7]

$$
\begin{array}{llllll}
(1 - a_{11})q_1 - & a_{12}q_2 & - \cdots - & a_{1i}q_i & - \cdots - & a_{1n}q_n & = q_{1F} \\
-a_{21}q_1 & + (1 - a_{22})q_2 - \cdots - & a_{2i}q_i & - \cdots - & a_{2n}q_n & = q_{2F} \\
\vdots & \vdots & \vdots & \vdots & \\
-a_{i1}q_i - & a_{i2}q_2 & - \cdots + (1 - a_{ii})q_i - \cdots - & a_{in}q_n & = q_{iF} \\
\vdots & \vdots & \vdots & \vdots & \\
-a_{n1}q_1 - & a_{n2}q_2 & - \cdots - & a_{ni}q_i & - \cdots + (1 - a_{nn})q_n & = q_{nF}
\end{array}
$$

This is a simple linear equation system with n equations in the n unknowns q_i. The theory is now that the technical coefficients are constant and invariant with respect to changes in the total outputs q_i and the final demands q_{iF}. We can therefore solve the system to determine the levels of output in the individual industries under alternative assumptions concerning final demands. When we have found the individual outputs necessary for the final demands to be satisfied, Equation 14.5 helps to calculate all the inputs, including the primary inputs, required for producing these outputs. It must then be determined whether sufficient quantities of primary resources are available; full employment, capacity limitations, or exhaustion of natural resources (land) may make an otherwise feasible production program impossible.

We would ask, however, whether a feasible production program exists at all. This is equivalent to asking whether Equations 14.7 have a meaningful solution with nonnegative outputs. It can be shown (Hawkins and Simon, 1949; see also Gale, 1960, Chapter IX, Section I) that such will be the case if and only if the system is "productive," which, generally speaking, means that commodities produced by the system should require less than one unit of itself, directly or indirectly, as inputs for producing one unit of output.[1] It can be shown that if the system fulfills this requirement, it will be well behaved in other respects, too. GNP (plus imports) will be positive, at least in some sectors, the prices implied by the system will be positive, and so forth. (See Dorfman, Samuelson, and Solow, 1958, pp. 255–256.)

Assuming that a solution actually exists, it can be written in the following form, where the A_{ij} are constants that can be calculated from the input coefficients of Equation 14.7. The number of units of output i needed, directly or indirectly, to produce one unit of the final demand j, that is, of output j, is A_{ij}. Equation 14.8 is then easy to understand.

$$q_1 = A_{11}q_{1F} + A_{12}q_{2F} + \cdots + A_{1n}q_{nF}$$
$$q_2 = A_{21}q_{1F} + A_{22}q_{2F} + \cdots + A_{2n}q_{nF}$$

[14.8]

$$q_n = A_{n1}q_{1F} + A_{n2}q_{2F} + \cdots + A_{nn}q_{nF}$$

The requirements for primary inputs can be expressed in an analogous manner.

3 / Prices and costs

It seems odd that a general equilibrium system that purports to be a descendent of the neoclassical system contains no prices. The open input-output

[1] This requirement seems rather obvious, but it is not really necessary from a purely technical point of view. Competitive imports may fill the gap and could be paid for by exports, even permanently. An industry that requires more than one unit input of itself (directly or indirectly) to produce one unit of output must operate at a loss, however. Unless society is prepared to subsidize it permanently, it would have to be closed down.

system, expressed entirely in physical units, might therefore be considered a technocratic, rather than an economic, system. Neither the (physical) input-output table nor the input-output model deals explicitly with prices and seemingly has nothing at all to do with price determination. Such is not the case, however. The system does, in fact, determine a set of equilibrium prices or, rather, relative equilibrium prices. It can be shown that the prices are equal to the marginal rates of transformation between outputs.

From Table 14.1, expressed in value terms, it follows that the value of total outputs is equal to the value of total inputs for any given industry (see Equation 14.3). Therefore, if we multiply the input coefficients for inter-mediary inputs in a certain industry by the prices of these inputs, and deduct their sum from the equilibrium price of the industry's outputs, we must obtain its value of primary inputs (including indirect taxes) per unit of output:

[14.9]
$$p_i - \sum_{j=1}^{n} a_{ji}p_j = y_i \qquad i = 1, \ldots, n$$

where p_i is the price of output i, and y_i is the value of primary inputs per unit of output i, estimated at zero net profits (we are looking for the equilibrium prices). Rearranging Equation 14.9, we can form the equation system

[14.9']
$$
\begin{aligned}
(1 - a_{11})p_1 - \quad a_{21}p_2 \quad - \cdots - \quad a_{n1}p_n \quad &= y_1 \\
-a_{12}p_1 + (1 - a_{22})p_2 - \cdots - \quad a_{n2}p_n \quad &= y_2 \\
\vdots \qquad\qquad \vdots \qquad\qquad\qquad \vdots \\
-a_{1n}p_1 - \quad a_{2n}p_2 \quad - \cdots + (1 - a_{nn})p_n &= y_n
\end{aligned}
$$

which can be shown to have the solution

[14.10]
$$
\begin{aligned}
p_1 &= A_{11}y_1 + A_{21}y_2 + \cdots + A_{n1}y_n \\
p_2 &= A_{12}y_1 + A_{22}y_2 + \cdots + A_{n2}y_n \\
\vdots \qquad \vdots \qquad \vdots \qquad\qquad \vdots \\
p_n &= A_{1n}y_1 + A_{2n}y_2 + \cdots + A_{nn}y_n
\end{aligned}
$$

Since A_{ij} as before is the total amount of commodity (output) i used in producing one unit of commodity (output) j, and y_i is the value of primary inputs per unit of i, $A_{ij}y_i$ is the cost of primary inputs at zero profits embedded in the amount of commodity i, directly and indirectly required for producing one unit of j. All these direct and indirect costs for use of primary inputs add up to the equilibrium price per unit of output. In other words, each output has been "dissolved" in primary inputs. (See Chapter 17.)

It is easily seen that the ratios between two output equilibrium prices must be equal to their marginal rates of transformation. Consider outputs 1 and 2. On the right side of Equation 14.10 we have the necessary costs in terms of primary inputs directly and indirectly needed to produce one unit of output 1. One dollar of primary input will thus suffice to produce $1/p_1$ units of output 1 (considering all the outputs indirectly required for production). Similarly, \$1 of primary inputs will suffice to produce $1/p_2$ of output 2. Giving up one unit of output 1 and using the saved costs to produce output 2, we can obviously obtain p_1/p_2 units of output 2. Thus, p_1/p_2 is equal to the marginal rate of transformation between outputs 1 and 2. It is true that the composition of the primary inputs required for production of the abandoned unit of output 1 may differ from the composition of the primary inputs required for producing the p_1/p_2 units of output 2. Their costs are the same, however, and through buying and selling primary inputs we can always acquire a basket of primary inputs of the composition needed, within the given costs. Since both the relative prices of the primary inputs and the input coefficients are constant and given, there is nothing ambiguous in this; we are applying a well-known theorem of Hicks, to the effect that a group of commodities (inputs) with constant relative prices can be treated as one commodity (Hicks, 1939, pp. 50f.).

Given the value of primary inputs per unit of output, y_i, Equation 14.10 determines the prices of all outputs. The y_i's are expressed in money terms and are the sum of the individual primary inputs necessary to produce one unit of output i, multiplied by their respective prices, that is, $y_i = a_{Li}p_L + a_{Ki}p_K + a_{Ri}p_R + a_{Mi}p_M + v_{Ti}$, where p_L, p_K, p_R, p_M are the prices of labor, capital services, land services, and imports, respectively, and $v_{Ti} = V_{Ti}/q_i$, that is, the amount of taxes in terms of money per unit of output. v_{Ti} cannot be divided into a quantity and a price component. Equation 14.10 thus determines the money prices of output, given the money prices of all primary inputs, including imports, and the tax in money terms per unit of output. Since there are no profits beyond necessary payments for primary inputs, the prices are equilibrium prices. Dividing Equation 14.10 through by p_L, for example, we obtain all prices of outputs (and primary inputs) in terms of the *numéraire*, labor. Therefore, we can also say that given the relative prices of all primary inputs (including the tax per unit in terms of the *numéraire*), the system determines the relative prices of outputs. It follows that a change in relative primary input prices will imply a change in relative output prices at given input coefficients. Only in this very limited sense does the open input-output system determine prices. On the other hand, it is clear that the system resembles the neoclassical system in that it determines, at most, a set of *numéraire* output prices, and that something more is needed to determine absolute money prices. Since the system determines the quantities of labor, capital, and land used, and their relative prices are given, we could, for instance, use the Cambridge equation to determine the money price of the *numéraire*, labor, and thus, by way of the quantity theory of money, arrive at the absolute money prices of the system.

In both the neoclassical and the other general equilibrium systems discussed so far, interdependence is the rule. Generally we must solve for all unknowns, prices as well as quantities, simultaneously. The open Leontief system falls into two systems, a quantity system and a price system, which can be solved independently. A study of the two systems reveals a close resemblance, however. Any coefficient row in the quantity system shown in Equation 14.7 is identical with the corresponding coefficient column in the price system shown in Equation 14.9'. The same applies to the solutions shown by Equations 14.8 and 14.10. We here encounter something that is characteristic for linear models: the price system appears as the "dual" of the quantity system, and vice versa, and the two can be studied independently.

4 / Extended input-output models

In the open input-output model, all final demands, consumption, investment, and exports, are exogenously determined. This applies also to the available quantities of primary resources, labor force, productive capacity, and land, which may or may not be completely used up. The open input-output model is thus a production model that only explains the demand for (and supply of) intermediary inputs and the demand for primary inputs, but leaves the demand for final use and the supply of primary inputs unexplained. It is natural, therefore, to extend the open Leontief system so that it explains at least some of the final demands and supplies of primary inputs.

Extended Leontief systems exist in great abundance. In most cases they combine the Keynesian model with Leontief's system. Ragnar Frisch's "repercussion systems" (1957) could be mentioned as a typical example. Final demands are then explained by a number of demand functions. For private consumption, n Keynesian consumption functions may be introduced with the (real) incomes generated by the production system as explanatory variables. The relative output prices could also be used as arguments in the consumption functions. Public consumption might still be considered to be determined exogenously. Private (and perhaps also public) investment could be made a function of output or capacity utilization, but incomes and relative prices could be introduced here, too. Finally, exports would presumably have to be treated as exogenously determined. The available supplies of primary inputs (apart from complementary imports) are usually taken as given in the short run, but supply functions with relative prices as arguments might be introduced. Proceeding as Keynesians, we would then have to let the money-wage rate and the other primary input prices be determined from outside. Excess supplies of primary inputs should exert no influence on prices, and factor owners' sales expectations would be assumed to adjust themselves to actual sales. We would thereby determine the absolute price level. The result would, of course, imply that the quantity theory could not be used for determining the absolute prices. We could instead add a liquidity-preference theory (such as Equation 11.4), which, given the quantity of money, would serve to determine the rate of interest, which in turn might appear as a determinant in the demand functions. Needless to say, real balances could also be introduced in both demand and supply functions.

The whole Keynesian machinery can thus be added to the Leontief system, or, stated another way: Leontief's production system can be inserted into the Keynesian model so that we arrive at a Keynesian model with intermediary goods. Keynes' and Leontief's systems are thus complementary rather than competing alternatives. It should be added that such a Keynesian-Leontief model would resemble Patinkin's rather than Klein's interpretation of Keynes' system. We would, namely, obtain a model wherein relative prices and wages exert no direct influence on the supply of goods, which is exclusively determined by and adjusts itself to effective demand.

But the Leontief system can also be extended to a perfect neoclassical system, without technical substitution, of course. Cassel actually assumed that the technical coefficients were constant (Chapter 3, Section 3). If we allowed for intermediary inputs in Cassel's system, we would have a neoclassical model with a built-in Leontief production system. If we proceed the other way and extend the open Leontief system to a neoclassical model, we must add demand equations for final demand and supply equations for the primary inputs. In form, these demand and supply functions might be the same as those added to the Leontief system to obtain a Keynesian system. The decisive factor in making the system neoclassical is to add equilibrium conditions for the primary inputs, and let their prices be endogenously determined. If the number of primary inputs is m this will furnish us with m new equations and m new unknowns, the money prices of primary inputs. We can then either proceed as neoclassicists and assume that Say's law holds, show that we have the same number of independent equations as unknowns, and add the exchange equation for determining absolute prices. Or, we can proceed à la Patinkin, introduce real cash balances in the demand and supply functions, discard Say's law, and thus obtain a system that directly determines the absolute prices.

5 / Empirical input-output models

The basic feature of the input-output model is the technical coefficients and their constancy. Input-output theory does not postulate that the coefficients cannot change, but only that they are invariant with respect to changes in final demands and outputs. Technical innovations will, of course, change the coefficients. In principle, changes in the relative prices of the primary inputs might result in substitution and thus lead to changes in the coefficients for both primary and intermediary inputs. To be true, even at a traditional smooth production function with unlimited substitution possibilities, the technical coefficients are, in fact, invariant to changes in final demands and outputs, provided that there is constant returns to scale and only one primary input (for instance, labor), or, what amounts to the same, that relative prices of all primary inputs are constant. This is the essence of N. Georgescu-Roegen's and P. A. Samuelson's so-called "nonsubstitution theorem" (Samuelson, 1951, 1961; and Dorfman, Samuelson, and Solow, 1958, Chapters 9-5 and 10-6). It is not very likely that all these conditions for constant coefficients to prevail should be fulfilled, either in the short or long run. Nevertheless, for most applications the hypothesis has been that observed coefficients remain approximately constant over time.

In measuring the coefficients, input-output tables in value terms must be taken as the starting point. The assumption of the model, that each industry or activity only produces one single well-defined commodity or service, cannot be upheld. Even at very detailed classifications, an industry will usually produce a multitude of commodities and services, and data for primary inputs can only be obtained as broad aggregates. The input coefficients must therefore be estimated as the value of inputs delivered to a certain industry from other industries, divided by the value of output of the industry concerned. Both inputs and outputs consist, then, of heterogeneous bundles of commodities and services. The coefficients observed for a certain period (usually a year) may be affected by a number of short-term factors related to prices, productivity, or composition of production within the individual industries, which could make the observed coefficients change substantially from one year to another, even if the underlying technology is unchanged. Moreover, since we have good reasons for assuming that in the long-run technical progress may change the coefficients radically, it is a common belief that the main field of application of the input-output model is in medium-term problems. For discussions of empirical problems related to the input-output models, and their applications, see, for example, Dorfman (1954), Christ (1955), Leontief (1951, 1966), Stone (1961), and U.N. (1968).

References

CHRIST, C.: "A Review of Input-Output Analysis," in N.B.E.R., *Input-Output Analysis: An Appraisal*, Princeton University Press, 1955.

DORFMAN, R.: "The Nature and Significance of Input-Output," *The Review of Economic Statistics*, vol. 36, no. 2, May, 1954.

—, P. A. SAMUELSON, and R. SOLOW: *Linear Programming and Economic Analysis*, McGraw-Hill, New York, 1958.

FRISCH, RAGNAR: *Oslo Decision Models*, Memorandum of June 4, 1957, University of Oslo, 1957.

GALE, D.: *The Theory of Linear Economic Models*, McGraw-Hill, New York, 1960.

HAWKINS, D., and H. A. SIMON: "Note: Some Conditions of Macroeconomic Stability,"
     Econometrica, vol. 17, no. 3–4, July–October, 1949.
HICKS, J. R.: *Value and Capital*, Clarendon Press, Oxford, 1939.
LEONTIEF, W. W.: "Quantitative Input-Output Relations in the Economic System of
     the United States," *The Review of Economic Statistics*, vol. 18, no. 3, August, 1936.
—:*The Structure of the American Economy*, Oxford University Press, Oxford, 1941.
     Second, enlarged edition, 1951.
—: *Input-Output Economics*, Oxford University Press, New York, 1966.
— (ed.): *Studies in the Structure of the American Economy*, Oxford University Press,
     New York, 1953.
MIERNYK, W. H.: *The Elements of Input-Output Analysis*, Random House, New York, 1965.
SAMUELSON, P. A.: "Abstract of a Theorem Concerning Substitutability in Open
     Leontief Models," in T. C. Koopmans (ed.), *Activity Analysis of Production and
     Allocation*, John Wiley & Sons, New York, 1951.
—: "A New Theorem on Nonsubstitution," in *Money, Growth, and Methodology, in
     honor of Johan Åkerman*, Gleerup, Lund, 1961.
STONE, R.: *Input-Output and National Accounts*, O.E.C.D., Paris, 1961.
—: *Quantity and Price Indexes in National Accounting*, O.E.C.D., Paris, 1956.
TASKIER, CHARLOTTE E.: *Input-Output Bibliography, 1955–1960*, United Nations, New
     York, 1961.
UNITED NATIONS: *Input-Output Bibliography, 1960–1963*, United Nations, New York, 1964.
—: *A System of National Accounts*, ST/STAT/SER.F/2/Rev. 3, United Nations,
     New York, 1968.

Input-output
and equilibrium growth

15

Modern theory of equilibrium growth was initiated by the famous equilibrium-growth model of John von Neumann (1938, 1945–46). Von Neumann's model is (logically) related to neoclassical equilibrium theory in Leontief's simplified version. To make it easier to comprehend von Neumann's model, we shall first show a dynamization of Leontief's closed model, which resembles von Neumann's model, but is simpler and easier to grasp for students acquainted with Leontief's input-output model. A rigorous treatment of the model is given by Samuelson and Solow (1953). See also Dorfman, Samuelson, and Solow (1958, Chapter 11), and Hahn and Matthews (1964, pp. 968 et seq.).

1 / Leontief's completely closed model

The first input-output model presented by Leontief (1936) is a closed model. There are no final demands or primary inputs. The household sector is considered an industry like any other industry, with a labor output (used as input by other industries), and using inputs (consumption) delivered from other industries. Assuming $n - 1$ other industries, and a household sector numbered as the nth industry, the input-output table is shown in Table 15.1.

The interpretation of the single elements of this input-output table is the usual one (Chapter 14, Section 2). All elements are measured in physical terms, thus excluding vertical summation. Each industry is assumed to produce one homogeneous commodity or service. The difference between this table and the traditional input-output table is that all outputs are used as inputs. The system, including the households, is self-perpetuating and

TABLE *15.1*

	Industry		n (households)	Total outputs
	1 $\cdots$ $n-1$			
Industry 1	q_{11} $\cdots$ $q_{1,n-1}$		$q_{1,n}$	q_1
$\cdot$	$\cdot$ $\cdot$		$\cdot$	$\cdot$
$\cdot$	$\cdot$ $\cdot$		$\cdot$	$\cdot$
$\cdot$	$\cdot$ $\cdot$		$\cdot$	$\cdot$
$n-1$	$q_{n-1,1}$ $\cdots$ $q_{n-1,n-1}$		$q_{n-1,n}$	q_{n-1}
n (households)	$q_{n,1}$ $\cdots$ $q_{n,n-1}$		$q_{n,n}$	q_n
Total inputs	— $\cdots$ —		—	

self-contained and reproduces itself continuously. We disregard capital. The national income generated by the system is q_n.

We define the technical coefficients as before:

[15.1] $$a_{ij} = \frac{q_{ij}}{q_j} \qquad \begin{array}{l} i = 1, \ldots, n \\ j = 1, \ldots, n \end{array}$$

They are considered given and constant, including those of the households, which are assumed to need inputs (consumption) in certain proportions; the total amount of labor output is determined by the scale of the inputs (consumption). The amount of commodity i needed as consumption to "produce" one unit of labor output is a_{in}. Double the scale of consumption and the labor force (labor output) will double. This is reminiscent of the population theories of Malthus and Ricardo. We shall return to this later.

By definition we have

[15.2] $$\sum_{j=1}^{n} q_{ij} = q_i \qquad i = 1, \ldots, n$$

or, inserting 15.1,

[15.3] $$\sum_{j=1}^{n} a_{ij}q_j = q_i \qquad i = 1, \ldots, n$$

In this equation system we consider the total outputs q_j as unknowns. Written fully, the system is:

[15.4]
$$\begin{array}{llll}
(1 - a_{11})q_1 - & a_{12}q_2 & - \cdots - & a_{1n}q_n & = 0 \\
-a_{21}q_1 + & (1 - a_{22})q_2 - & \cdots - & a_{2n}q_n & = 0 \\
\multicolumn{4}{c}{\cdots\cdots\cdots\cdots\cdots\cdots\cdots\cdots\cdots\cdots\cdots} \\
-a_{n1}q_1 - & a_{n2}q_2 & - \cdots + & (1 - a_{nn})q_n & = 0
\end{array}$$

Because of the zeros on the right side (there is no final demand), the q_j's can, at best, only be determined up to an arbitrary proportionality factor or, to state it differently, the system can only be solved for the relative outputs $q_1/q_n, \ldots, q_{n-1}/q_n$; that is, output per unit of labor. If the system has an equilibrium solution, it can be in equilibrium at any level of production.[1] But all such equilibrium solutions will be fully proportional; only the scale of activity will be different. Compare this indeterminacy of the absolute quantities with the indeterminacy of the absolute prices in the Walrasian and Hicksian systems. By itself, this static model is not very interesting. To determine the absolute level of $q_j, j = 1, \ldots, n - 1$, we must assume q_n given, which means simply that we return to the open input-output model. Move the last column to the right side and consider $a_{in}q_n$ as given final demands. Furthermore, disregard the last equation and we will have the usual open Leontief model in $n - 1$ sectors. We note finally that a "dual" price system can be established that will determine the relative equilibrium prices of the system. (Compare Chapter 14, Section 3.)

2 / The closed model and equilibrium growth

Leontief's closed model becomes interesting, however, when we ask how it may grow over time. To dynamize the model, we shall assume that production in all industries (including households) takes exactly one period, so that all inputs are made at the beginning of the period, and the outputs are ready for use at the end of the period. These assumptions mean that all the outputs from one period become inputs at the beginning of the next period, lead to outputs at the end of the following period, and so on. We thus arrive at an input-output table that is somewhat different from the traditional one. In this table $q_{ij}{}^t$ denotes input in industry j in period t delivered from industry i, and $q_i{}^t$ denotes total output in period t from industry i. (See Table 15.2.)

We have now, by assumption,

[15.5] $q_i{}^t = q_{i1}{}^{t+1} + q_{i2}{}^{t+1} + \cdots + q_{in}{}^{t+1} \qquad i = 1, \ldots, n$

that is, the total output from industry i in one period equals the sum of all inputs from industry i in the following period. Thus we do *not* in general have

$$q_i{}^t = q_{i1}{}^t + q_{i2}{}^t + \cdots + q_{in}{}^t \qquad i = 1, \ldots, n$$

Such will only be the case if the system is stationary. If the system is to grow, we must have $q_i{}^t > q_{i1}{}^t + \cdots + q_{in}{}^t.$[2] We assume again that the technical coefficients

[15.6] $$a_{ij} = \frac{q_{ij}{}^{t+1}}{q_j{}^{t+1}} \qquad \begin{matrix} i = 1, \ldots, n \\ j = 1, \ldots, n \end{matrix}$$

---

[1] Solution requires that the determinant of the system vanish. We disregard the zero solution, which is uninteresting.

[2] We could add a final demand, namely, investments; for example, q_{in+1}^t, to make $q_i{}^t = q_{i1}{}^t + \cdots + q_{in}{}^t + q_{in+1}^t.$

TABLE *15.2*

		Period *t*			Period *t* + 1			Period *t* + 2
		Industry	Total outputs		Industry	Total outputs		
		1 · · · *n* (households)			1 · · · *n* (households)			
	1	q_{11}^t · · · q_{1n}^t	q_1^t		q_{11}^{t+1} · · · q_{1n}^{t+1}	q_1^{t+1}		
Industry	·	· ·	·		· ·	·		
	·	· ·	·		· ·	·		*etc.*
	·	· ·	·		· ·	·		
	n (households)	q_{n1}^t · · · q_{nn}^t	q_n^t		q_{n1}^{t+1} · · · q_{nn}^{t+1}	q_n^{t+1}		
	Total inputs	— —	—	—	—	—		

are given and unchanged from period to period. There is no technical progress. Equations 15.5 can then be written as

$$[15.5']\quad q_i^t = a_{i1}q_1^{t+1} + a_{i2}q_2^{t+1} + \cdots + a_{in}q_n^{t+1} \qquad i = 1, \ldots, n$$

We shall now define the concept of equilibrium growth. The system is said to be in equilibrium growth if:

(1) All outputs constantly grow in the same proportion so that the relative outputs are constant over time.

(2) Sales revenues and costs are equal in each industry, which is the equilibrium condition used in the Walrasian system for the commodity markets (see Chapter 3, Section 2). Since we have no primary inputs here, we need no other equilibrium conditions.[1]

The first equilibrium condition means that, calling the rate of growth *g*,

$$[15.7]\qquad\qquad q_i^{t+1} = (1 + g)q_i^t \qquad i = 1, \ldots, n$$

It follows that we can write Equations 15.5' as

$$[15.8]\qquad\qquad q_i^t = (1 + g) \sum_{j=1}^{n} a_{ij}q_j^t \qquad i = 1, \ldots, n$$

Note that if $g = 0$, Equations 15.8 reduce to the stationary system of Equations 15.3 and 15.4.

Concerning the second equilibrium condition, we recall that production takes time. The inputs are made exactly one period's time before the outputs appear, meaning that in equilibrium the value of all inputs per unit of out-

---

[1] By its very construction, this model (in some unexplained way) assumes equality between demand for and supply of all goods. Otherwise, we would, of course, have to add this as a special equilibrium condition.

put, *plus* interests for one period, must be equal to the output price. Calling the prices $p_j{}^t$, $j = 1, \ldots, n$, and the rate of interest r, we have (assuming prices to be constant over time)

[15.9]
$$p_i{}^t = (1 + r) \sum_{j=1}^{n} a_{ji} p_j{}^t \qquad i = 1, \ldots, n$$

Equations 15.8 and 15.9 constitute the model. We have here $2n$ non-linear equations in $2n + 2$ unknowns, namely, the n q_i's, the n p_i's, g, and r. The number of unknowns is $2n$, however, because Equations 15.8 are homogeneous in the q_i's and Equations 15.9 in the p_i's. In Equations 15.8 we can therefore divide through by $q_n{}^t$, for example, and in Equations 15.9 by $p_n{}^t$, and obtain two systems of $2n$ equations to determine the $n - 1$ $q_i{}^t/q_n{}^t$, the $n - 1$ $p_i{}^t/p_n{}^t$, g, and r. Note that the system in Equations 15.8 determines $q_i{}^t/q_n{}^t$ and g, and the system in Equations 15.9 determines $p_i{}^t/p_n{}^t$ and r. Note also that in Equations 15.9, a_{ji} takes the place of a_{ij} in Equations 15.8. Equations 15.9 are the dual of Equations 15.8, and vice versa. At $r = 0$, Equations 15.9 become the price system corresponding to the stationary quantity system in Equations 15.4. (Compare also with Equations 14.9'.)

If we wish to determine absolute prices we must add an exchange equation; since Say's law holds, this can only be done in a formal definitional way. The quantity of money must grow at the rate g; otherwise absolute prices could not remain constant. If we want to determine the absolute level of output we must know the initial level at time zero.

3 / The rate of interest and the rate of growth

We shall now assume that the system has a solution in the relative prices, relative outputs, the rate of growth, and the rate of interest. Taking the existence of a solution for granted, we can show that in equilibrium growth the rate of interest is equal to the rate of growth; that is, $g = r$. To prove this we multiply Equations 15.8 on both sides with p_i and Equations 15.9 by q_i to obtain

[15.8']
$$p_i{}^t q_i{}^t = (1 + g) \sum_{j=1}^{n} a_{ij} p_i{}^t q_j{}^t \qquad i = 1, \ldots, n$$

[15.9']
$$p_i{}^t q_i{}^t = (1 + r) \sum_{j=1}^{n} a_{ji} p_j{}^t q_i{}^t \qquad i = 1, \ldots, n$$

Adding the left sides and the right sides, respectively, we obtain

[15.10]
$$\sum_{i=1}^{n} p_i{}^t q_i{}^t = (1 + g) \sum_{i=1}^{n} \sum_{j=1}^{n} a_{ij} p_i{}^t q_j{}^t$$

[15.11]
$$\sum_{i=1}^{n} p_i{}^t q_i{}^t = (1 + r) \sum_{i=1}^{n} \sum_{j=1}^{n} a_{ji} p_j{}^t q_i{}^t$$

from which it follows that

[15.12]
$$r = g = \frac{\sum\limits_{i=1}^{n} p_i{}^t q_i{}^t}{\sum\limits_{i=1}^{n} \sum\limits_{j=1}^{n} a_{ij} p_i{}^t q_j{}^t} - 1$$

The two double sums appearing in Equations 15.10 and 15.11 contain the same terms and are identical. The numerator of the fraction on the right side of Equation 15.12 is the total value of all outputs (including labor), and the denominator is the total value of all inputs (including labor). Since the difference between the two is equal to total profits before interest payments,[1] which we shall call "gross profits," we have the following proposition:

In our equilibrium-growth model the rate of interest is equal to the rate of growth, both being equal to the rate of gross profits (measured by total input value). To this we can add that the rate of savings and the rate of investments (measured by total input value) are also equal to the rate of growth, the rate of interest, and the rate of gross profits. It is unusual, however, to measure savings and investments by total input value. If we measure the rate of savings, the rate of investments, and the rate of profit on national income, they will still be equal, but will become much larger than the rate of interest and the rate of growth. (We can safely assume that the total value of intermediary inputs is much larger than total interest income.)

In period t, national income NI^t will be[2]

[15.13]
$$NI^t = \underbrace{\sum_{j=1}^{n} p_n{}^t q_{nj}{}^t}_{\text{Wages}} + \underbrace{\sum_{i=1}^{n-1} p_i{}^t q_i{}^t - \sum_{j=1}^{n-1} \sum_{i=1}^{n} p_i{}^t q_{ij}{}^t}_{\text{Gross profits in industry 1 to } n-1}$$

By virtue of Equations 15.5, 15.7, and 15.9, however, we have also

[15.14]
$$\underbrace{\sum_{j=1}^{n} p_n{}^t q_{nj}{}^t}_{\text{Wages}} = \underbrace{\sum_{i=1}^{n} p_i{}^t q_{in}{}^t}_{\text{Consumption}}$$

It follows that gross profits in industry 1 to $n - 1$ must be equal to total investments and savings.[3] Note that we have only circulating capital in this model. The total value of the circulating capital at the end of the period,

---

[1] In Equations 15.10, 15.11, and 15.12 the summations extend from 1 to n, which means that total inputs include consumption and total outputs include the labor to be used in the next period. It is not very suitable to include consumption and labor output in the calculation of the rate of gross profit, but in equilibrium this does not matter. As we shall see later $p_n q_n = (1 + g)\Sigma p_i q_{in}$. We can therefore omit the households in both Equations 15.10 and 15.11, without affecting the rate of gross profits.

[2] Profits in the households sector are not included in national income by traditional standard national accounting definitions. The household sector's "profits" are nothing but the value of the increase in labor input.

[3] Returning to note 2 on page 185, it is easily understood that for each sector investment $p_i{}^t q_{in+1}^t$ is equal to $g p_i{}^t q_i{}^t$, which is equal to the gross profits of the sector.

that is, total value of inputs in industry 1 to $n - 1$, including accruing interests, is equal to total output value from the same industries. In other words, the capital-output ratio in the model is equal to 1. Finally, we see that the net profits, or the gross profits minus interests on the capital, are everywhere equal to zero. Perfect competition is assumed and the rate of interest is implicitly assumed to be bidden up to the point where net profits are zero. It will be seen from Equations 15.9 that in principle the same reasoning is applied to households; that is, to the production of labor. This is a peculiar way of looking at the population and labor supply problem, of course, unless we are dealing with a slave economy. Therefore, to make the model more than a mere intellectual exercise, it would seem that there are a few assumptions that must be relaxed. As it happens, some of them can be relaxed without upsetting the main results.

4 / Population growth, extraneous consumption, and equilibrium growth

One way to abandon the treatment of labor supply as an ordinary production process with fixed input (consumption) coefficients is to assume that at the fixed real wages (the vector of "technical" coefficients a_{in} expresses the real wage per unit of labor) the labor supply grows at the same rate as the rest of the system. Then, however, the model would overcome in only a very artificial way a difficulty known from the more primitive growth model of Harrod and Domar (see Chapter 18, Section 3): there is no satisfactory built-in mechanism to ensure that the rates of production and employment growth are equal to the rate of population increase. This equality appears to be a natural requirement for an equilibrium-growth model.

The following consideration presents a possible solution, however. It has been shown in this kind of model that the lower the real wage of labor, that is, the smaller the coefficients a_{in}, the higher the equilibrium rate of growth. This is quite easy to understand. The less output that is needed to feed a unit of labor, the higher the input level can be in all other industries, and accordingly the higher the outputs of the next period. We can hereafter interpret the model as assuming a perfectly elastic labor supply at whatever level of real wages has been fixed. Alternatively, we can say that the model shows the labor requirements at a given real wage level. It is also clear that there may exist one level of real wages, that is, of a_{in}, which makes the rate of growth of the model equal to any exogenously given natural rate of population growth (provided that the latter is not too high). At that level of real wages per unit of labor, there may be continuous full employment in the model. The labor market is simply assumed to be competitive in the traditional sense so that real wages fall until full employment is ensured; we need no special assumptions about the determinants of population growth.

It is clear, however, that in this interpretation it is the exogenously given rate of population growth that sets the pace and determines the general growth rate.

The model is peculiar also in another respect. There is no final demand. We could, as we mentioned earlier, consider the increase in inputs from one period to the next as the final investment demand. With respect to consumption, however, it all appears as inputs in industry n (the labor-supplying households). An interesting modification, therefore, is to introduce a final, "extraneous" demand for consumer goods in addition to the input in the household sector, assuming, for example, that profit accrues to passive capitalists who may consume part of it, or that profit is taxed and the proceeds used to finance public consumption. Equations 15.5 change then to ($c_i{}^t$ being the extraneous consumer demand for commodities from sector i)

[15.5″] $$q_i{}^t - c_i{}^t = q_{i1}^{t+1} + \cdots + q_{in}^{t+1} \qquad i = 1, \ldots, n$$

We then have the equations

[15.8″] $$q_i{}^t - c_i{}^t = (1 + g) \sum_{j=1}^{n} a_{ij} q_j{}^t \qquad i = 1, \ldots, n$$

and

[15.9] $$p_i{}^t = (1 + r) \sum_{j=1}^{n} a_{ji} p_i{}^t \qquad i = 1, \ldots, n$$

Without elaborating on the problem of the existence of a solution to this system, it suffices to mention that if the $c_i{}^t$'s are certain linear functions of other variables in the system, it may still have a solution in the relative quantities, the relative prices, r, and g. For our limited purpose we do not need to concern ourselves with the precise determination of the $c_i{}^t$'s. Repeating the procedure leading to Equations 15.10 and 15.11 we find

[15.12′] $$r = g + \frac{\displaystyle\sum_{i=1}^{n} c_i{}^t p_i{}^t}{\displaystyle\sum_{i=1}^{n} \sum_{j=1}^{n} a_{ij} p_i{}^t q_j{}^t}$$

The rate of interest now exceeds the rate of growth by the ratio of total extraneous consumption to total inputs, both measured in terms of value. If the extraneous consumption consists exclusively of public consumption we can obtain a convenient expression for the relationship between interest and growth rates by letting c_{pub} denote the ratio of total public consumption over total output, both in terms of value. The last term on the right side of Equation 15.12′ then becomes $= (1 + r)c_{pub}$, and it reduces to

[15.12″] $$r = \frac{g}{1 - c_{pub}} + \frac{c_{pub}}{1 - c_{pub}}$$

This is a quantitatively very substantial modification of the original proposition, equality of interest and growth rates. At a rate of public consumption over total output of 7 per cent (this is the order of magnitude for the United States) an equilibrium growth rate of 4 per cent will be accompanied by an equilibrium interest rate of 12 per cent.

If, on the other hand, the extraneous consumption consists of capitalists' consumption out of profits, we can obtain another expression by defining c_{cap} as the ratio of extraneous consumption over total profits (in value terms), and $s_{cap} = 1 - c_{cap}$. Dividing through in both numerator and denominator of the last term on the right side of Equation 15.12′, and recalling that total value of inputs over total profits is equal to the inverted rate of interest, we obtain

$$r = g + \frac{1 - s_{cap}}{1/r}$$

or

[15.12‴]
$$r = \frac{g}{s_{cap}}$$

We find now that in equilibrium growth the rate of interest is equal to the rate of growth divided by the savings ratio of the capitalists. Since, generally, $s_{cap} < 1$, the rate of interest will exceed the rate of growth. If $s_{cap} = 0$ and capitalists consume all profits, the growth rate must be zero, of course, but this case is outside the above formulae. Total profits will, of course, also set an upper limit to public consumption.

We notice, further, that technical progress can be taken into account in a primitive way by assuming that all technical coefficients diminish at the same rate. This would not change the results in any significant way.

The equality of growth rate, interest rate, gross profits rate, and the rate of investments in a state of equilibrium growth was first formulated and proved by von Neumann (1938, 1945–46), although similar ideas can be found in earlier literature. In his theory of economic development, Schumpeter (1911, 1934) maintained that the rate of interest is related to the rate of growth via the rate of profits, and that the rate of interest would be zero in a stationary state. The modification whereby we allow for extraneous consumption is due to Malinvaud (1959), and Morishima (1960). The modification with respect to labor and wages is due to Morishima (1960).

The intimate, simple relationship between the rate of growth and the rate of interest that the present model discloses has caused much debate since Schumpeter proclaimed that in the stationary state, the rate of interest must be zero. The present model implies the same result. The zero rate of interest of the stationary state is, of course, dependent upon the underlying assumptions (Samuelson, 1943, 1958; Arvidsson, 1956). From Equation 15.12′ it would seem that the existence of extraneous consumption suffices to secure a positive interest rate at a zero rate of growth (provided that a solution with $c_i{}^t > 0$ and $g = 0$ exists). Be this as it may, it is important to note that this is not a question of a new theory for the determination of the rate of interest, as has sometimes been proclaimed. From the remarks to Equations 15.9 it is clear that the rate of interest is determined by demand for and supply of savings; since the model does not include money, this means, in fact, demand for and supply of loanable funds. Equality in growth and interest rates (in the simplest case) does not mean that the rate of growth determines the rate of interest or, more specifically, that population growth determines the rate of interest. Equality in the rate of growth and the rate of interest is an equilibrium property of the system as a whole and is dependent upon all the assumptions of the system.

The dynamized, closed input-output model contains some simplifications as compared to von Neumann's original model, and some of his results cannot be demonstrated by the simpler model. We must therefore turn to von Neumann's model.

References

ARVIDSSON, GUY: "On the Reasons for a Rate of Interest," *International Economic Papers*, no. 6, Macmillan, London, 1956.

DORFMAN, R., P. A. SAMUELSON, and R. SOLOW: *Linear Programming and Economic Analysis*, McGraw-Hill, New York, 1958.

HAHN, R. F., and R. C. O. MATTHEWS: "The Theory of Economic Growth: A Survey," *The Economic Journal*, vol. 74, no. 296, December, 1964. Reprinted in *Surveys of Economic Theory*, vol. 2, St. Martin's Press, New York, 1965.

KALDOR, N.: "A Model of Economic Growth," *The Economic Journal*, vol. 67, no. 268, December, 1957. Reprinted in *Essays on Economic Stability and Growth*, Gerald Duckworth and Co., London, 1960.

LEONTIEF, W. W.: "Quantitative Input-Output Relations in the Economic System of the United States," *Review of Economic Statistics*, vol. 18, no. 3, August, 1936.

MALINVAUD, E.: "Programmes d'expansion et taux d'intérêt," *Econometrica*, vol. 27, no. 2, April, 1959.

MORISHIMA, M.: "Economic Expansion and the Interest Rate in Generalized von Neumann Models," *Econometrica*, vol. 28, no. 2, April, 1960.

—: *Equilibrium, Stability, and Growth*, Clarendon Press, Oxford, 1964.

SAMUELSON, P. A.: "Dynamics, Statics, and the Stationary State," Essays in Honor of Joseph Schumpeter, *The Review of Economics and Statistics*, vol. 25, no. 1, February, 1943.

—: "An Exact Consumption-Loan Model of Interest with or without the Social Contrivance of Money," *The Journal of Political Economy*, vol. 66, no. 6, December, 1958.

—, and R. SOLOW: "Balanced Growth under Constant Returns to Scale," *Econometrica*, vol. 21, no. 3, July, 1953.

SCHUMPETER, J.: *The Theory of Economic Development*, Harvard University Press, Cambridge, Mass., 1934. Originally published as *Theorie der wirtschaftlichen Entwicklung*, 1911.

VON NEUMANN, J.: "A Model of General Economic Equilibrium," *The Review of Economic Studies*, vol. 13(1), no. 33, 1945–46. Originally published as "Über ein ökonomisches Gleichungssystem und eine Verallgemeinerung des Brouwerschen Fixpunktsatzes," in R. Menger (ed.), *Ergebnisse eines Matematischen Seminars*, Springer, Vienna, 1938.

Von Neumann's model

16

Von Neumann's model is remarkable in several respects. It introduced the concept of equilibrium growth, it provided the first proof that a solution to a general equilibrium model existed, and it was the first programming model. Here we are concerned only with the equilibrium-growth aspects of this path-breaking contribution (1938, 1945–46).

1 / The model

The main difference between von Neumann's model and the closed Leontief model discussed in Chapter 15 is that in Leontief's model the methods of production used were given *a priori*, and in von Neumann's model a larger number of possible production methods are available; one of the problems, then, is to choose the best techniques. Another difference is that Leontief's model works with sectors, each one producing a particular commodity (group of commodities), and von Neumann's model admits the possibility of joint production and allows the same commodity to be produced in several industries. Accordingly, von Neumann speaks about processes rather than industries.

We consider n different goods and m possible technical processes $m > n$. Each technical process may use several inputs and produce several outputs. Like the Leontief system, the technical possibilities are described by technical coefficients. Assume that process j is working at unit level (see below). The process is then characterized by the coefficients a_{ij}, which are the input quantities necessary, and b_{ij}, which are the output quantities produced.

$$a_{1j} \qquad b_{1j}$$

Inputs	.	.	Outputs
necessary	.	.	forthcoming
at unit	. $\longrightarrow$.		at unit
activity	.	.	activity
level	.	.	level

$$j = 1, \ldots, m$$

$$a_{nj} \qquad b_{nj}$$

Some of the a's and b's may be zero, but if $a_{ij} = 0$, then $b_{ij} \neq 0$ and vice versa, which means that every commodity appears in every process.[1] The same commodity may appear as both input and output. Constant returns to scale are assumed to prevail, which means that if the process is operated at a level of x_j, the necessary inputs will be $a_{1j}x_j, a_{2j}x_j, \ldots, a_{nj}x_j$, and the outputs will be $b_{1j}x_j, b_{2j}x_j, \ldots, b_{nj}x_j$. At $x_j = 1$ the process is operating at unit level. The choice of the unit level is entirely arbitrary; for example, it may be defined as the level of activity where an arbitrarily chosen $a_{ij} = 1$.

We assume as before that production takes one period. Fixed capital may exist; von Neumann included the fixed capital in both the inputs (a given machine) and the outputs (a one-period older machine, which is a different commodity than the given machine). To make production possible we must have

$$[16.1] \qquad \sum_{j=1}^{m} b_{ij}x_j{}^t \geqq \sum_{j=1}^{m} a_{ij}x_j{}^{t+1} \qquad i = 1, \ldots, n$$

Compare this set of n equations with Equations 15.5'. Two differences appear. The right sides are the same, but on the left side we now have a sum because commodity i may be produced in any of the m processes. (In Leontief's model it can only come from sector i.) Secondly, through the inequality sign we have allowed for the possibility that more is produced in period t than is needed in period $t + 1$. This may happen because we have joint production. To produce certain commodities in sufficient quantities, it may be that we find ourselves with a surplus of other commodities. Such commodities will be free goods and their price zero.

Defining equilibrium growth the way we did in Chapter 15, Section 2, and denoting the growth rate g, the first condition for equilibrium growth is

$$[16.2] \qquad x_j{}^{t+1} = (1 + g)x_j{}^t \qquad j = 1, \ldots, m$$

Inserting Equations 16.2 in Equations 16.1 we obtain (compare Chapter 15, Equation 15.8)

$$[16.1'] \qquad \sum_{j=1}^{m} b_{ij}x_j{}^t \geqq (1 + g) \sum_{j=1}^{m} a_{ij}x_j{}^t \qquad i = 1, \ldots, n$$

which is von Neumann's first set of equilibrium conditions. Turning our attention to the second set, which states that in no process must revenues

[1] This assumption may be discarded without changing the results in any essential way.

exceed costs, we have (at constant prices)

[16.3]
$$\sum_{i=1}^{n} p_i{}^t b_{ij} \leqq (1 + r) \sum_{i=1}^{n} p_i{}^t a_{ij} \qquad j = 1, \ldots, m$$

where r is the rate of interest. Compare with Equations 15.9, which differs from Equations 16.3 in two respects. On the left side of Equations 16.3 we have a sum of output values, whereas in Equations 15.9 we simply had the price of the sector's output. In von Neumann's model a process may have many outputs, and the left side gives us the total revenue when the process operates at unit level. The right side is the sum of input values necessary when the process operates at this level, plus interests for one period. Secondly, we have in Equations 16.3 an inequality sign to allow for the possibility that a process, if used, may operate at a loss. Such a process will obviously not be used at all, however, and its activity level (x) will be zero.

Equations 16.1' and 16.3 are the model. Von Neumann proved that a solution exists to this model. We shall not concern ourself with the proof itself; it requires advanced mathematics. We simply take for granted that a solution (at positive or zero prices, and positive or zero quantities) does exist. We will then show that the rate of interest is equal to the rate of growth. The proof follows the same pattern as in Chapter 15. Multiply Equations 16.1' on both sides by $p_i{}^t$, and Equations 16.3 on both sides by $x_j{}^t$, and then add the left and the right sides of both sets of equations. Recall that if in Equation 16.1' the inequality sign holds for a certain commodity, then the corresponding p will be zero and the equation will disappear in the summation. Also, if in Equations 16.3 the inequality sign holds, the process will not be used; that is, the corresponding x will be zero and the equation will disappear. In this way all inequalities disappear in the summations. We are left then with two equations. (Compare Equations 15.10 and 15.11.)

[16.4]
$$\sum_{i=1}^{n} \sum_{j=1}^{m} b_{ij} x_j{}^t p_i{}^t = (1 + g) \sum_{i=1}^{n} \sum_{j=1}^{m} a_{ij} x_j{}^t p_i{}^t$$

[16.5]
$$\sum_{j=1}^{m} \sum_{i=1}^{n} p_i{}^t b_{ij} x_j{}^t = (1 + r) \sum_{j=1}^{m} \sum_{i=1}^{n} p_i{}^t a_{ij} x_j{}^t$$

Solving Equation 16.4 for g and Equation 16.5 for r, we find $g = r$.

2 / Properties of von Neumann equilibrium growth

Once again we find that the rate of interest equals the rate of growth, which again is equal to the rate of gross profits. The economic reasons for this result were stated in our discussion of the Leontief model in Chapter 15. In each actually used process, net profits are zero in equilibrium; the interest payments must therefore be equal to the difference between revenues and (other) costs. Since revenues are equal to the value of outputs, and costs (other than interests) are equal to the value of inputs, this difference also measures the rate of growth. The modifications concerning labor supply and extraneous consumption carry over to this model.

Secondly, we have the important new result that the equilibrium-growth rate g is the maximal proportional[1] growth rate that the system is technically capable of achieving.[2] The mathematical proof for this (and the following) proposition depends on the proof for the existence of a solution and is too complicated for this discussion. To make it comprehensible that growth is maximal, however, imagine that the system is in equilibrium growth at a lower rate than that which is maximal. It would then be profitable at the given prices to use processes with higher rates of growth (such processes would by hypothesis exist), which makes it clear that equilibrium growth with less than maximal proportional growth is impossible in this profit-maximizing system.

Thirdly, the equilibrium-growth price system has the minimum property that it makes the rate of interest the smallest one at which zero net profits prevail everywhere. As a corollary, it follows that the level of consumption is maximal at equilibrium growth; we shall have a look at this corollary in the next section.

3 / The neo-neoclassical theorem of maximal consumption in equilibrium growth

That consumption is maximal in a state of von Neumann equilibrium growth was not noticed by von Neumann himself, although it is implicit in the minimum-rate-of-interest property of his system. It has played a large role in recent growth theory, however, and appears to have been discovered by T. Swan (1956). The theorem is considered to be one of the more profound results attained by modern growth theory. It is known under the nickname "neo-neoclassical theorem," and has also been called "the golden rule of accumulation" (Phelps, 1961).

Various formulations of the theorem have been presented, and there has been some confusion about what are the necessary and sufficient conditions for maximal consumption in equilibrium growth. A usual formulation is that a maximum level of consumption will be reached if the rate of interest is equal to the rate of growth. In ideal competitive systems where no risk exists, and where no limitations on competition imply monopolistic profits,

[1] Although all outputs and inputs increase at the same rate g, some outputs may continuously be larger than the required inputs; these goods will be free goods.
[2] The problem of maximal growth did not appear in the dynamized Leontief model because there the techniques employed were assumed to have been given in advance.

we can insert the words "the rate of profits" instead of "the rate of interest" in this formulation. Solow (1962) has shown the minimum assumptions on which this proposition can be proved. He argues that if there are

(a) constant returns to scale, and

(b) all inputs are growing in the same proportion,

then the maximal level of consumption will be reached if the rate of interest (profits) equals the rate of growth. We shall see, however, that a little more is actually needed by way of assumptions.

Solow's proof is as follows: Consider the following general (implicit) production function

[16.6] $$P(q_1, \ldots, q_m; \dot{K}_1, \ldots, \dot{K}_s; K_1, \ldots, K_s; L) = 0$$

where q_i, $i = 1, \ldots, m$ denotes quantities (produced) of m consumer goods; $\dot{K}_i$, $i = 1, \ldots, s$ denotes quantities produced of s capital goods; K_i, $i = 1, \ldots, s$ denotes the existing stocks of the s capital goods. L is labor. We naturally have the same number s of capital goods in stock and capital goods produced. The symbol $\dot{K}$ should be read as dK/dt, the *net* production of a certain capital good being equal to the increase in the stock of that capital good. Net outputs are q_i and $_i\dot{K}$; K_i and L are inputs. The production function in Equation 16.6 allows for joint production and is assumed to be homogeneous of degree 1 in all inputs and outputs, so that there are constant returns to scale. Let us solve Equation 16.6 for q_1 to obtain

[16.6'] $$q_1 = T(q_2, \ldots, q_m; \dot{K}_1, \ldots, \dot{K}_s; K_1, \ldots, K_s; L)$$

which is also homogeneous of degree 1.

We shall assume now that the supply of labor grows, and has always grown, so that at any point of time t the quantity of labor $L = le^{nt}$, where l is a constant (equal to the supply of labor at $t = 0$), e is the base of natural logarithms, and n is the exogeneously given rate of growth of labor supply. We assume also that all else is growing and has always grown in the same proportion, so that at any time we will have

[16.7]
$$L = le^{nt}$$
$$q_i = c_i e^{nt}$$
$$K_i = k_i e^{nt}$$
$$\dot{K}_i = nk_i e^{nt}$$

recalling that $\dot{K}_i = dK_i/dt = nk_i e^{nt}$. Inserting these expressions into Equation 16.6', and dividing through by e^{nt}, we obtain (see the definition of homogeneity in Chapter 5, Section 3):

[16.6''] $$c_1 = T(c_2, \ldots, c_m; nk_1, \ldots, nk_s; k_1, \ldots, k_s; l)$$

We shall now consider the composition of the other consumer goods; that is, $c_2, \ldots, c_m$, as given, and ask for conditions to maximize c_1 through changing the $k_i s$, the procedure being symmetric for the other consumer goods. Recalling that $K_i = k_i e^{nt}$, we find through differentiation

[16.8]
$$n \frac{\partial T}{\partial \dot{K}_i} + \frac{\partial T}{\partial K_i} = 0 \qquad i = 1, \ldots, s$$

or

[16.9]
$$n = - \frac{\partial T / \partial K_i}{\partial T / \partial \dot{K}_i} = \frac{\partial \dot{K}_i}{\partial K_i} \qquad i = 1, \ldots, s$$

The right sides of the s expressions are the marginal productivities of capital goods (stocks) in terms of themselves, the so-called "own-rates of interest." We have thus found that a necessary condition for consumption to be a maximum is that the own-rates of interest, that is, the physical productivities of capital, must be equal to the rate of growth of the labor supply. For these own-rates to be equal to the money rate of interest (the rate of interest on money loans), however, we must add an assumption of perfect competitive equilibrium with constant prices over time (Dorfman, Samuelson, and Solow, 1958, p. 318). It is easily seen that these assumptions are fulfilled by von Neumann's model which must accordingly imply maximal consumption.

References

CHAMPERNOWNE, D. C.: "A Note on J. von Neumann's Article," *The Review of Economic Studies*, vol. 13(1), no. 33, 1945–46.

DORFMAN, R., P. A. SAMUELSON, and R. SOLOW, *Linear Programming and Economic Analysis*, McGraw-Hill, New York, 1958.

HAHN, R. F., and R. C. O. MATTHEWS, "The Theory of Growth: A Survey," *Economic Journal*, vol. 14, no. 296, December, 1964.

KOOPMANS, T.: "Economic Growth at a Maximal Rate," *The Quarterly Journal of Economics*, vol. 78, no. 3, August, 1964.

PHELPS, E.: "The Golden Rule of Accumulation: A Fable for Growth Men," *American Economic Review*, vol. 51, no. 4, September, 1961.

SWAN, T.: "Economic Growth and Capital Accumulation," *The Economic Record*, vol. 32, no. 63, November, 1956.

"Symposium on Production and Economic Growth," with contributions by Arrow, Kaldor and Mirrlees, Samuelson, Solow, Joan Robinson, Meade, Champernowne, Black, Stone, and Brown, in *Review of Economic Studies*, vol. 29, no. 80, June, 1962.

VON NEUMANN, J.: "A Model of General Economic Equilibrium," *The Review of Economic Studies*, vol. 13(1), no. 33, 1945–46.

Walrasian model with capital à la Wicksell

17

Both Leontief's dynamized, closed model and von Neumann's model are offsprings of neoclassical equilibrium theory. Von Neumann's model is powerful and deals with several problems that traditional neoclassical theory was unable to handle. Yet its linear form, treatment of households, consumption, and supply of labor, and other special features, make it natural despite Malinvaud's and Morishima's amendments to seek more generalized equilibrium-growth models. One of the basic problems is the treatment of capital and capital accumulation in such processes. Leontief's closed model could only deal with this problem in a rudimentary way; it did not include fixed capital. Von Neumann solved the problem of fixed capital ingeniously by considering durable producers' goods as both inputs and outputs of the production processes in which they participate. Intertemporal general equilibrium systems, such as, for example, Hicks' futures economy (Chapter 7, Section 5), incorporate demand for and supply of durable producers' goods and cause no problems in explaining both purchases and sales, and holdings of those goods (see, e.g., Malinvaud, 1953, 1965). The real problems arise when theory insists on working with the concept of capital as a factor of production analogous to labor, land, raw materials, and other well-defined, easily measurable inputs. A heated discussion has been going on during the last two decades about the possibilities of defining a concept of aggregate real capital to which marginal productivity theory applies (see the survey by Harcourt, 1969). Of the two neoclassical models we shall consider in this and the following chapter, the first avoids the problem by abstaining from working with the concept of total real capital, the second, simply by ignoring it.

In the present chapter we consider the general equilibrium system that was presented by Erik Lindahl (1929, 1939) and could be characterized as a Walrasian system with capital à la Wicksell. It is completely disaggregated and does not need the concept of aggregate real capital; in this respect it resembles von Neumann's system. Instead of treating the individual durable producers' goods as inputs (and outputs) in the production process, however, they are conceived of as stored services of land and labor. This way of analyzing capital goods was introduced by E. von Böhm-Bawerk (1888, 1921) and further developed by Wicksell (1907, 1934). It is reconciled with marginal productivity theory through ascribing productivity to the passage of time, that is, to the process of storage. Its major disadvantage is that it classifies capital goods in an abstract way that does not easily lend itself to empirical application and measurement. Lindahl developed his model mainly for the stationary state, but it is easily carried over to the problem of equilibrium growth.

1 / The concept of capital as stored services

Capital goods may be conceived of as stored services of land and labor (that is, primary, original services) that are invested in an investment process. After a number of years t they mature into commodities for final consumption, perhaps in direct cooperation with original services, or with other stored services. The existing technology is assumed to permit many different processes with t varying from zero, if we include processes using no stored services, to T, which may be any large, finite number. In equilibrium, each process must be used to a point where the value of its marginal product is equal to the value of the original inputs plus accrued interest. In each line of investment, which is characterized by the original service it uses as input, and by its t, new investments take place concurrently with capital consumption ("maturing").

The investment process, with the stocks of stored services and their composition on various processes and age groups, can be illustrated by Wicksell's "triangle." In Figure 17.1 we assume that t runs from zero to 3. The figure applies to an arbitrarily chosen original service j; there are m different original services so that m diagrams such as in Figure 17.1 could be drawn.

$Q_j{}^{t,\tau}$ denotes quantities of original services, j being the number of the service, t the investment process (characterized by the length of the investment period) in which Q_j is used as input, and τ the age of the input. The price of current original service j (expressed in terms of a *numéraire*) is Π_j, assumed to be constant over time. Thus, $Q_j{}^{2,1}$ is the quantity of service j invested (stored) one year ago in an investment process that lasts two years. The original investment costs of $Q_j{}^{2,1}$ were $Q_j{}^{2,1}\Pi_j$, and its present value, including accrued interests, is $Q_j{}^{2,1}\Pi_j(1 + r)$, where r is the rate of interest per period.

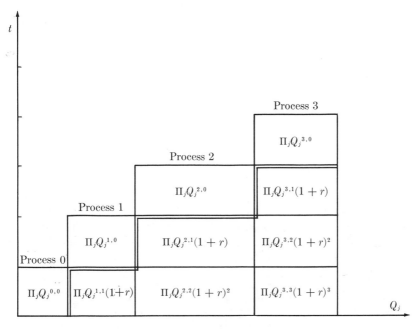

FIGURE *17.1*

The investments made this year consist of the quantities $Q_j^{3,0}$, $Q_j^{2,0}$, and $Q_j^{1,0}$. The original services are also used in direct production, process zero, without being stored; the input here is $Q_j^{0,0}$. We have then

$$Q_j = Q_j^{0,0} + Q_j^{1,0} + Q_j^{2,0} + Q_j^{3,0}$$

where Q_j is the total quantity of service j available. The total income from sales of the original service is $Q_j \Pi_j$.

All processes result in outputs of consumer goods. The total cost value, including accrued interest, of the service j, maturing in a given period, is

$$Q_j^{0,0}\Pi_j + Q_j^{1,1}\Pi_j(1+r) + Q_j^{2,2}\Pi_j(1+r)^2 + Q_j^{3,3}\Pi_j(1+r)^3$$

that is, the total value of the lower row in Figure 17.1.

The value of the stock of capital, that is, of all stocks of the stored service j at the beginning of the period just before consumer goods mature and investments are made, is the value-sum of all the elements in the "triangle" under the double line. For example, the value of stored services in investment process 3 is

$$Q_j^{3,1}\Pi_j(1+r) + Q_j^{3,2}\Pi_j(1+r)^2 + Q_j^{3,3}\Pi_j(1+r)^3$$

and for all the three storing processes the capital value is

$$\sum_{t=1}^{3} \sum_{\tau=1}^{t} Q_j^{t,\tau} \Pi_j (1+r)^\tau$$

Immediately after the consumer goods have matured and investments have been made, the capital value will be

$$\sum_{t=1}^{3} \sum_{\tau=1}^{t} Q_j^{t,\tau-1} \Pi_j (1+r)^{\tau-1}$$

During the following period interest is accruing, and at the end of the period capital value is again expressed by the previous formula.

Similar formulae hold for each individual original service.

In the general case we assume that $j = 1, \ldots, m$, and t and $\tau = 1, \ldots, T$. If we now let K_{00} and K_{01} denote capital value at the beginning of period zero, before and after maturing of consumer goods and investment of original services, respectively, we have

[17.1]
$$K_{00} = \sum_{j=1}^{m} \sum_{t=1}^{T} \sum_{\tau=1}^{t} \Pi_j Q_j^{t,\tau} (1+r)^\tau$$

and

[17.2]
$$K_{01} = \sum_{j=1}^{m} \sum_{t=1}^{T} \sum_{\tau=1}^{t} \Pi_j Q_j^{t,\tau-1} (1+r)^{\tau-1}$$

Total income from capital during the period is then

[17.3]
$$rK_{01} = r \sum_{j=1}^{m} \sum_{t=1}^{T} \sum_{\tau=1}^{t} \Pi_j Q_j^{t,\tau-1} (1+r)^{\tau-1}$$

In the stationary state where $Q_j^{t,0} = Q_j^{t,1} = \cdots = Q_j^{t,t}$ for all j and t, we can simplify Equations 17.2 and 17.3 to

[17.2']
$$K_{01} = \sum_{j=1}^{m} \sum_{t=1}^{T} \Pi_j Q_j^{t} \frac{(1+r)^t - 1}{r}$$

and

[17.3']
$$rK_{01} = \sum_{j=1}^{m} \sum_{t=1}^{T} \Pi_j Q_j^{t} [(1+r)^t - 1]$$

in which the expression Q_j^t denotes the quantity of original service j invested in process t at each period.

2 / Lindahl's model for a stationary state

Lindahl's model is easily recognized as an amended version of the original Walrasian model, which we discussed in Chapter 3. There are no intermediary inputs, but we have now stored services of primary factors. There are no cash holdings, but saving and investment as well as borrowing and lending may take place.

The number of consumer goods is n. The demand equations correspond to those in the original Walrasian system (Equations 3.1), except that the rate of interest now enters the demand function as a determinant. Money is not incorporated into the system, and we therefore choose service m as *numéraire*, π_i and Π_j being the *numéraire* prices of consumer goods and original services, respectively. We have then

[17.4] $q_i = q_i(\pi_1, \ldots, \pi_n; \Pi_1, \ldots, \Pi_{m-1}; r)$ $i = 1, \ldots, n$

The equilibrium condition for consumer goods is, as usual, equality of price and costs; that is, zero profit. (Compare Equations 3.2 and 15.9.) We assume that current original services and stored services of all ages cooperate in the process of production, and that original services of all kinds and ages may thus be used to produce any particular consumer good. The technical coefficient $a_{ij}{}^t$ denotes the quantity of original service i of age t needed for producing one unit of consumer good j. Since stored services only mature the last year of their storage period, we need only one time superscript. The equilibrium conditions then, are (compare Equations 14.10)

[17.5] $$\pi_i = \sum_{j=1}^{m} \sum_{t=0}^{T} a_{ji}{}^t \Pi_j (1 + r)^t \qquad i = 1, \ldots, n$$

Technical substitution is possible and the technical coefficients depend upon factor prices and the rate of interest, but not upon commodity prices. Thus there are constant returns to scale (see Equation 3.3). This assumption is not essential in the case of the stationary state, but we need it when we extend the model to equilibrium growth.

[17.6] $a_{ij}{}^t = a_{ij}{}^t(\Pi_1, \ldots, \Pi_{m-1}; r)$ $\begin{array}{l} i = 1, \ldots, n \\ j = 1, \ldots, m \\ t = 0, \ldots, T \end{array}$

When compared with the Walrasian system, two differences are apparent: the rate of interest appears as a determinant of the choice of technique, and we have a new dimension—time.

The supply equations for primary, or original, services also correspond closely to the Walrasian system (see Equations 3.4), the only difference being the inclusion of the rate on interest.

[17.7] $Q_j = Q_j(\pi_1, \ldots, \pi_n; \Pi_1, \ldots, \Pi_{m-1}; r)$ $j = 1, \ldots, m$

The equilibrium conditions for the market of original services express that total supply equals demand, and that such services are demanded partly for direct use in current production and partly for storage in time-consuming processes. With a notation already explained we have

[17.8] $$Q_j = \sum_{t=0}^{T} Q_j^{t,0} \qquad j = 1, \ldots, m$$

where the right side is the demand for original services from the $m(T+1)$ processes.

As a condition of stationarity, there is the further requirement that the same quantity of each kind of original service be invested in the various investment processes as used in current production; that is, that mature as consumer goods.

[17.9] $$Q_j^{t,0} = \sum_{i=1}^{n} a_{ji}{}^t q_i \qquad \begin{aligned} t &= 0, 1, \ldots, T \\ j &= 1, \ldots, m \end{aligned}$$

Equations 17.9 secure that all stocks of stored services remain unchanged in physical terms, which obviously implies that net investment, both physically and in value terms, be zero. We must make sure, however, that net savings are also zero. Thus far we have written no equations for the credit market. Since there are no cash holdings in the system, however, the credit market can be dealt with in terms of savings and investments. (See Equation 12.1.) To complete the system we must therefore write an equation that expresses the equality of investments and savings. Since we know that the stationarity conditions in Equation 17.9 imply zero net investment, it is simpler to use the condition net saving equals zero. Accordingly, we have

[17.10] $$\sum_{j=1}^{m} \Pi_j Q_j + r K_{01} - \sum_{i=1}^{n} \pi_i q_i = 0$$

or, inserting Equation 17.3', and utilizing Equation 17.9, recalling that in the stationary state all $Q_j^{t\tau}$, $\tau = 1, \ldots, t$, are equal, we have

[17.10'] $$\sum_{j=1}^{m} \Pi_j Q_j + \sum_{j=1}^{m} \sum_{t=1}^{T} \sum_{i=1}^{n} \Pi_j a_{ji}{}^t q_i [(1+r)^t - 1] - \sum_{i=1}^{n} \pi_i q_i = 0$$

which states that total factor income plus interest income from capital, minus total value of consumption, equals zero. It would be a mistake to think that this is the budget restriction of the households. Since enterprises are assumed to pay all gross profits to households-owners as interests, enterprises can only expand; that is, increase the value of the stocks of stored services if the households deliver the necessary finance through net savings. If we had introduced the credit market explicitly instead of working with investments and savings it would have been necessary to introduce some kind of claims on enterprises to be kept by the households. The total value of these claims (= total capital value) could then be introduced as a separate argument in the demand and supply functions. But we shall not elaborate on this hypothesis, however.

We are now prepared to count equations and unknowns. Equations 17.4, 17.5, 17.6, 17.7, 17.8, 17.9, and 17.10' furnish us with $2n + 2m +$

$m(T + 1) + nm(T + 1) + 1$ equations. Altogether, the unknowns q_i, π_i, Π_j, r, $a_{ij}{}^t$, Q_j, and $Q_j{}^{t,0}$ are $2n + 2m + m(T + 1) + nm(T + 1)$. By Walras' law, one equation follows from the rest and we thus have the same number of equations and unknowns. We shall not write Walras' law, but it is easy to show, for example, that if the rest of the system is in equilibrium, Equation 17.10′ is automatically fulfilled. Multiply Equation 17.5 on both sides by q_i and sum over i. Then multiply Equation 17.8 on both sides by Π_j, insert Equation 17.9, and sum over j. Inserting the expressions for $\Sigma \pi_i q_i$ and $\Sigma \Pi_j Q_j$ thus obtained in Equation 17.10′, the left side of this equation vanishes. We could therefore have omitted Equation 17.10′. Indeed, we could have omitted any one of the equations.

The model determines, among other things, all the stocks of stored services; that is, all the component parts of what is loosely called "the stock of real capital" are thus endogenously determined. We do not work with such a concept, however, and it is entirely superfluous. We do work with the concept of the total value of capital (in terms of the *numéraire*). (See Equations 17.1 and 17.2.) In contradistinction to "total real capital," total current value of capital is a clear, well-defined concept.

There is nothing to indicate that the rate of interest should be zero in this model for the stationary state, although the possibility cannot be excluded, of course. In this respect the model differs from the von Neumann model.

To conclude our discussion of the stationary state we observe that the absolute money prices can, as usual, be determined by adding the equation of exchange and assuming the quantity of money to be given. The model could easily be extended in the direction of the Patinkin model, but this would add nothing new to the picture.

3 / Lindahl's model in equilibrium growth

The stationary state is interesting and useful, not because stationary societies are very common nowadays, but because they are a convenient starting point for the discussion of evolutionary economies. Lindahl indicated (1939, p. 318) that his model could easily be extended to a situation wherein "the supply of all factors and the demand for consumption goods show a *proportional* growth or diminution, while the technical coefficients remain unchanged . . . prices will also evidently be unchanged . . ."

Lindahl's statement can hardly be correct. In a growing economy, savings must be positive and the time structure of capital must be different, which must affect relative demands for consumer goods and original services, and influence relative prices and, hence, the technical coefficients. Lindahl did not develop the growth model explicitly, but it seems worthwhile to have a brief look at it.

If the driving force in the growth process is an autonomous increase in population at a rate of μ per period, we may assume that at given prices and interest rates, both demand for consumer goods and supply of original services will grow at the same rate. This amounts to assuming that individuals in the population are identical with respect to preferences; we disregard the effects on consumption and factor supply that may follow from a change in the age structure of population. Using prefixes 0 and 1 to denote the period considered, we assume

[17.11] $^1q_i = (1 + \mu)^0 q_i(\pi_1, \ldots, \pi_n; \Pi_1, \ldots, \Pi_{m-1}; r)$

$$i = 1, \ldots, n$$

and

[17.12] $^1Q_j = (1 + \mu)^0 Q_j(\pi_1, \ldots, \pi_n; \Pi_1, \ldots, \Pi_{m-1}; r)$

$$j = 1, \ldots, m$$

At this point we must obviously disregard land and other natural resources, or consider them free services available in unlimited quantities. Incidentally, this is one of the assumptions that deprives the concept of equilibrium growth of much of its interest. Equilibrium growth may have applied to the United States before the time of the last frontier!

The system must be affected in another way, as well. If production of consumer goods is to grow proportionately, the amount of stored services that mature in a period must be 100 μ per cent larger than in the previous period. At constant returns to scale, this is possible only if the amount of original services stored one period earlier are 100 μ per cent larger than the latest maturing services. Turning again to Wicksell's triangle, and concentrating for example on process 3, we see that proportional growth requires amounts of stored services in the pipeline as shown in Figure 17.2.

This figure is a picture of the stocks of stored services at the beginning of period zero, where the top cell is the investment of original services and the bottom cell is the maturing consumer goods originating from this process and this service in period zero. The expression in the top cell can also be written $\Pi_j a_{ji}^3 \, ^0q_i(1 + \mu)^3$. It follows that instead of the condition of stationarity in Equation 17.9, we now have the equilibrium-growth condition

[17.9'] $Q_j^{t,0} = \sum_{i=1}^{n} (1 + \mu)^t a_{ji}{}^t q_i \qquad \begin{matrix} j = 1, \ldots, m \\ t = 0, \ldots, T \end{matrix}$

The equilibrium-growth system thus consists of Equations 17.4, 17.5, 17.6, 17.7, 17.8, and 17.9'. They contain the same number of equations and unknowns, given the rate of population growth μ. Inspection shows immediately that if the system has a solution in *numéraire* prices and interest rate, and quantities of consumer goods and original services, the solution will be unaffected if we multiply all q_i and Q_j by $1 + \mu$. Hence, it holds for any period, and the prices and interest rates will be unchanged over time. But

Process 3

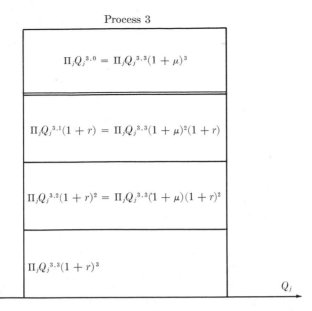

$$\Pi_j Q_j{}^{3,0} = \Pi_j Q_j{}^{3,3}(1 + \mu)^3$$

$$\Pi_j Q_j{}^{3,1}(1 + r) = \Pi_j Q_j{}^{3,3}(1 + \mu)^2(1 + r)$$

$$\Pi_j Q_j{}^{3,2}(1 + r)^2 = \Pi_j Q_j{}^{3,3}(1 + \mu)(1 + r)^2$$

$$\Pi_j Q_j{}^{3,3}(1 + r)^3$$

Q_j

FIGURE *17.2*

the solution certainly depends on μ because of Equations 17.9'. Since money prices are assumed to be constant, the quantity of money must grow at the same rate μ. We could also add the equilibrium conditions for the demand for and supply of loans. Since investments are now positive, the equilibrium condition is savings equals investments; that is, $S = I$. With our earlier notation this equilibrium condition can be written for period zero as

[17.10″] $$\sum_{j=1}^{m} \Pi_j{}^0 Q_j + rK_{-1,1} - \sum_{i=1}^{n} \pi_i{}^0 q_i = \mu K_{-1,1}$$

where $K_{-1,1}$ is the value of capital at the beginning of period -1 immediately after maturing of consumer goods and investments in that period. Interests are paid at the end of the period so that income from capital at the beginning of period zero is $rK_{-1,1}$. Since all component parts of the stock of capital increase in proportion to population, and money prices are constant, investments must be $\mu K_{-1,1}$. Forming the expression for the value of capital with Figure 17.2 as a starting point, and inserting this expression with Equations 17.8, 17.9', and 17.4, we are able to show that Equation 17.10″ vanishes identically and thus follows from the rest of the system.

4 / Interest rate and growth rate again

Assume now that the model has a meaningful solution. The rate of interest will in general differ from the rate of (population) growth. So far, the Lindahl model differs from the von Neumann model. Nevertheless, there is a striking similarity between the two models. Rewrite Equation 17.10″ as

$$[17.10''']\qquad \sum_{j=1}^{m} \Pi_j{}^0 Q_j - \sum_{i=1}^{n} \pi_i{}^0 q_i = (\mu - r)K_{-1,1}$$

From Equation 17.10‴ it follows that if in our equilibrium solution the rate of interest is equal to the rate of growth $r = \mu$, then the left side of the equation must be zero; that is, the total value of consumption is equal to total factor income, with the implication that savings are equal to total profits (interest income of capital). If the rate of growth exceeds the rate of interest, then savings must exceed profits; and vice versa, if the rate of interest exceeds the rate of growth, consumption exceeds factor income, and profits are partly consumed; in other words, there is "extraneous" consumption. The logics are reversed, but otherwise the results are identical to those obtained on the basis of the von Neumann model. Von Neumann assumed that all profits are saved and that consumption equals factor income, and showed then that growth and interest rates are equal. We do not need von Neumann's model to prove this, however, since it follows from Equation 17.10‴. If the left side of Equation 17.10‴ is zero, the right side must also be zero; that is, $r = \mu$. Moreover, if we denote the difference between total consumption and factor income C_{cap}, then we can immediately rewrite Equation 17.10‴ as

$$[17.10^{IV}]\qquad r\,\frac{rK_{-1,1} - C_{cap}}{rK_{-1,1}} = \mu$$

The fraction on the left side is the ratio of savings over profits. We have thus arrived at the same expression we found in the dynamized Leontief and von Neumann models in Equation 15.12‴.

There is nothing surprising in this result. The point here is that we do not need the rest of the system to write Equations 17.10″ and 17.10‴. The assumption of equilibrium growth implies, by definition, that savings are equal to investments. It also implies that there are no profits over and above interests on capital. We know, moreover, that at constant returns to scale all stocks of capital goods (stored services) must increase at the equilibrium-growth rate; that is, investments must be equal to the growth rate times the total value of capital. These assumptions hold true for any equilibrium-growth system. This is all we need by the way of assumptions to write Equation 17.10″. We need the rest of the model to know whether we shall argue from the left side of Equation 17.10‴ to the right side, or vice versa, or from the model to both sides simultaneously.

References

BÖHM-BAWERK, E. VON: *Positive Theorie des Kapitales*, 4th ed., Gustav Fischer, Jena, 1921. First edition, 1888.

HARCOURT, G. C.: "Some Cambridge Controversies in the Theory of Capital," *The Journal of Economic Literature*, vol. 1, no. 2, June, 1969.

LINDAHL, ERIK: *Studies in the Theory of Money and Capital*, George Allen and Unwin, London, 1939. Part 2, "The Rate of Interest and the Price Level," was originally published as *Penningpolitikens medel*, Gleerup, Lund, 1930. Part 3, "The Place of Capital in the Theory of Price," appeared first as "Prisbildningsproblemets uppläggning från kapitalteoretisk synpunkt," *Ekonomisk Tidskrift*, vol. 31, no. 2, 1929.

MALINVAUD, E.: "Capital Accumulation and Efficient Allocation of Resources," *Econometrica*, vol. 21, no. 2, April, 1953.

—: "Interest Rates in the Allocation of Resources," in F. H. Hahn and F. P. R. Brechling (eds.), *The Theory of Interest Rates*, Macmillan, London, 1965.

WICKSELL, K.: *Lectures on Political Economy*, vol. 1, Routledge and Kegan Paul, London, 1934. First Swedish edition, 1907.

Aggregated
growth models

18

The equilibrium-growth models considered in the previous chapters were completely disaggregated. Much of the discussion of this topic has, however, been conducted in terms of highly aggregated models, one- or two-sector models, a host of which has come to light during the past two decades. They can be classified into two main groups, labeled the "neoclassical" and "Keynesian" growth models. The neoclassical models are based on all the standard neoclassical assumptions; their most influential representative is a model presented by R. Solow (1956). The Keynesian models are loosely related to certain ideas in Keynes' *Treatise on Money* and discard neoclassical marginal productivity theory; they assume full employment and the equilibrating mechanism is based on shifts in the income distribution and differences between the propensities to consume of wage earners and profit earners (Kaldor, 1957; see also Kaldor and Mirrlees, 1962).

Here we shall concentrate upon the neoclassical, aggregated models in Solow's version. First it may be useful, however, to consider which kinds of changes and extensions are needed to convert a typical aggregated, static equilibrium model into a growth equilibrium model. When we have seen how this is done, Solow's model—more concentrated and less explicit—is easier to comprehend. We return, therefore, to Klein's static, neoclassical model which was used in Chapter 11 for the comparison with static Keynesian unemployment theory.

1 / The stationary state

Klein's neoclassical model as described by Equations 11.1 to 11.9 is essentially a short-term model. Its short-term nature manifests itself primarily in the treatment of productive capital, which is considered given and constant and does not appear explicitly in the equations. Investments do take place, however, and the model determines their size. If net investments are positive, the stock of capital must increase, which seems to contradict the assumption of a given stock of capital. This "paradox" is usually cleared up by assuming that investments do not add instantaneously to productive capacity. Assuming the gestation lag of investments to be one period of time, the stock of capital can be considered given within each single period. The production function in Equation 11.6 could, of course, be written as $q = \varphi(K,N)$ instead of $\phi(N)$, K being the physical stock of capital; but at a constant K this would make no difference to the short-term equilibrium solution. At the beginning of the following period, the stock of capital must, however, increase from K to $K + \Delta K$, where ΔK is the (net) investments embarked upon during the previous period; the short-term equilibrium position changes accordingly. In this way a process over time will be generated. This process may have a stationary solution with a constant stock of capital, production, income, and so forth; or, it may end in a state of equilibrium growth with all physical quantities increasing at the same rate, and with constant prices and interest rate. Solow's model describes this dynamic process in a simplified way. Our present concern is only to describe the final long-term equilibrium state and this can be done by simpler devices that relate the growth theory directly to short-term static theory.

Let us first consider a possible stationary state. Such a state can, of course, only exist if there are no exogenous changes in the labor force, technical knowledge, and so forth. A further condition for a stationary state is that the stock of capital is constant, requiring that no net investments take place. For convenience, assume that Klein's model is dealing with net savings, investments, and income. Since our aim is only to set out the conditions for a stationary state, we replace the investment behavior equation (11.2) by the stationarity condition $I/p = 0$. We must, however, also make sure that the size of the stock of capital is such that profits are at their maximum. Otherwise the enterprises will have no motive for keeping this particular stock of capital; in the short run the stock of capital cannot be changed and no such condition was necessary. Total profits may be written as $pq - wN - vK$, v being the money rental per period, that is, the price of hiring one unit of physical capital during one period. The necessary conditions for a profit maximum become $w/p = \varphi'_N(K,N)$, which replaces Equation 11.7, and $v/p = \varphi'_K(K,N)$, which states that the real rental of capital is equal to its marginal productivity. We have thus two new unknowns K and v, but only one additional equation $v/p = \varphi'_K$. Since real capital can be substituted for financial capital, equilibrium also requires that the rate of return on real capital equals the rate of return on financial assets. Assuming a constant price level and disregarding depreciation, this means that $r = v/p$, which, incidentally, ensures zero net profits in production (after payment or imputation of interest on capital), as we should have it in a truly competitive equilibrium. The number of equations is hereby brought up to match the number of unknowns.

We have thus transformed Klein's neoclassical static short-term equilibrium model into a long-term stationary state model which determines the stock of capital and the price of its services, the rental, in addition to the other endogenous variables.

2 / The state of equilibrium growth in a monetary economy

The stationary state is a limiting case of equilibrium growth with the growth rate at zero. The starting point for the construction of a neoclassical aggregated growth model with a positive growth rate is the assumption that, *ceteris paribus*, the supply of labor is growing at a certain natural rate μ, so that Equation 11.8 must be replaced by

[11.8a] $$N^s = e^{\mu t}\psi(w/p)$$

The natural growth of labor supply may be related to population growth but may also be interpreted as an increase of labor efficiency due to technical progress. The supply of labor at time $t = 0$ is $\psi(w/p)$.

In a state of equilibrium growth all volume entities change by definition at the same rate. Productive capital thus must grow at the same rate as labor supply, that is $\Delta K/K = \mu$. Letting I/p denote real investments in productive equipment, we have $\Delta K = I/p$, or $I/p = \mu K$. We replace Equation 11.2 by this expression. We must also allow for a possible increase in the supply of money M. Assuming that it increases through income transfers from the government to the private sector, disposable income may be written as $Y + \epsilon M$, where ϵ is the rate of increase of the quantity of money M. It follows that the savings function $f(r, Y/p)$ should be replaced by $f[r, (Y + \epsilon M)/p]$. Likewise, part of the savings must now be used for financing the increase of cash balances. Instead of $I = S$, Equation 11.3 becomes $I + \epsilon M = S$. In Equation 11.4 the supply of money M could alternatively be written as $e^{\epsilon t}M_0$, where M_0 is the quantity of money at $t = 0$. The production function is as above $\varphi(K,N)$ and the necessary conditions for profit maximum $w/p = \varphi'_N$ and $v/p = \varphi'_K$. Adding the equilibrium condition $r = v/p$, we have all that we need by way of formal changes to transform Klein's static, neoclassical model into an equilibrium-growth model. To ensure that the model thus arrived at really is capable of being in equilibrium growth at constant prices, some further specifications are needed, however. To understand why this is so, it may be helpful to write the complete modified system:

[11.1a] $$\frac{S}{p} = f\left(r, \frac{Y + \epsilon M}{p}\right)$$

[11.2a]
$$\frac{I}{p} = \mu K$$

[11.3a]
$$S = I + \epsilon M$$

[11.4]
$$\frac{M}{p} = L\left(r, \frac{Y}{p}\right)$$

[11.5]
$$Y = pq$$

[11.6a]
$$q = \varphi(K,N)$$

[11.7a]
$$\frac{w}{p} = \varphi'_N(K,N)$$

[11.7b]
$$\frac{v}{p} = \varphi'_K(K,N)$$

[11.7c]
$$r = v/p$$

[11.8a]
$$N^s = e^{\mu t}\psi\left(\frac{w}{p}\right)$$

[11.9]
$$N = N^s$$

The system now consists of eleven equations in the eleven endogenous variables Y, S, I, K, q, r, p, w, v, N, N^s. The equations for the credit market are left out by virtue of Walras' law, the usual method in Keynesian models. The parameter t indicates time; μ and ϵ are given constants. For $\mu = 0$ and $\epsilon = 0$ the system describes the stationary state discussed in the previous section. We assume now that μ is positive. The value of ϵ is given, too; we shall find that for the system to be in equilibrium growth at constant prices we must have $\mu = \epsilon$. This is, of course, also what intuition tells us; indeed, as we shall see in Section 6, the system is only well specified for this particular case.

Assume now that we have solved the system and found all the equilibrium values of the endogenous variables at a certain arbitrary moment of time $t = t_0$. At the equilibrium values w and p, the supply of labor N^s is growing at the rate μ according to Equation 11.8a. Recalling that we are looking for an equilibrium solution in which all volume entities increase at the same rate over time, all prices and the rate of interest being constant, the question is now what will happen to the other endogenous volume variables when the supply of labor is growing autonomously at the rate of μ, granted that w, v, p, and r are kept at their initial equilibrium values? By Equation 11.9 actual employment will also grow at the rate μ, and by Equation 11.2a we have in advance ensured that productive capital K is growing at the same rate, too. From Equation 11.6a it follows that total output q will grow at the same rate, provided we assume that the production function is homogeneous of degree 1, which is our first additional assumption. With employment and capital growing at the same rate, Equations 11.7a and 11.7b will then be fulfilled at unchanged w/p and v/p because the first derivatives of a function homogeneous of degree 1 are homogeneous of degree zero. It follows, furthermore, from Equation 11.5, that at given p, Y will increase with q at the rate μ. Consider then the savings-investments relations in Equations 11.1a to 11.3a.

Investments in productive equipment were assumed to increase at the rate μ, because the capital stock is required to increase at that rate (Equation 11.2a). If we now make our second additional assumption, that the quantity of money M increases at the same rate as I, that is $\epsilon = \mu$, total investments (investments in productive capital plus hoarding) increase at the rate μ. To ensure that real savings increase at the same rate, we must make our third additional assumption, that the savings function is homogeneous of degree 1 in disposable income. If at given r and p, both Y and M increase at the rate of μ, savings must then do the same, and since in the initial equilibrium situation savings and total investments were equal, they must continue to be so. We are then left with the money market as described by Equation 11.4. We shall now make our fourth additional assumption, that the liquidity-preference function is homogeneous of degree 1 in Y. With Y growing at the rate μ, r and p being constant, the demand for money will then grow at the same rate, and Equation 11.4 will be fulfilled at unchanged r and p. The supply of money has already been assumed to be increased by the monetary authorities at the rate μ, that is, $M = e^{\mu t} M_0$.

With our four additional assumptions we can thus be sure that if at an arbitrary point of time t_0 the system has an equilibrium solution, it will continue to be in equilibrium with all real quantities increasing over time at the rate of μ, all prices and the interest rate remaining constant; indeed, the system must then always have been in equilibrium growth at constant prices.

The additional homogeneity assumptions we were compelled to adopt to make the system "work," not only with respect to the production function but also for some behaviorial equations, are characteristic of equilibrium-growth models. If we choose to specify the model so that both real capital and real balances appear in the savings and liquidity-preference functions—in accordance with the generally accepted hypothesis that total wealth and its composition influence demand and supply—we would obviously have to extend the homogeneity assumption to include Y/p, K, and M/p. (Obviously, this assumption cannot be applied to the labor supply function.) Through division by N^s or K the system may be expressed exclusively on a per capita or per unit of capital basis; this may be convenient for analytical purposes (see below, Sections 4 and 5). The majority of models presented in the literature have actually been formulated in this way.

The model can be studied for the effects of disturbances, for instance, a change in the savings function. The rate of growth μ is given exogenously and cannot be affected by such disturbances, but crucial variables such as income per capita Y/N, or capital intensity K/N will take on new equilibrium values. The effects can be calculated by straightforward differentiation, but without additional assumptions about the signs or values of partial derivatives we may not be able to determine even the signs of the effects. The situation is the same as in traditional multiplier theory. We notice, incidentally, that since the system is homogeneous of zero degree in the quantity of money, money income, prices, wage rate, and money rental of capital, a discrete increase in the quantity of money will lead to a corresponding increase in price, wage rate, money rental, and money income, leaving all real variables and the rate of interest unchanged. We shall continue our discussion of the effects of money on the state of equilibrium growth in Section 6 below.

3 / Neoclassical equilibrium growth and the Harrod-Domar model

An important feature of neoclassical equilibrium-growth models is that both the stock of capital and real output (income) are endogenously determined variables. The capital-output ratio is therefore endogenously determined, too. If at time t_0, the equilibrium solutions for real income and capital are Y_0/p_0 and K_0, respectively, we can calculate the capital-output ratio as $\sigma = K_0/(Y_0/p_0)$, which is not an *a priori* given constant but depends upon the solution of the system as a whole. Nevertheless, in equilibrium growth σ is in fact constant over time because Y and K expand at the same rate, and p is constant. We find something similar for the savings ratio measured upon disposable income $s = S/(Y + \epsilon M)$. Savings depend, *inter alia*, upon the rate of interest, and so does the savings ratio, of course. In equilibrium growth, however, both r and p are constant; thanks to the assumed homogeneity of the savings function in the disposable income, and the assumption that the quantity of money increases at the rate of μ, savings increase at the same proportion as disposable income, and their ratio remains constant over time. The constancy of σ and s over time is an equilibrium property of the system as a whole.

Moreover, since in equilibrium growth $S = I + \mu M$, and $I/p = \mu K$ (Equations 11.3a and 11.2a), we have $S = \mu p K + \mu M$ and, hence $s = (\mu p K + \mu M)/(Y + \mu M)$ from which we get (for normal values of μ)

[18.1]
$$\mu = \frac{s}{\sigma + k/(1 + \mu k)} \sim \frac{s}{\sigma + k}$$

in which k denotes the ratio between cash holdings and income (the Cambridge k). k is constant over time, but is endogenously determined. If k were equal to zero, Equation 18.1 would reduce to $\mu = s/\sigma$. All this resembles somewhat the Harrod-Domar model, but the two should not be confused.

In the Harrod-Domar model (Lundberg, 1937; Harrod, 1939, 1946; Domar, 1946, 1947), the rate of growth g of national income is determined by the *a priori* given savings and capital-output ratios. The rate of growth thus determined may differ from the rate of growth of population and there is nothing to ensure full employment and equilibrium in the labor market. Defining $g = \Delta Y/Y$, and assuming $s = S/Y$ and $\sigma = K/(Y/p)$ to be predetermined constants, it is easy to show that in so-called "steady growth," that is, a state where capital and real income permanently increase in the same proportion, we must have

[18.1']
$$g = \frac{s}{\sigma}$$

From the definition of σ we have $\Delta(Y/p) = \Delta K/\sigma$, or, since $\Delta K \equiv I/p = S/p$, $\Delta(Y/p) = (S/p)/\sigma$, or $\Delta Y/Y = (S/Y)/\sigma$, from which Equation 18.1' directly follows. Thus determined, g is sometimes called the "warranted" rate of growth. If population growth is μ, there is obviously nothing to ensure equilibrium growth in the sense that $g = \mu$ at full employment. In the Harrod-Domar model equilibrium growth will only occur per chance in a "razor's edge" case.

The basic difference between our neoclassical model and the Harrod-Domar model is thus that (disregarding money) in the former both the savings ratio and the capital-output ratio adjust so as to make equilibrium growth at full employment possible. Partially, the adjustment takes place through an adjustment of the capital employed per worker, the so-called "capital intensity." How this adjustment occurs is shown by Solow's model.

4 / Solow's dynamic model

Comparison between Solow's model, to which we turn now, and the neoclassical equilibrium-growth model of Section 2, based on Klein's static short-term model, shows immediately that the former may be viewed as a primitive dynamization of the latter with money left out of the picture.

Only one commodity is produced, and the only inputs are capital and labor. Total output at time t, $Y(t)$, is therefore equal to total income. Prices are assumed constant and we do not distinguish between income in money terms and real terms. The average savings ratio s is given and constant. Denoting the total capital stock at time t by $K(t)$, the rate of net investment will be $dK/dt = \dot{K}$. In equilibrium, we must therefore have

[18.2]
$$\dot{K} = sY$$

The production function, assumed to be homogeneous of degree 1 in capital and labor is

[18.3]
$$Y = \varphi(K,N)$$

where N denotes total labor input.

From Equations 18.2 and 18.3 we obtain

[18.4]
$$\dot{K} = s\varphi(K,N)$$

a differential equation in two variables, K and N, both being functions of t. (If $\varphi(K,N)$ is simplified to K/σ, Equation 18.4 is reduced to $\dot{K}/K = s/\sigma$, which is equivalent to Equation 18.1′.) The growth of labor is considered exogenously given, and at any moment of time t we have

[18.5] $$N(t) = N_0 e^{\mu t}$$

where N_0 is total supply of labor at time 0 and μ is the natural growth rate of labor supply. In Equation 18.4, N means total labor input. In Equation 18.5, it means total supply. Thus we assume that all labor supply is used as input; in other words, there is full employment. From Equations 18.4 and 18.5 we then get, finally

[18.6] $$\dot{K} = s\varphi(K, N_0 e^{\mu t})$$

which is a differential equation of the first order in one variable, K. Solving Equation 18.6, we should find the stock of capital as a function of time $K(t)$, and from $N(t)$ and $K(t)$ we could calculate the time path of output $Y(t)$. We could then study whether it has a solution with proportional growth. (See below.) If in Equation 18.6 we replace $\dot{K}$ by μK we could, of course, solve directly for K.

From the model we can calculate the real returns to the factors; that is, the real-wage rate $w/p = \partial Y/\partial N$, and the real rental $v/p = \partial Y/\partial K$. The price of one unit of output is p, the money-wage rate is w, and v is the money rental. The model functions as follows:

> At any moment of time the available labor supply is given by [Equation 18.5] and the available stock of capital is also a datum. Since the real return to factors will adjust to bring about full employment of labor and capital we can use the production function [Equation 18.3] to find the current rate of output. Then the propensity to save tells us how much of net output will be saved and invested. [See Equation 18.2.] Hence we know net accumulation of capital during the current period. Added to the already accumulated stock, this gives the capital available for the next period, and the whole process can be repeated. (Solow, 1956, p. 68.)

In principle this is, of course, the way in which Klein's modified model in Section 2 worked, disregarding money.

Hahn and Matthews (1964) presented a simple illustration of the equilibrium state at a certain moment of time: Since in equilibrium growth we must have $g = s/\sigma$[1] and $\mu = g$, the equilibrium capital-output (income) ratio must be $\sigma = s/\mu$, where both μ and s are exogenously given. The

---

[1] We have as a definition of the capital-income ratio $\sigma = K/Y$, which can be written as $\sigma = KS/\dot{K}Y = s/g$.

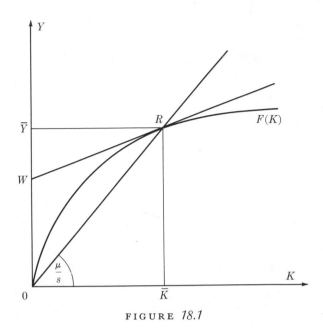

FIGURE *18.1*

capital-output (income) ratio is an endogenous variable. In Figure 18.1 we measure on the ordinate total income Y and on the abscissa total capital K. At the given moment of time, labor input is given (exogenously) as $\bar{N}$, at which time the production function may be written as $Y = \varphi(K,\bar{N}) = F(K)$, which is shown in Figure 18.1.

Assuming equilibrium growth, the capital-output ratio K/Y is at any point of time equal to s/μ, which is measured by the inverse of the slope of the ray OR. Total income is thus $\bar{Y}$ and the stock of capital $\bar{K}$ at the given moment of time. The rate of profit $\partial Y/\partial K$ is equal to the slope of $F(K$ at) R. Total profits $\bar{K}(\partial Y/\partial K)$ are equal to $W\bar{Y}$, and the rest of income $0W$ represents total wages. The capital-output ratio is independent of the actual production function. No matter what the form of $F(K)$, the capital-output ratio is s/μ. The rate of profits and income distribution depends on the precise form of $F(K)$, however.

To solve Equation 18.6, we must know the form of the production function in Equation 18.3. Solow, however, has shown us a device for studying the properties of Equation 18.6 without an explicit solution.

We call the capital-labor ratio $k = K(t)/N(t)$. From Equation 18.5 it follows that $K = kN_0e^{\mu t}$. Differentiation with respect to time gives

[18.7] $$\dot{K} = \dot{k}N_0e^{\mu t} + \mu k N_0e^{\mu t}$$

where $\dot{k} = dk/dt$. With Equation 18.6, this gives us

[18.8] $$(\dot{k} + \mu k)N_0e^{\mu t} = s\varphi(K,N_0e^{\mu t})$$

Dividing through by $N_0 e^{\mu t}$ and recalling that φ is homogeneous of degree 1, we obtain

[18.9] $$\dot{k} = s\varphi(k,1) - \mu k$$

which is a differential equation in the capital-labor ratio k. Equation 18.9 is equivalent to Equation 18.6, which was expressed in terms of total capital, but has the advantage of being susceptible to geometrical analysis. In Figure 18.2 we measure the components of $\dot{k}$; that is, the change in the capital-labor ratio along the ordinate, and k, the ratio itself, on the abscissa. We then draw in the diagram the two curves μk, being a straight line through the origin, and $s\varphi(k,1)$.

The curve $s\varphi(k,1)$ is drawn to pass through the origin, to be concave as seen from the x axis, and cut μk from above at a value of $k = \bar{k}$. This shape of the curve is natural, taking into account the economic meaning of $s\varphi(k,1)$. The function $\varphi(k,1)$ shows production at increasing values of the stock of capital per unit of labor k at employment of one unit of labor. The curve $s\varphi(k,1)$ thus shows actual savings and, hence, investments per man at the actual capital-labor ratio k. The line μk shows the investments required to keep the capital-labor ratio unchanged at its actual level. Now at $\bar{k}$ we have $\dot{k} = 0$, in other words, the capital-labor ratio will be constant. Therefore, if this capital-labor ratio is attained, it will remain unchanged forever, capital and labor growing in the same proportion. The circumstance that $s\varphi(k,1)$ may cut μk implies that the system may have an equilibrium-growth solution (with full employment). If the capital-labor ratio k should be larger

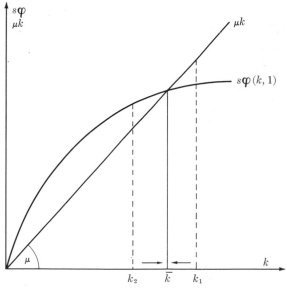

FIGURE 18.2

than $\bar{k}$, that is, equal to k_1, we see that $\mu k > s\varphi(k,1)$, which means that $\dot{k}$ is negative (see Equation 18.9). At k_1 the capital-labor ratio is accordingly falling and will approach $\bar{k}$. In the same way, at k_2 the capital-labor ratio is increasing toward $\bar{k}$. It follows that the system may have not only an equilibrium- (i.e., proportional) growth solution, the equilibrium solution may also be stable so that no matter what capital stock we begin with, the system will finally approach a state wherein the stock of capital increases in the same proportion as the supply of labor. Note, however, that cases with unstable equilibrium growth, with multiple equilibria, or with no equilibrium solution, are all possible, depending upon the shape of $s\varphi(k,1)$.

The dynamic system now discussed is primitive insofar as it only relaxes the equilibrium-growth condition in Equation 11.2a in Section 2, and assumes the other equilibrium conditions are fulfilled instantaneously.

Solow has shown various extensions of the model, taking into account technical progress, elasticity in the supply of labor, interest elasticity of savings, and so forth. None of these extensions alters the fact that the system may have a stable equilibrium-growth solution at full employment, however. By adding a Phillips' relation to Solow's model, Rose (1966) has shown how it may be extended to the case with (monopolistic) unemployment. The system of equations in Section 2, that is, Equations 11.1a to 11.9, could easily be changed in the same way (see also Chapter 11, Section 7).

5 / A simple proof of the neo-neoclassical theorem

Let us finally return to the neo-neoclassical theorem of maximal consumption in equilibrium growth, which we dealt with generally in Chapter 16, Section 3. Using Solow's model as a background, we shall now show a simple geometrical proof of the theorem at the macroeconomic level. The proof is due to J. Fei (1965).

Since the production function is homogeneous of degree 1, we can write

[18.10] $$y = \varphi(k,1)$$

which gives us the product per man $y = Y/N$ as a function of capital per man $k = K/N$. In equilibrium growth, both capital and labor grow in the same proportion μ; that is, $\Delta K/K = \mu$, or $I = \mu K$, from which

[18.11] $$i = \mu k$$

In other words, the investment requirements per man $i = I/N$ must be equal to the rate of population growth times capital per man. The consumption possible per man $c = C/N$ is the difference between product and investment requirements per man; that is

[18.12] $$c = y - i = \varphi(k,1) - \mu k$$

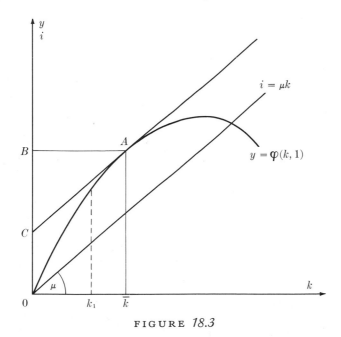

FIGURE *18.3*

In Figure 18.3 we have capital per man k on the abscissa, and production, as well as investments i per man on the ordinate. Both Equations 18.10 and 18.11 are drawn in the diagram, and both pass through the origin.

For a given k, for example, k_1, the vertical distance to the curve $\varphi(k,1)$ will measure the total product (national income) per man; the distance to the straight line μk will measure the investments per man necessary to keep capital per man unchanged. The vertical difference between $\varphi(k,1)$ and μk will then measure the possible consumption per man c on the assumption that capital per man remains unchanged despite the population increase. It will immediately be seen that consumption per man reaches a maximum at the capital-labor ratio $\bar{k}$. In other words, of all available techniques (capital-labor ratios), there is one in particular that will ensure a maximal consumption per man in equilibrium growth. A condition for this result is, of course, that the curve φ be concave (seen from below), reach a maximum, and then turn downward. This condition, however, is nothing but the traditional assumption of decreasing marginal productivity of capital, and the assumption that, at any given labor input, an increase in capital will sooner or later lead to zero marginal productivity of capital and that after that will follow a direct fall in the total product.

Now draw the tangent to $\varphi(k,1)$ at A, where we have maximum consumption per man. The slope of this tangent is the marginal rate of profit on capital, and is equal to the slope of the straight line μk; indeed, this is the maximum condition. It follows that at maximal consumption per man, the rate of profit is equal to the rate of population growth, which is equal to the general rate of growth. Conversely, at a rate of profit equal to the rate of growth, consumption per man will be maximal. Note that if we draw the curve $s\varphi$ (see Figure 18.2) in Figure 18.3, it will, of course, cut μk at $\bar{k}$.

If we add that we are concerned with a risk-free competitive economy in equilibrium, and that prices are considered constant, the rate of interest must be equal to the marginal rate of profit on capital. This concludes the proof.

Note that when the rate of interest (profit) equals the rate of growth, profits per man CB are equal to investments and, accordingly, savings per man. Wages per man $0C$ are equal to consumption per man. Against the background of the von Neumann model, this result does not surprise us. Von Neumann's model implies maximal consumption in this sense. It is clear, also, that if we have "extraneous" consumption, or if savings exceed profits so that the rate of interest (profits) exceeds or falls short of the rate of growth, consumption per man will be lower than maximal consumption.

6 / Money and equilibrium growth

All the equilibrium-growth models described in Chapters 15 to 17 treat money in much the same rudimentary way. Although there are credit markets with demand for and supply of loans, cash holdings and their changes do not appear. Investments and savings may differ *ex ante* (at least in Lindahl's model), but demand for and supply of money seem to be identically equal. The role of money is simply left unspecified. Money prices could be determined, however, through the addition of an exchange equation. Thus a common feature of these models is that the equilibrium-growth solution is invariant with respect to the existence of money and to the absolute level at which prices are kept constant. A sudden change in the quantity of money, over and above the increase needed to maintain constant prices, would lead to a proportional jump in the price level but would have no other effects on the system and its equilibrium solution. Growth would continue at the same rate as before at unchanged relative prices, interest rate, techniques used, and so forth.

The situation is thus remarkably similar to what we found in relation to the original and the simplified Walrasian systems. (See Chapter 5, Section 1.) Natural questions, therefore, are: What will happen to the equilibrium-growth process if money is integrated into the models? Are the systems still invariant to isolated changes, once and for all, in the quantity of money? What will happen if the quantity of money is allowed to change continuously at a rate differing from the equilibrium-growth rate? In the latter case there must be permanent inflation or deflation in the system. Will this affect the growth rate, relative prices, interest rates, techniques, and so forth? It must be recalled that in equilibrium growth everything, including the price changes, must be fully and correctly foreseen and taken into account by households and enterprises.

To each one of these three questions there is a corresponding definition of neutral money. The first two we have already met in connection with the static general equilibrium models, but they apply to equilibrium-growth models as well. They are: (1) Money is neutral if the solutions of the models for a nonmonetary and a monetary economy are identical with respect to relative prices, interest rates, and quantities in demand and supply. (2) Money is neutral if in an established monetary economy a change in the quantity of money, once and for all, leaves relative prices, interest rates, and quantities in demand and supply unchanged and only affects the absolute level of money prices. We know that in the first definition money is not neutral in relation to static general equilibrium (Chapter 5, Section 1). And in the second definition money is neutral only under highly artificial assumptions (Chapter 8, Section 5).

In relation to equilibrium-growth models the situation is the same. The modified Klein model presented in Section 2 helps us to see why this is so. The solutions of the models for equilibrium growth in nonmonetary and monetary economies should be expected to be radically different for the same reasons as in the static case. In particular, if the private sector holds cash, during an equilibrium-growth process at constant prices these cash holdings must be increased along with output and income, and part of the savings must be used to accumulate cash rather than real capital (see Equation 11.3a). The accumulation of cash must affect the process. The precise effects will depend upon the assumptions of the model. Tobin (1965) has concluded that the very existence of cash holdings for that reason will lower the capital intensity in equilibrium growth. Levhari and Patinkin (1968) have shown, however, that with other assumptions this does not necessarily apply. Be this as it may, it is clear that money is generally not neutral to equilibrium growth in the first definition.

That money may be neutral in equilibrium growth in the second definition follows also in the same way as in the static case. We called attention to this circumstance in connection with the modified Klein model in Section 2 of this chapter. In a neoclassical growth model that disregards public debts and other complications, demand and supply functions are homogeneous of zero degree in absolute money prices and the quantity of money, as they are in Patinkin's static system. In monetary equilibrium-growth models, however, demand and supply are usually also assumed to be dependent upon the expected rate of price change (this feature was not incorporated in the modified Klein model in Section 2). On the condition, therefore, that the expectations with respect to the future rate of change of prices are not affected, a sudden increase of the quantity of money, combined with a proportional change in prices, leaves all real demand and supplies unaffected, thus leaving relative prices, the real rate of interest, relative quantities, and the rate of growth unchanged. There appears to be agreement in the literature about both of these cases. (See, for instance, Levhari and Patinkin, 1968, p. 733.)

In relation to equilibrium growth we meet, however, a third definition of neutral money which has no counterpart in static theory. It is: (3) Money is neutral if in relation to a growth process where future price changes are fully foreseen, a change in the rate of change of the quantity of money leaves the "real" growth process unchanged and only affects the rate of change of prices.

It was a well-established neoclassical view that if future changes in the price level are fully foreseen by everyone, money contracts can be written accordingly, and if the money rate of interest on loans is increased according to the rate of price increase so that the real rate of interest is unchanged, nothing will change in real terms. Lindahl (1929, 1939, pp. 147–150 and 328) took this position although he was reserved regarding "possible changes in cash holdings and other complications connected with a monetary economy," which of course, leaves the question open. The consensus seems now to be that on reasonable assumptions money is not neutral in this sense of the word. The implication is that inflation and deflation do have effects on the "real" economy. A number of authors (Tobin, 1965; Johnson, 1967; Sidrauski, 1967; Levhari and Patinkin, 1968; Stein, 1969; and others) argue that since the opportunity costs of holding cash balances are influenced by the rate of change of the price level, a change in the rate of change of the price level will lead to substitution between real capital and cash balances—this, indeed, is nothing but the well-known phenomenon of "flight" from (or, to) money— and other financial assets which in turn must have consequences for the equilibrium-growth solution. Exactly how the solution is affected depends upon the specifications of the concrete models considered; generally, it does not seem possible to predict even the signs of the effects.

The model presented in Section 2 includes money but assumes a constant price level and is not adequately specified for discussing permanent inflation or deflation. We shall briefly consider which amendments are needed to adapt the model for this purpose. The quantity of money was assumed to increase at the same rate as output, that is, $\epsilon = \mu$. We assume instead that $\epsilon \gtrless \mu$. In equilibrium growth the current rate of price change must be equal to the difference between the rate of change of the supply of money and the growth rate of output, that is $dp/dt = \epsilon - \mu$. In a state of permanent inflation (or, deflation), it is natural to assume that the current rate of price change is expected to continue forever. We assume thus that prices are expected to increase at the rate $\epsilon - \mu$. Expectations of future price changes influence the current demand for consumer goods and savings, and lead to a "flight" from (or, to) money and financial assets with fixed interest payments. To account for such effects we must introduce the expected rate of price change as a new argument in the savings and liquidity-preference functions.

Exactly how these functions should be formulated now depends upon the way in which they are derived. If they are based on a model of household utility maximization, their form would follow from the maximum conditions. In Chapter 7, Section 3, we gave an example of the derivation of demand functions in an intertemporal setting. We found there (see Equation 7.16) that all demand functions contain, among other things, both the real rate of interest (that is, the money rate of interest minus the expected rate of price change) and the expected rate of price change. If, on the other hand, the demand and supply functions of the system are postulated on the basis of *ad hoc* considerations, we may proceed similarly. Apart from an isolated instance (Sidrauski, 1967), the usual procedure has been to postulate the functions. Another problem that arises is related to the equilibrium condition $r = v/p$ in Equation 11.7c. To make financial and real investments equally attractive we must now have $r = v/p + (\epsilon - \mu)$, that is, money rate of interest must equal the real rental plus the rate of price increase of real assets. This condition can also be written in the more familiar form $r - (\epsilon - \mu) = v/p$, that is, the real rate of interest must equal the real rental (recall that we disregard depreciation). It has, moreover, been maintained that the real disposable income entering as an argument in the savings function should be adjusted for the loss (or gain) involved in the change of the real value of the existing stock of money following the price change. Instead of $Y + \epsilon M$, disposable income should thus be redefined as

$$Y + \epsilon M - (\epsilon - \mu)M = Y + \mu M$$

(Tobin, 1965). Some authors have proposed that in addition disposable income be adjusted for the imputed value of the services of the stock of money (Johnson, 1967; Levhari and Patinkin, 1968), but we shall not discuss this rather subtle point.

The conclusion is that if, in the equilibrium-growth model described by Equations 11.1a to 11.9 in Section 2 of this chapter, we interpret r, the rate of interest, as the real rate of interest, and replace Equations 11.1a and 11.4, respectively, by

[11.1a']
$$\frac{S}{p} = f\left(r, \epsilon - \mu, \frac{Y + \mu M}{p}\right)$$

and

[11.4a]
$$\frac{M}{p} = L\left(r, \epsilon - \mu, \frac{Y}{p}\right)$$

we arrive at a system of equilibrium growth with permanent inflation or deflation. (At $\epsilon = \mu$ we return to the system of Section 2 with constant prices.) In this system both the rate of growth and the rate of inflation are exogenously determined. Fixing t, ϵ, and μ at arbitrary values, we can solve the system for given rates of growth and inflation. Inspection of the system shows that if it has a solution for arbitrary values of t, ϵ, and μ, it is capable of staying in equilibrium with all real quantities increasing at the rate μ, and all prices at the rate $\epsilon - \mu$, all relative real quantities, all relative prices, and the rate of interest remaining constant over time. This property of the system, to be able simultaneously to grow at one rate in the real quantities and at another rate in the prices, is closely related to the homogeneity properties of the system: homogeneity of degree zero in prices and quantity of money, and homogeneity of degree 1 in real quantities (real capital, labor, real income, etc.). Having solved the system at given t, ϵ, and μ, we can then study the effects on the equilibrium values of the endogenous variables of a change in the rate of inflation, that is, a change in ϵ. We have no reasons for expecting the system to be invariant in the relative physical quantities, the relative prices, and the rate of interest at changes in the rate of expansion of money supply. The total derivatives with respect to ϵ are relatively complex, however, and even if we were able to make assumptions about the signs of all the partial derivatives of the system, and to make use of stability conditions, we would in general be unable to determine the signs of the total derivatives. It is interesting to notice that once more (compare with the *quasi*-equilibrium systems in Chapter 10) we are studying inflation and its effects in what formally appears as a completely static arrangement.

In these neoclassical growth models, the rate of growth is given exogenously and is unaffected by changes in the rate of inflation. This particular feature deprives, of course, this kind of theory of money and growth of some of its interest inasmuch as one of the most burning issues in development policy is whether the rate of growth itself is accelerated or retarded by inflationary monetary policies.

References

DOMAR, E.: "Capital, Expansion, Rate of Growth, and Employment," *Econometrica*, vol. 14, no. 2, April, 1946.

—: "Expansion and Employment," *American Economic Review*, vol. 37, no. 1, March, 1947.

FEI, J.: Unpublished paper read at First World Congress of the Econometric Society, Rome, 1965.

HAHN, F. H., and R. C. O. MATTHEWS: "The Theory of Economic Growth: A Survey," *The Economic Journal*, vol. 74, no. 296, December, 1964.

HARROD, R.: "An Essay in Dynamic Theory," *The Economic Journal*, vol. 69, no. 193, March, 1939.

—: *Towards a Dynamic Economics*, Macmillan, London, 1946.

JOHNSON, H. G.: *Essays in Monetary Economics*, George Allen and Unwin, London, 1967.

KALDOR, N.: "A Model of Economic Growth," *The Economic Journal*, vol. 67, no. 268, December, 1957.

—, and J. MIRRLEES: "A New Model of Economic Growth," *Review of Economic Studies*, vol. 29, no. 80, June, 1962.

LEVHARI, D., and D. PATINKIN: "The Role of Money in a Simple Growth Model," *The American Economic Review*, vol. 58, no. 4, September, 1968.

LINDAHL, E.: *Studies in the Theory of Money and Capital*, George Allen and Unwin, London, 1939.

LUNDBERG, ERIK: *Studies in the Theory of Economic Expansion*, Chapter IX, Section 2, P. S. King and Son, London, 1937.

ROSE, H.: "Unemployment in a Theory of Growth," *International Economic Review*, vol. 7, no. 3, September, 1966.

SIDRAUSKI, M.: "Rational Choice and Patterns of Growth in a Monetary Economy," *American Economic Review*, Papers and Proceedings, vol. 57, no. 2, May, 1967.

—: "Inflation and Economic Growth," *The Journal of Political Economy*, vol. 75, no. 6, December, 1967.

SOLOW, R.: "A Contribution to the Theory of Economic Growth," *The Quarterly Journal of Economics*, vol. 70, no. 1, February, 1956.

STEIN, J.: " 'Neoclassical' and 'Keynes-Wicksell' Monetary Growth Models," *Journal of Money, Credit and Banking*, vol. 1, no. 2, May, 1969.

TOBIN, J.: "Money and Economic Growth," *Econometrica*, vol. 33, no. 4, October, 1965.

Index